American Society and Culture
美国社会文化

王恩铭 编

图书在版编目(CIP)数据

美国社会文化/王恩铭编. ——北京:北京大学出版社,2010.4
(21世纪英语专业系列教材)
ISBN 978-7-301-16643-7

Ⅰ. 美… Ⅱ. 王… Ⅲ. ①英语－阅读教学－高等学校－教材 ②文化－概况－美国 Ⅳ. H319.4:G

中国版本图书馆 CIP 数据核字(2010)第 059703 号

书　　　名:	美国社会文化
著作责任者:	王恩铭　编
责任编辑:	黄瑞明
标准书号:	ISBN 978-7-301-16643-7/G·2828
出版发行:	北京大学出版社
地　　　址:	北京市海淀区成府路 205 号　100871
网　　　址:	http://www.pup.cn　电子信箱:zpup@pup.pku.edu.cn
电　　　话:	邮购部 62752015　发行部 62750672　编辑部 62755217
	出版部 62754962
印　刷　者:	北京大学印刷厂
经　销　者:	新华书店
	650 毫米×980 毫米　16 开本　20.75 印张　400 千字
	2010 年 4 月第 1 版　2017 年 3 月第 4 次印刷
定　　　价:	38.00 元

未经许可,不得以任何方式复制或抄袭本书之部分或全部内容。
版权所有,侵权必究
举报电话:(010)62752024　电子信箱:fd@pup.pku.edu.cn

《21世纪英语专业系列教材》编写委员会

(以姓氏笔画排序)

王守仁　王克非　申　丹
刘意青　李　力　胡壮麟
桂诗春　梅德明　程朝翔

总　　序

北京大学出版社自 2005 年以来已出版《语言学与应用语言学知识系列读本》多种，为了配合第十一个五年计划，现又策划陆续出版《21 世纪英语专业系列教材》。这个重大举措势必受到英语专业广大教师和学生的欢迎。

作为英语教师，最让人揪心的莫过于听人说英语不是一个专业，只是一个工具。说这些话的领导和教师的用心是好的，为英语专业的毕业生将来找工作着想，因此要为英语专业的学生多多开设诸如新闻、法律、国际商务、经济、旅游等其他专业的课程。但事与愿违，英语专业的教师们很快发现，学生投入英语学习的时间少了，掌握英语专业课程知识甚微，即使对四个技能的掌握也并不比大学英语学生高明多少，而那个所谓的第二专业在有关专家的眼中只是学到些皮毛而已。

英语专业的路在何方？有没有其他路可走？这是需要我们英语专业教师思索的问题。中央领导关于创新是一个民族的灵魂和要培养创新人才等的指示精神，让我们在层层迷雾中找到了航向。显然，培养学生具有自主学习能力和能进行创造性思维是我们更为重要的战略目标，使英语专业的人才更能适应 21 世纪的需要，迎接 21 世纪的挑战。

如今，北京大学出版社外语部的领导和编辑同志们，也从教材出版的视角探索英语专业的教材问题，从而为贯彻英语专业教学大纲做些有益的工作，为教师们开设大纲中所规定的必修、选修课程提供各种教材。《21 世纪英语专业系列教材》是普通高等教育"十一五"国家级规划教材和国家"十一五"重点出版规划项目《面向新世纪的立体化网络化英语学科建设丛书》的重要组成部分。这套系列教材要体现新世纪英语教学的自主化、协作化、模块化和超文本化，结合外语教材的具体情况，既要解决语言、教学内容、教学方法和教育技术的时代化，也要坚持弘扬以爱国主义为核心的民族精神。因此，今天北京大学出版社在大力提倡专业英语教学改革的基础上，编辑出版各种英语专业技能、英语专业知识和相关专业知识课程的教材，以培养具有创新性思维的和具有实际工作能力的学生，充分体现了时代精神。

北京大学出版社的远见卓识，也反映了英语专业广大师生盼望已久的心愿。由北京大学等全国几十所院校具体组织力量,积极编写相关教材。这就是说,这套教材是由一些高等院校有水平有经验的第一线教师们制定编写大纲,反复讨论,特别是考虑到在不同层次、不同背景学校之间取得平衡,避免了先前的教材或偏难或偏易的弊病。与此同时,一批知名专家教授参与策划和教材审定工作,保证了教材质量。

  当然,这套系列教材出版只是初步实现了出版社和编者们的预期目标。为了获得更大效果,希望使用本系列教材的教师和同学不吝指教,及时将意见反馈给我们,使教材更加完善。

  航道已经开通,我们有决心乘风破浪,奋勇前进!

胡壮麟

北京大学蓝旗营

前　言

　　目前,我国外语教学界正日渐形成这样一种共识,即外语教学与外国文化教育密切相关,不可割离。围绕语言教学与文化教育的关系问题,学术界主要有三种观点。一种观点认为,语言与文化是一种从属关系,即语言为主,文化为辅,英语表述为 language teaching with a cultural dimension。另一种观点提出,语言教学与文化教育应齐头并进,不分主次,互为补充,英语表述为 culture teaching as a parallel to language teaching。还有一种观点主张,语言教学与文化教育构成一个不可割裂的整体,英语表述为 culture teaching as an integral part of language teaching。尽管这三种观点侧重点相异,对文化在语言教学过程中的权重认识不一,但它们的共同点还是显而易见的,即三者都强调文化教育对语言教学的影响和作用。以此推论,即便了解和掌握一国文化不是学好其语言的必要条件,至少也是有助于语言学习和运用的。

　　正是基于这一认识,本人用英语编写了这本《美国社会文化》,旨在为中国的英语学习者和美国文化爱好者提供一幅以美国文化理念和价值观为主线、以美国人民族特性和行为方式为内容、以美国社会结构和地区特色为衬托的"美国社会文化全景图"。众所周知,语言的背后是文化,文化的背后是良知,良知的背后是人性。因此,无论是从现实主义或者实用主义,还是从道德良知或者人文精神的角度来说,知晓和领悟美国文化不仅有助于我们对英语(至少是美国英语)的切实掌握和灵活运用,而且有助于我们人文素养的提升和思想情操的修炼。毋庸说,我们不必把美国文化"照单全收",更没有必要仿而效之,而应该采取取其精华、去其糟粕的态度,一方面探寻美国人的文化精神,另一方面寻求全人类的共同关怀。在了解和诠释美国文化的精神之旅中,我们不仅可以解读英语文字中的文化信息,更可以英语文字为载体透视美利坚民族之魂。

　　长期以来,本人在讲授英语语言技能的同时教授美国文化课程。近三十载的教学实践告诉我,英语语言教学必须辅以文化内容,即 language teaching with a cultural dimension。这是最基本的要求,否则语言学习只能流于表面,无法深入内层。事实上,对英语国家文化的生疏和无知不仅阻碍语言习得过程,而且影响甚至制约对语言的准确理解和完整掌握。然而,比辅助方法更有效和更理想的方式无疑是把文化教育看作语言教学不可分割的一部分,即 culture teaching as an integral part of language teaching。专门讲授某一英语国家的文化,如美国文化,可以使英语学习者较为系统、完整地理解和把握该国文化,进而在理性层面对英语语言既"知其然",又"知其所以然",最终自觉使用正确、地道的英语。本人历时一年编写《美国社会文化》之目的即在于此。这不仅是英语语言学习的需要,也是人文素质培养的需要。

《美国社会文化》以美利坚民族的发展足迹开篇,为全书奠定历史演进和社会变化的背景,之后各章逐一展开美利坚民族的文化价值观念、政治宗教信仰、社会制度机构、少数民族群体、大众文化媒介、流行文化传播、社会福利服务和习俗信念体系等问题,使全书具备一定的历史纵深度,并显现出美国文化的丰富性和独特性。为了便于使用和学习,本教程在每一章节的开头都设有"Learning Objectives"一栏,意在提纲挈领地把本章节的要点(highlights)突显出来,帮助使用者一目了然地得知该章节所涉及的范围及必须掌握的基本内容。同样,为了帮助使用者掌握核心信息和主要观点,本教程的每一章后面都编写了"Summary"一栏,旨在言简意赅地概括出该章节的主要成分。最后,为了帮助本教程使用者巩固所学内容和批判性地解读美国文化,每一章的最后部分还提供了"Essay Questions"一栏,以激发读者对该章节所涉及问题的思考和探究。总之,本教程编者殷切地期望,此书能使喜爱英语语言和美国文化的读者有所收获,并深深地期待他/她们以此为基础深入钻研下去,精益求精,更上一层楼,共同把我国的英语学习和美国文化研究推向一个新的高度。

王恩铭
上海外国语大学
英语学院 美国研究中心
2009 年 6 月 28 日

Contents

Chapter One Out of the Past
Learning Objectives ·· (2)
1.1　The Birth of a New Nation ································ (3)
1.2　The Growth of the New Republic ······················ (8)
1.3　The Civil War and the Reconstruction ················ (16)
1.4　Growth and Transformation ······························ (22)
1.5　The Progressive Thrust ····································· (28)
1.6　War, Prosperity, and Depression ······················· (33)
1.7　World War II and Its Impact ····························· (39)
1.8　Decades of Change: 1960—1980 ······················· (45)
1.9　America at the Turn of the Century ··················· (51)
Summary ·· (58)
Essay Questions ·· (58)

Chapter Two The American Identity
Learning Objectives ·· (62)
2.1　The Anglo-Saxons ·· (62)
2.2　White Ethnic Americans ···································· (64)
2.3　African Americans ·· (66)
2.4　Latinos/Hispanics ··· (68)
2.5　Asian Americans ·· (70)
2.6　Native Americans ··· (72)
Summary ·· (74)
Essay Questions ·· (75)

Chapter Three Religion in America
Learning Objectives ·· (78)
3.1　Religion in America: A Brief History ··················· (78)
3.2　"In God We Trust" ··· (80)
3.3　Church, State and Politics ································· (82)
3.4　Popular Religion ·· (85)

  3.5 Civil Religion and Beyond ······················· (86)
  Summary ··· (88)
  Essay Questions ····································· (89)

Chapter Four American Beliefs
  Learning Objectives ································ (92)
  4.1 Primary Beliefs of American Culture ············ (92)
  4.2 Immigrant Beliefs ······························ (94)
  4.3 Frontier Beliefs ································ (95)
  4.4 Religious and Moral Beliefs ···················· (97)
  4.5 Social Beliefs ·································· (100)
  4.6 Political Beliefs ······························· (102)
  4.7 Beliefs on Human Nature ······················· (105)
  Summary ··· (107)
  Essay Questions ····································· (108)

Chapter Five American Values and Assumptions
  Learning Objectives ································ (110)
  5.1 Individualism and Privacy ······················ (111)
  5.2 Equality ··· (112)
  5.3 Informality ····································· (114)
  5.4 Achievement, Action, Work, and Materialism ······ (115)
  5.5 Directness and Assertiveness ···················· (117)
  5.6 Cooperation and "Fair Play" ···················· (119)
  Summary ··· (120)
  Essay Questions ····································· (121)

Chapter Six Cultural Regions in America
  Learning Objectives ································ (124)
  6.1 New England ···································· (124)
  6.2 The South ······································· (126)
  6.3 The Midland ···································· (129)
  6.4 The Midwest ···································· (131)
  6.5 The Far West ···································· (133)
  Summary ··· (136)
  Essay Questions ····································· (137)

Chapter Seven Education in America

Learning Objectives ········· (140)
7.1　Initial Efforts in Promoting Education ········· (140)
7.2　Education as Philanthropy ········· (143)
7.3　The Birth of Public Schools ········· (144)
7.4　The Emergence of the Academies ········· (146)
7.5　Colleges: Private and Public ········· (148)
7.6　The Arrival of the University ········· (150)
7.7　Progressivism in Education ········· (152)
Summary ········· (154)
Essay Questions ········· (155)

Chapter Eight The American Family

Learning Objectives ········· (158)
8.1　European Origins of the American Family ········· (159)
8.2　Separate Spheres and the Birth of the Modern American Family ········· (160)
8.3　Private Lives and Paradoxes of Perfection ········· (163)
8.4　The Contemporary American Family ········· (165)
8.5　Upper, Middle, and Working-Class Families ········· (168)
Summary ········· (171)
Essay Questions ········· (172)

Chapter Nine Mass Media

Learning Objectives ········· (174)
9.1　Books ········· (174)
9.2　Newspapers ········· (177)
9.3　Magazines ········· (179)
9.4　Films ········· (182)
9.5　Radio and Sound Recording ········· (185)
9.6　Television ········· (189)
9.7　The Internet and the World Wide Web ········· (192)
Summary ········· (195)
Essay Questions ········· (196)

Chapter Ten Popular Culture

Learning Objectives ········· (200)
10.1　Comic Art ········· (200)

10.2	Advertising	(204)
10.3	Automobile Culture	(207)
10.4	Dance	(210)
10.5	Music	(213)
10.6	Sports	(216)
Summary		(219)
Essay Questions		(220)

Chapter Eleven Capitalist Economy and Business Civilization

Learning Objectives		(224)
11.1	American Capitalism	(225)
11.2	The Cult of the Businessman	(228)
11.3	The Corporate Empire	(231)
11.4	Business and Its Satellites	(234)
11.5	Capital and Labor	(238)
Summary		(241)
Essay Questions		(242)

Chapter Twelve Social Services

Learning Objectives		(246)
12.1	American Values in Social Welfare	(247)
12.2	Social Services: A Brief History	(250)
12.3	Public Social Services	(252)
12.4	Health Care Services	(255)
12.5	Housing	(258)
Summary		(260)
Essay Questions		(261)

Chapter Thirteen Law and Legal System

Learning Objectives		(264)
13.1	The Sources of the Law	(265)
13.2	The Federal Judicial System	(267)
13.3	The State Judicial System	(269)
13.4	The Criminal Court Process	(271)
13.5	The Civil Court Process	(275)
Summary		(279)
Essay Questions		(279)

Chapter Fourteen   American Women

- Learning Objectives ·· (282)
- 14.1 Founding Mothers ·· (282)
- 14.2 Women in the New Republic ································ (285)
- 14.3 Women's Rights Movement ································· (287)
- 14.4 The Cult of Domesticity and New Women ············· (289)
- 14.5 Housewifery and Domesticity ······························· (291)
- 14.6 A New Wave of Feminism ···································· (293)
- 14.7 Gains and Uncertainties ······································ (296)
- Summary ··· (298)
- Essay Questions ·· (299)

Chapter Fifteen   Who Is an American?

- Learning Objectives ·· (302)
- 15.1 The Puritan Thesis ·· (303)
- 15.2 The Frontier Thesis ··· (305)
- 15.3 The Melting-Pot Thesis ······································· (307)
- 15.4 The Salad Bowl Thesis ·· (310)
- 15.5 Multiculturalism ·· (313)
- Summary ··· (315)
- Essay Questions ·· (316)

Bibliography ·· (317)

American Society and Culture
美 国 社 会 文 化

Chapter One
Out of the Past

American Society and Culture
美 国 社 会 文 化

LEARNING OBJECTIVES

- Understand a series of triggering events that led to the birth of the United States of America
- Know the democratization process of the new Republic
- Be aware of the rapid development of industrialization and urbanization
- Learn the ways the United States shifted from non-engagement to engagement in world affairs, especially in the two world wars and the cold war
- Make sense of the social reform movements of the 1960s

    To understand the society and culture of any nation, we need to, first and foremost, build a reasonable amount of knowledge about the nation's past, for it is out of the past that the nation has traveled to its present, and it is also out of the past that the nation has developed its social institutions and formulated its cultural values.

    In this chapter, we will probe into the American past, examining its evolutionary process from the early colonial period to the forging of the republic, from the outbreak of the Civil War to the development of industrialization and urbanization, and from the arrival of the post-industrial society to the emergence of the superpower. Sketchy in style, it is largely designed to furnish the historical background for the discussion of American social and cultural fabrics in the following chapters.

Chapter One
Out of the Past

1.1 The Birth of a New Nation

The First Americans

In 1492, North America was not an empty wasteland. As many as 7 to 10 million lived north of present-day Mexico, unevenly scattered in small tribes from the warlike Iroquois hunters of the Northeast to the pueblo dwellers of the Southwest. These people, nowadays called Native Americans (also known as Indians), had crossed from Asia to Alaska some 20,000 years earlier, making good use of the land and its resources to lead a nomadic life on this vast continent. Sparse populations of nomads inhabited the Great Basin, the high plains and the northern forests. Fairly dense concentrations, however, thrived along the Pacific coast, in the Southwest and Southeast, in the Mississippi, and along the Atlantic coast. All these peoples grouped themselves in several hundred nations and tribes, speaking many diverse languages and dialects. But the most important Indian social groups were the family, the village, and the clan. Within these spheres, Native Americans fed themselves, reared their children, and tried to sort out the mysteries of life.

By all accounts, Native American society in North America was closely tied to the land. Identification with nature and elements was integral to their religious beliefs. Their life was essentially clan-oriented and communal, with children allowed more freedom and tolerance than was the European custom of the day. Although some Native Americans developed a type of hieroglyphics to preserve certain texts, their culture was primarily oral, with a high value placed on the recounting of tales and dreams. Killing only for food, traveling by water and forest paths, making their weapons and tools from stone and wood, and using animal skins and bark for their shelters, they had left a beautiful virgin landscape largely untouched. Clearly, however, there was a good deal of trade among various groups and strong evidence exists that neighboring tribes maintained extensive and formal relations, sometimes friendly, and sometimes hostile.

Most Indians explained the origin and destiny of the human race in myths told by storytellers during religious ceremonies. In the beginning, said the Iroquois, was the sky world of unchanging perfection. From it fell a beautiful pregnant woman, whom the birds saved from plunging into the limitless ocean.

American Society and Culture
美 国 社 会 文 化

On the back of a tortoise who rose from the sea, birds created the earth's soil, in which the woman planted seeds carried during her fall. From these seeds sprang all nature; from her womb, the human race. Based on such myths, Native American religions revolved around the conviction that all nature was alive, pulsating with a spiritual power. A mysterious, awe-inspiring force that could affect human life for both good and evil, such power united all nature in a unbroken web. Their belief in supernatural power led most Indian peoples to seek constantly to conciliate all the spiritual forces in nature: living things, rocks and water, sun and moon, even ghosts and witches. To the Indians, humanity was only one link in the great chain of living nature. The Judeo-Christian view that God had given humanity domination over nature was very strange to them.

The Coming of the English

The early 1600s saw the beginning of a great tide of emigration from Europe to North America, with Englishmen making their first permanent settlement at Jamestown, Virginia in 1607. The encounter of these two peoples, the one a hunting society that depended on game and the other an agricultural people who cleared the forests for planting, was often tragic and sometimes brutal. In the short span of less than two hundred years, for example, the Atlantic seaboard that the Indians had known was scarcely recognizable. Vast forest regions had been cleared to build self-sufficient English communities, inter-colonial roads were being constructed to facilitate trade and commerce, the port towns were developing into bustling cities, and a growing number of adventurers were passing through the mountain gaps to settle the Ohio Valley. In short, with the influx of European settlers, Native Americans not only found it difficult to maintain their tribal life, but after the seizure of land by whites, they were literally driven out of the homeland they had had lived in for centuries.

Most European emigrants left their own countries to escape political oppression, to seek the freedom to practice their religion, or to find opportunities denied them at home. Between 1620 and 1635, for example, economic difficulties swept England, with many people thrown out of work without any foreseeable hope in sight. Even skilled artisans could not earn enough to make a decent living. Moreover, the Commercial Revolution had created a burgeoning textile industry, which demanded an

Chapter One
Out of the Past

ever-increasing supply of wool to keep the loom running. In response, landlords enclosed farmlands and evicted the peasants in favor of sheep cultivation. Thus, colonial expansion became an outlet for this displaced peasant population. Similarly, on the British throne from 1603 and 1688 sat four Stuart kings, each in his way attempting to maintain a strong monarchial control over the country. They supported the Church of England and vigorously enforced the laws that required religious conformity. In the short run, they silenced many religious dissenters and, in the long run, they drove many intensely religious-minded people like Puritan separatists out of the country.

Being the first to come and raising large families despite a frightful mortality, the English element secured a dominant influence for their language and culture, playing a pivotal role in shaping the political, social and cultural life of colonial America. Not only were English political and legal institutions brought to the New World, but their cultural customs and social habits were transplanted to the newly-found land as well, leaving a long and enduring impress on the future direction of this young colony. However, while recognizing the importance of English influence, we must be fully aware that immigration to the future United States during the 17th century was primarily English, but largely non-English during the 18th century. Indeed, by the end of 18th century, half of the population living in the then newly-established Republic was made up of continental Europeans, Africans and Native Americans. Their languages, customs, and cultures not only modified English institutions, practices and beliefs, but also contributed to the rich variety of American society, creating, with English settlers, a unique culture—a blend of English and continental European culture conditioned by the environment of the New World.

The Daily Lives of European-Americans

The basic unit of colonial society was the household. Headed by a white male, the household was the chief mechanism of production and consumption. Its members—bound by ties of blood and servitude—worked together to produce goods for consumption or sale. The white male head of the household represented it to the outside world, occasionally serving in the militia or political posts and casting the household's sole vote in elections. Also, he managed the finances and held legal authority over the rest of the family—his wife, his children, and his servants or slaves. Such households were considerably larger than American families today; in 1790, the average home housed 5.7 whites. Most big families were nuclear, that is, they did not include extended kin like aunts, uncles, and grandparents.

The vast majority of colonial families lived in rural areas. As a result, nearly all adult white men were farmers, and nearly all adult white women were farm wives. In colonial America, household tasks were allocated by sex. The master, his sons and his male servants or slaves performed one set of chores; the mistress, her daughters, and her female servants or slaves, an entirely different set. So rigid were these gender classifications that in households without a master or mistress, no one did those chores. Only in emergencies and for brief periods of time would women do men's work or men do women's.

The mistress of the rural household was responsible for what were termed indoor affairs. She and her female helpers prepared food, cleaned the house, and did laundry, and often made clothing. In 18th-century America, these basic chores were complex and time-consuming. Preparing food involved planting and cultivating a garden, harvesting and preserving vegetables, salting and smoking meat, drying apples and pressing cider, milking cows and making butter and cheese, not to mention cooking and baking. Making clothes meant processing raw wool and flax fibers, spinning thread, weaving cloth, dyeing and softening the cloth, and finally cutting out and sewing garments by hand.

The head of the household and his male helpers, responsible for outdoor affairs, also had heavy workloads. They had to plant and cultivate the fields, build fences, chop wood for the fireplace, harvest and market crops, care for livestock, and butcher cattle and hogs to provide for the household with meat. Only on southern plantations and in northern cities could a few adult white males lead lives free from arduous physical labor. As a rule, the father of the family was the dominant figure in the household, whose legal and customary authority extended to both his wife and children. He set the general standards by which children were raised and usually had the final word on such matters as education and vocational training for the children and the way money was spent for the family.

Chapter One
Out of the Past

The Road to Independence

  In much of colonial history, a striking feature was the lack of controlling influence by the British government. Consequently, most of the colonies were able to enjoy a considerable measure of self-autonomy in their political and economic life. Such being the case, the colonies tended to consider themselves chiefly as commonwealths or states, having only a loose association with the authorities in London. This was largely the result of the so-called "salutary neglect" policy by the British government, which, among other things, allowed the enforcement of trade relations laws to be lenient. According to most historians, this policy, which lasted from 1607 to 1763, was a large contributing factor to the outbreak of the American Revolutionary War, because when the imperial authority did not assert the power it had, the colonists were left to govern themselves. As time went by, these virtually sovereign colonies soon became accustomed to the idea of self-control, and the effects of such prolonged isolation eventually resulted in the emergence of a collective identity that considered itself separated from the mother country. However, such a "salutary neglect" policy did not mean that these British colonies and the ruling country enjoyed a harmonious relationship, free from frictions or trouble. Indeed, in the long history of British settlement in North America, considerable tension had at times marred the relationship between individual provinces and Great Britain. Still, for various reasons, that tension had rarely been sustained for long, nor had it been widespread, except during the crisis that followed the Glorious Revolution in 1688.

  In the 1750s, however, a series of events began to draw the colonists' attention from domestic matters to their relations with their mother country. The turning point came when the British Parliament attempted to enforce English policies after the Seven Year's War (also known as French and Indian War), which would involve not only more centralized control but also more equitable share of costs of empire. Such an attempt, however, immediately met with resistance from the colonies, because the latter, long accustomed to a large measure of self-autonomy, expected more, not less, freedom and independence. Thus, Great Britain, having gone heavily into debt for the Seven Year's War, was anxious to reduce the debt by imposing revenue-raising taxes on the colonies in addition to the customs duties that had long regulated trade. The colonies, by contrast, resenting the new direction Great Britain was taking regarding its colonial policy, were eager to preserve and indeed assert their autonomy in relation to the mother country. Eventually, with contempt growing in Britain toward the Americans and indignation rising high in the colonies toward the British, the two sides could find little room for reconciliation, moving slowly at first but later irreversibly toward confrontation and hostility.

During the 1760s and early 1670s, a broad coalition of white Americans, men and women alike, rose up in protest against new tax levies and attempts by British officials to tighten controls over the provincial governments. America's elected leaders became ever more suspicious of Britain's motives as the years passed. They laid aside intercolonial antagonisms to coordinate their response to the new measures, and slowly began to reorient their political thinking. Still, however, as late as the summer of 1774, most were seeking a solution within the framework of the empire, and only a few harbored thoughts of independence. Indeed, when independence rather than loyal resistance became the issue, the coalition broke down. But what later happened, such as the battles of Lexington and Concord, the meeting of the Second Continental Congress, and particularly King George's declaration of the colonies in the state of rebellion, escalated the tension between the colonies and the mother country, pushing the former faster onto the road toward independence. On July 4, 1776, the Declaration of Independence was adopted by the Second Continental Congress, announcing to the world the birth of a new nation.

1.2 The Growth of the New Republic

Creating a Virtuous Republic

When the colonies declared their independence from Great Britain, there was no question concerning the form of government, that is, other than the republican form, they would have none. When the Independence was achieved, however, three different definitions of republicanism emerged in the new nation. The first, held chiefly by members of educated elites, was based directly on ancient history and political theory,

Chapter One
Out of the Past

believing that republics could succeed only if they were small in size and homogenous in population. Unless the citizens of a republic were willing to sacrifice their won private interests for the good of the whole, the government would inevitably collapse, In return for sacrifices, a republic offered its citizens equality of opportunity. Under such a government, society would be governed by a "natural aristocracy" of men whose rank would be based on merit rather than inherited wealth and status.

A second definition, advanced by other members of the elite but also by some skilled craftsmen, drew more on economic theory than on political thought. Instead of perceiving the nation as an organic whole composed of people nobly sacrificing for the common good, this version of republicanism followed the English theorist Adam Smith in emphasizing individuals' pursuit of rational self-interest. When republican men sought to improve their economic and social circumstances, the entire nation would benefit. Republican virtue would be achieved through the pursuit of private interests rather than through their subordination to some communal ideal.

The third notion of republicanism was more egalitarian than the other two, both of which contained considerable potential for inequality. This view was less influential, because many of its proponents were illiterate or barely literate and this wrote little to promote their beliefs. Americans who advanced this version of republicanism, the most prominent of whom was Thomas Paine, called for widening men's participation in the political process. They also wanted government to respond directly to the needs of ordinary folk and openly rejected any notion that the lesser sort should automatically defer to their betters. They were, in fact, democrats in the modern sense.

It is important to recognize that the three strands of republicanism were part of a unified whole and shared many of the same assumptions. For example, all three contrasted a virtuous, industrious America to the corruption of England and Europe. In the first version, that virtue manifested itself in frugality and self-sacrifice; in the second version, it would prevent self-interest from becoming vice; and in the third, it was the justification for including even propertyless white men in the ranks of voters. At any rate, since they complemented more than excluded each other, all three of them were incorporated into the making of the republican form of government for the new nation. Indeed, as the citizens of the United States set out to construct their republic, they believed they were embarking on an unprecedented enterprise. With great pride in their new nation, they expected to replace the vices of monarchial Europe with the sober virtues of republican America, embodying republican principles not only in their government but also in their society and culture. The great importance they attached to literature, arts, education and republican motherhood all testified to their strong commitment to what they understood to be the republican virtues that the new republic needed so badly for its healthy growth.

Forming a National Government

The success of the American Revolution gave Americans the opportunity to give legal form to their ideas as expressed in the Declaration of Independence. Following the advice of the Second Continental Congress in May 1776, some states immediately passed their constitutions, but most states adopted their constitutions within a year after the Declaration of Independence. On the whole, the new constitutions showed the impact of democratic ideas, reflecting the spirit of republicanism of the era. For the framers of these constitutions, the first objective was to secure those "unalienable rights" whose violation had caused the former colonies to repudiate their connections with Britain in the first place. Thus, each constitution began with a declaration or a bill of rights. Virginia's, for example, explicitly included a declaration of principles: popular sovereignty, freedom of elections, freedom of the press and conscience, and the right of the majority to reform the government. The Virginia constitution later served as a model for all the others.

However, the constitutional theories that Americans applied at the state level did not at first influence their conception of national government. Because American political leaders had little time to devote to legitimizing their de facto government while organizing the military struggle against Britain, the power and structure of the Continental Congress evolved by default early in the war. Not until late 1777 did Congress send the Articles of Confederation to the states for ratification. Under the Articles of Confederation, the chief organ of national government was a unicameral (one-house) legislature, in which each state had one vote. Its powers included the conduct of foreign relations, the settlement of disputes between states, control over maritime affairs, the

Chapter One
Out of the Past

regulation of Indian trade, and the valuation of state and national coinage. However, the Articles did not give the national government the ability to tax effectively or to enforce a uniform commercial policy. More significantly, since each state retained its sovereignty and every power not expressly delegated to the United States, the national government under the Articles had neither independent income nor authority to compel the states to accept its rulings. Clearly, such a government could never function effectively.

Precisely because of its ineffectiveness in exercising its authority over either domestic or international issues, particularly its inability to deal with commercial matters and social upheavals, political leaders of the early republic recognized the need and urgency of strengthening the power of the national government. In mid-May 1787, fifty-five delegates, most of whom were men of property and substance, convened in Philadelphia to hammer out the U. S. Constitution to replace the Articles of Confederation. The Constitution, as finally approved in September 1787, was an extraordinary document, incorporating in it the organization of the most complex government yet devised, one that would be supreme with a clearly defined and limited sphere. For instance, the Constitution augmented national authority in several ways, vesting in Congress the authority to lay and collect taxes, and to regulate interstate commerce, and to conduct diplomacy. States could no longer coin money, interfere with contracts and debts, or tax interstate commerce. Also, the national government was authorized to raise and maintain an army and navy, manage Native American affairs, and wage war. Yet, still concerned about too strong a federal government, the Constitution's framers devised two ways to restrain the power of the new national government. First, they established three distinct branches—executive, legislative, and judicial—within the national government, and second, they designed a system of checks and balances to prevent any one branch from dominating the other two. To further ensure the independence of each branch, the Constitution provided that the members of one branch would not choose those of another, except for judges, whose independence was protected by lifetime appointment. In addition to checks and balances, the founders improvised a novel form of federalism, a system of shared power and dual lawmaking by the national and state governments, to place limits on central authority. In short, while the national government was granted enough power to be functional and effective, a series of checks and balances had also been designed to promote individual liberty and public virtue. The ideals embodied in the U. S. Constitution remain an essential element of the American national identity.

The Rise of Nationalism and Democracy

The half a century that followed the end of the War for Independence is a remarkable period in American history. Seldom has there been a time in America when the future seemed so promising and the problems so profound. Having broken from the mother country, Americans thought of themselves as in something of a state of nature, with a clean slate on which they could draw the grandest blueprint for their new-found nation. With the political institutions established and their first president George Washington elected, those with great ambitions for themselves and for their country began to push for something to turn the United States into a great and powerful country equal to the then European powers.

The person who pushed hardest for nationalism for the young republic was the first Secretary of Treasury in American history, Alexander Hamilton, then thirty-two years old with extraordinary intelligence and remarkable executive ability. In a series of brilliant reports, he urged upon Congress the measures he considered necessary to set the national economy in order, such as establishing sound public credit and a stable currency, developing manufacturing through bounties and tariffs, and encouraging commerce and trade. More importantly, he believed these measures could be advanced only by a strong central government, which based its support primarily upon politically influential citizens and economically powerful groups. Clearly, democracy had no charm to Hamilton. However, while Hamilton was not able to muster the popular appeal for his programs, he brought to public life a love of efficiency, order, and organization. To a great extend, it is exactly through efficient organization and orderly management that Hamilton, together with other national leaders, helped to create a strong and stable government that could eventually be directed to democratic ends.

However, democracy does not come easily, much less automatically. But the United States is lucky to have Thomas Jefferson as their champion of democracy. If Hamilton preferred elitism, Jefferson trusted ordinary people; if Hamilton was in favor of a strong national government, Jefferson was fearful of national authority; if Hamilton advocated banking, industry and commerce as a way of developing the new Republic, Jefferson favored agrarian life and agricultural values, believing

Chapter One
Out of the Past

that freedom and democracy would flourish best in a rural society. Of course, as a champion of democracy, Jefferson's greatness lay less in his statesmanship than in his fundamental attitudes toward government and society. He had that faith in the basic goodness of men which people like Hamilton lacked. He once remarked: "I am not among those who fear the people, for they, not the rich, are our dependence for continued freedom." Still, Jefferson's democracy was subject to qualification. For one thing, the ignorance and vice of the masses in Europe, he admitted, provided a poor basis for popular government; it was America's good fortune to have a society in which the people could be trusted with power. For another, in his actual suggestions for broadening the franchise, Jefferson did not advocate universal suffrage but favored giving the vote to all men who paid taxes or served in the militia. Besides this minimum stake in society, he believed that voters should have an elementary education, for government would be rendered safer when people's minds are improved to a certain degree.

If Thomas Jefferson demonstrated his passion for democracy by his faith in the perfectibility of human beings, Andrew Jackson displaced his commitment to democracy by his trust in the ordinary people as essentially virtuous. When he was inaugurated President on March 4, 1829, for example, the event was regarded by both his supporters and opponents as a significant victory for democracy. In many ways, much of the Jacksonian philosophy was borrowed directly from Jefferson. Like his famous predecessor, Jackson avowed again and again his faith in the people, his hatred for aristocracy, his fear of consolidated power, and his respect for the sovereignty of the states. "Equal rights for all, and special privileges for none," was probably the most memorable slogan that people of his and later generations associated with Andrew Jackson. In essence, however, Jacksonian democracy was more thoroughgoing than Jeffersonian democracy. If the latter had pinned its hopes almost exclusively on the virtues of the yeoman farmers, the former broadened its faith to include planter, farmers, merchants, and laborers—all whose livelihood was based on honest industry. Indeed, the Jacksonians denied that the only function of the average voter was to use his ballot to entrust power to the natural aristocrat. Rather, according to Jackson, "the duties of all public officers are made so plain and simple that men of intelligence may readily qualify themselves for their performance," thereby pushing the door open for common people to participate in the running of government.

Jeffersonian or Jacksonian, between 1800 and 1840, a variety of democratic movement, inspired by these democratic ferments, sprang in American rural and urban areas, bent on improving the lot of the people. Consequently, workingmen's parties and trade unions were organized, and earnest reformers agitated for public schools, for free homesteads, for utopian socialism, and for many other humanitarian causes involving the interests of common people. For this and many other reasons, this period in American history is regarded as the era of nationalism and democracy, which got further promoted as the nation accelerated its pace of westward movement.

Western Expansion

At the time of the founding of the United States, the boundaries of the country had been set at the Mississippi River on the west and along the 31st parallel on the south. However, by 1853, the United States had added the huge territory of the Louisiana Purchase, acquired Florida from Spain, and swept westward over Texas, California, and Oregon into every square mile of territory that was to make up the continental United States. This breath-taking acquisition of territory had involved American intrigue in Florida, conflicts in Texas, and a blustering threat of force in Oregon, and full-scale war against Mexico. Generally, however, the American people were in advance of their government. Land—to settle on or speculate in—rather than gold, was the chief lure that drew Americans westward into lands beyond the borders of their own country.

Throughout American history, few movements have captured the imagination as has the settlement of the great American West. The image of the sturdy pioneer, plodding beside his lumbering covered wagon, driving away Indians from their land, fording swift streams, and finally looking out upon the blue Pacific, has become enshrined not only in American folklore, but also in Hollywood movie industry. In all of this, there is much that is sheer myth, but there is also much that is true.

Historically speaking, the earliest opening of some American frontiers was accomplished by lone trappers and hunters who, because the game was there or because they weren't comfortable in more settled communities, turned their paths westward. Though such men served as guides and added to the scant geographical knowledge of nineteenth-

Chapter One
Out of the Past

century America, they were relatively unimportant in western settlement. Even in the case of the fur trader, the single hunter was rapidly supplanted by the business organization. Indeed, settlement of the West in large numbers required careful planning, substantial equipment and supplies, organization, and community effort. Whether seeking gold in California, land in Oregon, or religious Eden in Utah, the pioneers usually went west in group. They chose their leaders cautiously, assembled supplies carefully, and laid down laws of the trail strictly. Still, while pioneer life was that of an organized community, rather than that of the lone scout, this does not mean that the stories of struggle and hardship are entirely mythical.

The process of westward movement started from the northeast. Conditions along the entire Atlantic seaboard stimulated migration to the newer regions. From New England, whose soil was incapable of producing grain competitively with the cheap and fertile western lands, came a steady stream of men and women, who left their coastal farms and villages to take advantage of the rich interior of the continent. Then, people in the back settlements of the Carolinas and Virginia, handicapped by the lack of roads and canals giving access to coastal markets, and suffering from the political dominance of the tidewater planters, also joined the growing ranks of pioneers. Shortly afterwards, attracted by the abundant opportunities in the West, people from the mid-Atlantic states jumped onto the westbound wagon train as well. Together, these three streams of people moved across the American continent, writing a new and important chapter in American history, while at the same time leaving a trail of murdered Native Americans and slaughtered buffalo.

The movement profoundly affected the American scene: it encouraged individual initiative; it fostered political and economic democracy; it roughened manners; it broke down conservatism; and it bred a spirit of local self-determination, coupled with respect for the "common person." In the West, men and women were valued not for family background, inherited money, or years of schooling, but for what they were and what they could do. Farms were easy to acquire, and opportunities were abundant. It was a time when, as the journalist Horace Greeley said, young men could "go west and grow up with the country." However, just as people poured into the West in hot pursuit of millions of acres of land beyond the Mississippi, tension started to build up over the issue of slavery—should it be allowed to expand to the West, or should it be contained where it was? This issue became one of the crucial factors in accentuating the sectional conflict between the North and the South.

1.3 The Civil War and the Reconstruction

The Clash of Interests and Ideals

By 1850, American territory stretched over forest, plain, and mountain. Within its far-flung limits dwelt 23 million people in a Union comprising 31 states. In the East, industry boomed, with New England and Middle Atlantic states becoming the centers of manufacturing, commerce, and finance. In the Midwest and the South, agriculture flourished, the South featuring an economy centered on agriculture, and the Midwest concentrating its production on wheat crops. Apparently, by then the nation had already moved in two directions: the North would welcome the Industrial Revolution and the South would reject it. The fact that the North would go one way and the South another would surely lead the two sections to collide with each other, resulting in the bloodiest war ever on the American soil.

Why did North and South lock grips in four years of desperate warfare? To this simple question, historians have given a dozen different answers. Some argue that it was a war of rival theories of government, i.e., state sovereignty against national supremacy. Others believe that it was a war of rival economic interests, that is, agrarian South against commercial and industrial North. Many people are convinced that it was a war of rival nationalisms, for instance, loyalty to the South against loyalty to the United States as a whole. Still others think that it was a war of different social ideas, namely, aristocratic South against democratic North. To be fair, all these elements were present when the Civil War broke out. Yet, no matter how other issues complicated the quarrel, the basic difference between North and South was in their attitudes toward slavery. Abraham Lincoln put his finger on it when he said: "One section of our country believes slavery is right, and ought to be extended, while the other believes it is wrong, and ought not to be extended. This is the only substantial dispute."

Under the Constitution, slavery in the states could not be touched by

Chapter One
Out of the Past

federal government; but slavery might be prohibited in the territories, and blacks accused of being fugitive slaves might be assured of fair trial. From the Republican point of view, this was essentially defensive, aimed at preventing the federal government from continuing to be the tool of the slavery power. When the Republican party won victory in the election of 1860, it made its position unequivocally clear that slavery was wrong. But Republican opposition to the extension of slavery was, from the Southern point of view, aggressively hostile to the South. They reasoned if slaves were perfectly a legitimate form of property, it violated the slave owner's rights to deny him the privilege of taking his property with him into the territories. Moreover, even if the Republicans respected the constitutional bars to legislating against slavery in the states, Southerners feared that their peculiar institution would have a short life if no new lands were opened to plantation agriculture, if agitation and assistance from outside the South made it ever easier for slaves to escape, and if, through the admission of new free states to the Union, the political climate became increasingly hostile to slave-holding.

Thus, it was to preserve the institution of slavery that the South seceded from the Union, established a new government, and fought to maintain its independence. If the Lincoln administration had been willing to let the seceding states go, there would have been no Civil War. Hostilities began when Lincoln held to the symbols of federal authority and the Confederates challenged those symbols by attacking and capturing Fort Sumter in Charleston harbor. When the South fired upon the US flag, it resolved the doubts that had been paralyzing Northern policy. Lincoln's call for troops met enthusiastic response and the nation steeled itself for a conflict that most men had hoped to avoid. The summons was not a crusade against slavery but to a war to uphold the authority of the national government, to suppress "rebellion," and to preserve the Union. In many ways, it was only through such a statement of objectives that Lincoln could hope to hold the support of the slave-holding states, and of large sections of the Northwest where migration from the South was reflected in a public opinion violently opposed to abolitionism. However, the fact that the ideal of Union was an expedient standard did not detract from its potency. After all, the Northerners possessed all the beloved symbols of nationhood. For example, the flag carried by the Union forces was the flag that had flown over American troops in the War of 1812 and the Mexico War. To Lincoln, maintenance of the Union meant more than the continuance of a political state with its historic boundaries. He insisted that it was a test of democracy itself—of whether a nation "conceived in Liberty, and dedicated to the proposition that all men are created equal" could long endure.

Impact of War

National authority was significantly strengthened during the long struggle. Never before had the Presidential powers been so vigorously exerted. To save the Union, Lincoln proclaimed a blockade of the Southern ports, enlarged the army, and authorized the arrest and imprisonment of many Northerners engaged in disloyal activities. Congress also established new precedents. It issued legal-tender currency, levied an income tax, and passed a conscription law. Even more important than this emergency legislation was the extension of national authority into areas where military needs were involved only indirectly, if at all. Additionally, war also made its imperative demands upon Northern business and agriculture. For instance, coal mining and the making of iron and steel expanded with the demands of war industry, and agriculture soon expanded production through an increased use of machinery to meet the needs of the army. At any rate, the basic economic strength of the North was impressively demonstrated by the ability of industry and agriculture to cope with these disruptive conditions.

In the South, the war's economic consequences were different. Only in rudimentary form was there an industry capable of weaving cloth, making uniforms and shoes, and manufacturing arms and ammunitions. Newspapers there were full of ambitious projects for establishing factories in every section of the Confederacy. But, despite all these big talks, Southern industrial production fell far short of meeting the total needs of the section. Many civilians were reduced to dependence on homespun textiles and crude tools hammered out on the forge of the village blacksmith. Indeed, the Confederacy never found any adequate solution for the shortage of certain raw materials like wool and leather. Any large-scale building of factories was precluded by the difficulty of getting machinery. Even existing factories were hard pressed to maintain production, cut off as they were from the machine shops of the North and of England. Worst of all, the South's precarious war economy was eventually ruined by the invasion of Northern troops as the war proceeded, which soon hastened the collapse of the Confederacy.

Chapter One
Out of the Past

Apart from the impact of war on industry and agriculture in the North and the South, morals in both areas had also deteriorated to a shocking extent. Northern cities struggled with outbreaks of rowdiness, drunkenness, and increased prostitution. Dishonest contractors often found their accomplices in dishonest public officials. Many of the newly rich indulged in a conspicuous luxury that aroused natural resentment on the part of those to whom the war had brought not money but bereavement and sacrifice. Nor was the South free from similar scandals. Indeed, it was a notorious fact that the blockade runners favored trade in luxuries and fine liquors over the less profitable carrying of needed military supplies. Trading with the enemy was widespread, as unscrupulous Northerners conspired with their Southern counterparts to exchange manufactured goods for cotton. In short, both sides found morals on the decline in the wake of the war.

Emancipation Proclamation

Throughout the first year of the war, Lincoln handled the slavery with extreme caution, believing it imperative to preserve unity in the North, avoid offense to the border states, and leave the door open for reconciliation with the South. No thought was given to the incitement of the slaves to rebel against their masters. Negroes attempting to enlist in the Union army were rejected, and Southern slaves seeking refuge behind the Northern lines usually met a cool reception. This policy brought down upon Lincoln's head a deluge of criticism from disappointed abolitionists. Partially in response to this pressure, and partially in recognition of new elements in the situation, the Lincoln administration step by step changed its policy. One important consideration was the diplomatic advantage to be gained by identifying the cause of the Union with that of human freedom. Another major objective was to strengthen the Union armies by addition of black workers and soldiers. Still, such steps were too moderate. Not until Congress took action in April, 1862, did the pace to terminate slavery pick up. On September 22, 1862, President Lincoln himself took the boldest step in the direction of abolition, issuing on that day the famous Emancipation Proclamation, which stated, among other things, that all persons held as slaves within any state or designated part of a state in rebellion against the United States should be thenceforward, and forever free.

From the legal point of view, the Emancipation Proclamation was indeed an extraordinary document, since by its very terms it applied only to those slaves whose location within the Confederacy made it impossible for them to claim freedom. Yet, far from being a futile gesture, the Proclamation actually marked a turning point in the war. All confusion of military policy was now ended. As the Union armies fought their way through the South, more and more slaves sought protection in claiming their rights as freedmen. Since emancipation was fixed as an objective of the war, the peculiar institution (slavery) disintegrated rapidly during the following years. All the border states except Delaware and Kentucky abolished slavery, and in December, 1865, the Thirteenth Amendment to the Constitution, prohibiting slavery or involuntary service, went into effect throughout the United States.

Meanwhile, Blacks were making a large contribution to the Union war effort. In 1862, the Northern army to the Union began accepting black enlistments. By 1865, some 186,000 blacks had enrolled. At first, the black soldiers were subject to discrimination. They were paid less than whites and were used mostly as labor battalions, but they won distinction in combat and very late in the war gained equal pay. Confederate authorities watched these developments with dismay. At first, they greeted the news that the North planned to use black troops with assertions that members of "the inferior race" would never fight and that if they did, they would, when captured, be treated as slave insurrectionists. But even the South was compelled to acknowledge that the balance of military power might hinge on the black soldiers. Soon, a growing demand was heard that the Confederacy itself use black troops. Even General Robert E. Lee urged that Blacks be recruited with a promise of freedom at the end of the war. In March, 1965, the desperate Confederacy gave official sanction to the conscription and recruitment of black troops.

Reconstruction and the Freedmen

Long before the war was over, the growing multitude of Blacks freed by the advancing Union army constituted a serious problem. Destitute blacks, uprooted by the conflict, attached themselves to the Union army, pleading for food and clothing. With no general policy to guide them, officers on the spot were left to deal with the problem as best they could.

Chapter One
Out of the Past

As the war approached its end, the problem of aiding the freedmen became increasingly acute. In March, 1865, Congress established the Bureau of Refugees, Freedmen, and Abandoned Lands, usually known as the Freemen's Bureau. The new organization undertook a multiplicity of tasks. As a relief agency, it gave out about 22 million rations to desperately needy people in the devastated South. As an employment agency, it helped the freed blacks to secure work and supervised the writing of contracts between freedmen and their employers. As an educational agency, it encouraged the establishment of black school and granted them financial aid. In addition to all this, it maintained special courts in which both civil and criminal cases involving the ex-slaves were dealt with.

Throughout the summer of 1865, President Johnson, who had succeeded Lincoln after his assassination, tried to carry out Lincoln's reconstruction program, with minor modifications. Radical Republicans in Congress, however, were suspicious that the Southern leopard had not changed his spots—that the Southern state governments established under the lenient reconstruction policy inaugurated by Lincoln and continued by Johnson could not be relied upon to deal just with the freed Blacks. To protect the freedmen against discriminatory legislation, Radical-controlled Congress passed the Civil Rights of 1866, which bestowed United States citizenship on all persons born in the United States and granted to citizens "of every race and color" the same rights to make and to enforce contracts, to sue and to testify in courts and to convey property, and to be subject to the same punishment and penalties.

Following this, Congress passed the Fourteenth Amendment to the Constitution, stating that "all persons born or naturalized in the United States" are citizens. In the Reconstruction Act of March 1867, Congress, ignoring the governments that had been established in the South, divided the South into five districts and placed them under military rule. Escape from permanent military government was open to those states that established civil governments, took an oath of allegiance, ratified the Fourteenth Amendment, and adopted black suffrage. The Fifteenth Amendment, passed by Congress the following year and ratified in 1870 by state legislatures, provided that "The rights of citizens of the United States to vote shall not be denied or abridged by the United States or any state on account of race, color, or previous condition of servitude."

As time went by, it became increasingly obvious that the problems of the South were not being solved by harsh laws and continuing rancor against former rebel states. In 1877, President Hays removed those harsh and punitive measures, thereby admitting the failure of the radical reconstruction policy. With this, Northern rule in the South came to an end. By then, however, the South was not only devastated by war, but also burdened by debt caused by misgovernment and demoralized by a decade of racial warfare. Apparently, after twelve years of "false" reconstruction, from 1865 to 1877, real efforts to rebuild the South had to be made in a new direction.

1.4 Growth and Transformation

The Last Frontier

In 1912 when New Mexico and Arizona became the forty-seventh and forty-eighth states of the United States, the event provided the final chapter in an American story that had started at Jamestown three hundred years before. Although Americans continued to be a rootless people, moving from one section of their country to another, the frontier movement was basically over. The last great wave of settlement and state building after 1860 had created fourteen commonwealths west of the Mississippi River. The lure of precious metals, vast grazing lands, and fertile soil had brought thousands of settlers into the great region between the Missouri River and the Sierras—an area ignorantly designated "the great American desert" by earlier generations.

The new West was a land of paradoxes. Through the miracle of railroads, it was more accessible to the urban East than any previous frontier had been. Yet, the contrast between West and East had never been so striking. To Easterners, pale from work in urban offices and factories, the deeply tanned Westerners—prospectors, cowboys, and homesteaders—seemed like characters from another planet. To Westerners, busy with exploring and settling the wild land, the established lifestyle of the Easterners seemed to be too routine and too unchallenging. Nevertheless, the America of mass industry and mechanized agriculture delighted in business adventure of every kind, pushing the frontier-line all the way to the West Coast. In this sense, the process of westward movement, initiated by explorers and hunters and followed by miners, farmers, cowboys and ranchers, was completed by agribusiness and industrial interests.

Chapter One
Out of the Past

In 1890, the U. S. Census Bureau declared that, with no more unsettled area in the West, the American frontier was now officially closed, marking the end of an epoch that had excited the nation for almost a century.

However, although the frontier line had disappeared, the frontier itself was far from forgotten. As farmers, miners, ranchers and Indian agents had pursued their varied activities in the real West, a parallel legendary West had taken deep roots in the American imagination. In the 19th century, for example, this mystic West was a product of novels, songs, and paintings. Dime novels, originating about 1860 and exceedingly popular during the 1870s and 1880s, discovered in the Western cowboys and bad men stock characters certain to delight their juvenile readers. In the 20th century, it would be perpetuated by movies, radio programs, and television shows. The legend deserves attention, for its evolution is fascinating, and its influence far-reaching.

While millions of moviegoers and magazine readers experienced vicarious adventure in the West of imagination, serious scholars pondered the extent and nature of the frontier's influence on American civilization. The problem was first clearly stated by Frederick Jackson Turner, when he presented his paper entitled "The Significance of the Frontier in American History." To the influence of the frontier, Turner attributed the rise of American nationalism, the promotion of democracy, and the growth of ruthless individualism. He suggested that America's relative freedom from serious class conflict might have resulted from the existence of the frontier as a "safety valve of discontent." Inspired by his writings and teachings at Wisconsin and Harvard, a new generation of scholars explored every aspect of the frontier movement. While the central thrust of Turner's thesis was accepted, i. e., the frontier had exerted enormous impact on the growth of American civilization, many of his specific arguments were challenged and modified. After all, American civilization has been the product of many forces rather than one. Immigration, the interplay of European and American ideas, changing technology, the growth of capitalism, sectionalism, the rise of cities, the aspirations of preachers and idealists—all had their impact on American social development. Along with all this, the existence of the frontier had its share, and must be given prominent attention.

Rise of Big Business

The victory of the North in the Civil War ensured more than the preservation of the Union. While the conflict was in progress, the national government gave strong encouragement to the investing classes through enactment of high tariffs, establishment of national banks, and grant of generous subsidies for building railroads. Spurred by such favorable policies, masterful men started to pitch in to build larger and larger business units. Consequently, a host of giant businesses sprang up in the United States during the late 19th and early 20th centuries, which ranged from railroad industry to financial institutions, from oil companies to iron and steel corporations. As these big businesses kept expanding, many of them eventually turned into monopolies or trusts, holding a significant amount of control over the nation's economy. Such successful businessmen as Commodore Vanderbuilt, J. P. Morgan, Edward Harriman, John D. Rockefeller, and Andrew Carnegie have all become legendary figures in American history.

How did big business become the fixtures of modern American business? Generally speaking, there were at least four dominating features that marked the birth of modern industrial America after the Civil War. To begin with, the rapid spread of technological innovation and the factory system had laid the solid foundation for the growth of big companies. Secondly, the constant pressure on firms to compete tooth and nail by cutting costs and prices had pushed small and medium-sized companies to form larger and more competitive corporations. Thirdly, the relentless drop in price levels (a stark contrast to the inflation of other eras) had driven all companies to consolidate their share of market by improving efficiency and expanding scope of business. Finally, the failure of the money supply to keep pace with production had helped raise interest rates on the one hand, and restrict the availability of credit on the other, making it not only necessary but also urgent to stabilize banking and financial institutions of the country.

All these factors were closely interrelated. Technological change enormously increased productivity and gave impetus to the breathtaking industrial expansion. Also, technology enabled manufacturers to cut costs and hire cheap unskilled or semi-skilled labor. The cost cutting, in turn, drove firms to undersell each other, leaving weaker companies by the wayside and promoting stronger, more efficient (and more ruthless) ones

Chapter One
Out of the Past

to consolidate. At any rate, until the mid-1890s, cost reduction, new technology, and fierce competition forced down overall price levels. Farmers and industrial workers suffered chronically low agricultural commodity prices and wages, but in their capacity as consumers, they benefited as store-bought goods cheapened. Meanwhile, high interest rates and the difficulty of obtaining credit added to the burdens of farmers and small entrepreneurs, driving many of them out of the market eventually. Indeed, business tycoons' unflagging drive to maximize efficiency both created colossal fortunes at the top of the economic ladder and forced millions of wage earners to live near the subsistence level.

Out of the new industrial system poured dismal clouds of haze and soot, making the environment increasingly polluted. At the same time, the first tantalizing trickle of what would become an avalanche of consumer goods also manifested itself. In turn, mounting demands for consumer goods stimulated heavy industry's production of "capital goods"—machines to boost farm and factory output. Together with the railroads and financial institutions, the corporations that manufactured capital goods, refined petroleum, and made steel became the main driving force in the economic growth of the United States at the turn of the century.

Urban Growth

Along with the expansion of modern economy in post-Civil-War America, the physical appearance of American cities also went through significant transformations. Responding to a critical need for factory sites, housing, and offices, land speculators, developers, and builders broke up urban space into residential neighborhoods, parks, downtown business districts, and commercial and manufacturing areas. Opportunistic business leaders pioneered transportation systems that moved thousands of urban commuters from home to work and back again by means of streetcars, trains, and eventually electric trolleys and subway cars. Working feverishly to keep pace with the demand for new housing, local carpenters and construction companies expanded the cities' boundaries by developing suburban communities along railroad lines in the countryside, where land was cheaper and residents could enjoy a more pleasant environment than what the bustling downtown afforded.

The immense growth of cities was not peculiar to America. During the second half of the 19th century, London and Paris doubled in population, and Berlin more than quadrupled. Viewed in this context, the rise of American cities reflected the play of similar economic forces like the rapid expansion of industrial economy, accentuated perhaps by such peculiarly American factors as large-scale migration and massive immigration. In the latter part of the 19th century, for example, the growing concentration of industries in urban settings produced demands for thousands of new workers. The promise of good wages and a broad range of jobs draw numerous rural and small-town dwellers to the cities. In many cases, young farm women led the exodus cityward, because with the growing commercialization and specialization of farming in the late 19th century, farm work was increasingly male work. Meanwhile, the prospect of a better life also attracted nearly 10 million northern European immigrants to East Coast and midwestern cities, where they joined the more than 4 million who had settled there in the 1840s and 1850s. In the 1890s, these recent arrivals from northern and western Europe, the so-called "old immigrants," were joined by swelling numbers of "new immigrants." These comprised Italians, Slaves, Greeks, and Jews from southern and eastern Europe.

The overwhelming majority of both old and new immigrants, together with most of migrants from rural areas, settled in cities in the northeastern and north-central states. While some immigrants found it hard to make a living in a strange land, for many the stress of adjusting to urban life in a new society was eased by the fact that they could settle among compatriots who had preceded them. Indeed, despite all the adversity, many immigrant families managed to live a satisfying and pleasant life, maintaining their accustomed way of life through such devices as church, newspaper, school and benevolent association. However, other immigrants were not so lucky. For a great variety of reasons, but mostly due to racial discrimination, some ethnic groups were excluded from the prosperity of this urban development. During the 1890s, for example, Italians in New York, Blacks in Philadelphia and Chicago, Mexican-Americans in Los Angeles, and Chinese in San Francisco all became increasingly locked in segregated, run-down, and over-crowded ghettos.

Chapter One
Out of the Past

Social Transformations

The city had many faces. Slums, criminals, beggars, and grafters displayed one side of urban life. Beautiful parks, broad avenues lined with smart stores and find mansions, great churches, theaters, museums, and libraries showed another. The best hospitals and the best schools were to be found in the cities, as were also the intellectual nerve centers of the country—the offices of the leading magazines, newspapers, and book publishers. It was part of the centralization of American life that the more sophisticated manners and morals of the city should exert a steadily widening influence over the country as a whole.

The city was the home of the rich no less than of the poor, but the rich were enjoying their golden hour in the city as the poor could not. For women, however, the city gave them new opportunities for independence that were nerve dreamed of. The narrow alternatives of earlier days—school-teaching, domestic service, factory work—now broadened to offer employment to women doctors, lawyers, typists, telephone operators, librarians, journalists, and social workers. Particularly interesting were the opportunities in nursing. Excerpt in a few Catholic hospitals, female nurses before the Civil War were an untrained and little-respected group. But by 1883, with the radical alteration of public attitudes, there were twenty-two training schools in the country.

Urban conditions, the growing independence of women, and many other economic and social factors exerted their influence on American family life. Between 1860 and 1910, the birth rate declined from about 41 per thousand to about 27. Smaller families were particularly characteristic of the urban professional and business classes, who found it increasingly expensive to give children the educational and other advantages that were considered necessary. Even more alarming to many moralists was the steady increase in divorce. In 1867, fewer than 10,000 divorces were granted in the whole country—0.3 divorce per thousand of population. In 1914, there were over 100,000 divorces and the rate had risen to 1.0 per thousand inhabitants.

Despite feminine progress in other lines, men held to their monopoly of voting and office holding with surprising tenacity. In 1848, a group of radical and far-sighted women launched the first feminist movement in the United States, but throughout much of the 19th century, they had a bitter disappointment. During the 1870s, a number of feminists attempted

27

to vote, arguing that the franchise was one of the privileges and immunities of citizenship guaranteed by the Fourteenth Amendment. But with firm male logic, the U. S. Supreme Court rejected this proposition in 1875. To most of the 19th-century Americans, males in particular, equal rights for women were just too disturbing to be legally recognized. Still, through their persistent efforts, women's suffrage cause did win a few significant victories. The territorial legislature of Wyoming voted to give equal franchise to men and women in 1869, and that of Utah took the same step in 1870. In 1893, Colorado women received the vote after a popular referendum on the issue; in 1896, the same thing happened in Idaho. Meanwhile, women had been given the right to vote in school elections and on other municipal issues in thirteen states. All these changes represented the new direction of the country, as it went through radical transformations from a rural to an increasingly urbanized society.

1.5 The Progressive Thrust

Progressivism: An Overview

At the start of the 20th century, intellectuals increasingly challenged the ideological foundations of a business-dominated social order, and writers and journalists published the human toll of industrialization and urbanization. Soon, reform thundered over the nation as progressive activists sought to make government more democratic, eradicate unhealthful and dangerous conditions in cities and factories, and curb corporate power. A vigorous protest movement was thus launched, known in history as the progressive movement.

What was progressivism? This is a quite controversial issue, but on a few points, all students of the movement agree. First, it was a political response to industrialization and its social by-products: immigration, urban growth, the concentration of corporate power, and the widening of class divisions. Second, it was distinct from populism, the reform movement that preceded it. Whereas populism attracted aggrieved farmers, progressivism's strength lay in the cities, enlisting far more journalists, academics, and social theorists than did populism. Finally, the progressives were reformers, not radicals or revolutionaries. They wanted to remedy the social evils spawned by capitalism, not destroy the

Chapter One
Out of the Past

system itself.

But which aspects of the new urban-industrial capitalist order most needed attention, and what remedies were required? These basic questions stirred deep disagreements. Indeed, progressivism never constituted a cohesive movement with a unified program, but rather a diverse array of reform activities that sometimes overlapped and sometimes diverged sharply. Many reformers insisted that the preservation of democracy required stricter regulation of business, from local transit companies to the almighty trusts. Other reformers emphasizing the humanitarian theme called for legislation to protect workers and the urban poor. Still other progressives concentrated on schemes for reforming the structure of government, especially at the municipal level. Finally, some reformers, regarding immigration, urban immorality, and incipient social disorder as the central problems, fought for immigration restriction, the abolition of prostitution and saloons, and other social strategies. All this contributed to the mosaic of progressive reform.

And then, who were the progressives? Like the movement itself, they comprised a diverse lot, aligned in shifting coalitions that might unite on one issue and then divide on another. The native-born Protestant middle class, including the new white-collar professionals, was certainly central, but on issues affecting the welfare of factory workers and slum dwellers, the urban-immigrant political machines provided critical support. Even corporate leaders at times endorsed and helped shape business-regulation measures, especially when the pressure for such regulation became irresistible. Altogether, be they corporate leaders, gifted journalists, earnest ministers, energetic organizers or party leaders, they all made their share of contribution to the progressive movement in their own special way.

Trustbusting and Corporate Regulation

With the formation of big corporations in the late 19th century, America found itself confronting with the issue of monopoly. If left alone, big corporations would dominate any given industry, leaving little space for small or medium-sized businesses to compete on an equal basis, much less to develop in a fair and healthy environment. Obviously, monopoly needed to be challenged, and if necessary, busted.

The one who led the busting was President Theodore Roosevelt.

American Society and Culture
美 国 社 会 文 化

With his privileged social background, Theodore Roosevelt neither feared nor much respected the capitalists who had clawed their way to the top in Gilded Age America. Conservative at heart, he had no desire to abolish big corporations, which he believed essential to national greatness. Nevertheless, as President, he embraced the progressive convictions that corporate behavior must be carefully regulated. A strict moralist, he believed that corporations, like individuals, must be held to a high standard of virtue. Out of all these considerations, President Roosevelt first took on the United States Steel Company, the nation's first billion-dollar corporation, charging it with violation of the Sherman Anti-Trust Act. Shortly afterwards, the Roosevelt administration sued forty-three other companies for violating the anti-trust law. As a gesture of support for Roosevelt, the U.S. Supreme Court in 1904 ordered another monopoly, the Northern Securities Company, to be dissolved.

After defeating his Democratic rival in 1904, Roosevelt turned to one of his major goals: railroad regulation. He had come to regard corporate regulation, rather than dramatic trustbusting, as a more promising long-term role for government, and this shift of outlook was reflected in the central role that he played in the passage of the important Hepburn Act (1906). Previously, a similar act had stiffened the penalties against railroad rebates to favored shippers, and the Hepburn Act further tightened existing railroad regulation. This measure empowered the Interstate Commerce Commission to set maximum railroad rates and to examine railroad's financial records. It also standardized bookkeeping to make such inspection easier and curtailed the railroads' distribution of free passes. Although the measure did not entirely satisfy reformers for business regulation, it did significantly increase the government's ability to regulate the railroads.

When Woodrow Wilson became President, he, too, took up the business regulation issue. Although as a candidate Wilson had shown little sympathy for the regulatory approach, as President, Wilson shepherded through Congress two important regulatory measures. The first, the Federal Trade Commission Act (1914), created a five-member federal "watch-dog" agency, with power to investigate suspected violations of federal regulatory statutes, to require regular reports from corporations, and to issue "cease and desist" orders when it found unfair methods of business competitions. The second, the Clayton Antitrust Act (1914), took the more traditional approach of listing specific illegal

Chapter One
Out of the Past

activities. The Sherman Anti-Trust Act of 1890, although outlawing business practices in restraint of trade, had remained vague about details. The Clayton Act spelled out a series of such illegal practices, such as selling at a loss to monopolize a market. Thus, with the added clout of the Clayton Act, the Wilson administration filed antitrust suits against nearly a hundred corporations.

Consumer Protection and the Conservation Movement

No progressive reform aroused a more popular response than the campaign against unsafe and falsely labeled food, drugs, and medicine. Upton Sinclair's *The Jungle* (1906) turned Americans' stomachs by describing the foul conditions under which their sausages and cold cuts were produced. Other muckrakers exposed useless and even dangerous medicines. Many popular nostrums, including children's medicines, contained cocaine, opium, or a large percentage of alcohol. In response to all this, Congress in 1906 passed the Pure Food and Drug Act and the Meat Inspection Act. The former outlawed the sale of adulterated foods or drugs and required accurate labeling of ingredients; the latter imposed strict sanitary requirements for meatpackers, set up a meat-quality rating system (still in effect today), and created a program of federal meat inspection. By 1906, the large food-processing, meatpacking, and medicinal companies, eager to regain public confidence, supported regulatory measures as well.

Speaking more directly to the present was the Conservation Movement led by President Roosevelt, whose commitment to conservation has recently been given a great deal of credit. As we all know, by 1900, decades of urban-industrial growth and western expansion had taken a heavy toll on the land. In the West, controversies over land use burst into the political arena as mining and timber interests, farmers, ranchers, sheep growers, city officials, and preservationists advanced competing claims. Whereas western business interests and boosters preached maximum exploitation of the region's resources, groups such as the Sierra Club sought to preserve large wilderness areas of their pristine beauty and aesthetic appeal. Also, socially prominent easterners embraced the wilderness cause. Thanks to their efforts, Congress in 1891 authorized the president to designate public lands forest reserves. In the early 20th century, a wilderness vogue swept America, and, riding on the wave of wilderness vogue, President Roosevelt, a preservationist by temperament, planned and regulated use of the nation's land for various public and commercial purposes. In 1907, for example, Roosevelt designated twenty-one national forests totaling 16 million acres in the six states.

Equally significant, the Progressive Era saw environmental issues become for the first time matters of intense national concern. Again, Roosevelt played a crucial part in this process. Along with millions of areas of national forests, he created fifty-three wild-life reserves, sixteen national monuments, and five new national parts. Indeed, Roosevelt kept environmental concerns constantly in the public mind. Declaring conservation "the most vital internal question" facing America, he gave priority to an issue that would reverberate through the rest of the century. "We are not building this country of ours for a day," Roosevelt said, "It is to last through the ages."

Imperialism's Siren Song

Progressives did not always exhaust their zeal in domestic affairs. Many became convinced that the United States had a mission to extend its beneficent influence far beyond its own borders. They readily allied themselves with imperialists of a more conservative philosophy to urge the acquisition of colonies and protectorates. But other progressives fought these tendencies. They deplored American imperialism as a denial of the American principle of government by the consent of the governed. They opposed military preparedness and involvement in war as certain to weaken the domestic reform movement and to strengthen control of the American economy by big business.

The Spanish-American War marked the beginning of American imperialism. With a minimum of casualties it lifted America from long-held isolation to overseas expansion. In a few months, it was all over, and the American flag flew over Puerto Rico, Guam, and the Philippines. Thus set in motion, the expansionist surge soon led to additional annexations in Hawaii and Samoa. Nominally independent but placed under American protection were such countries as Cuba, Panama, the Dominican Republic, Haiti, and Nicaragua. In still other countries like China and Mexico, the United States sought to exert influence through economic and diplomatic channels.

Why did the United States turn to imperialism? Some people emphasize economic causation, arguing that the rapid expansion of

Chapter One
Out of the Past

American industry and the need for new markets and fields for investment served as the driving force of American expansion. Other people single out the religious-minded as the strong advocators of U. S. imperialism. Josiah Strong, a clergyman, for example, admonished his fellow Christians to reform America in preparation for the extension of Christian civilization throughout the world. Still others believe that such tough-minded characters as Alfred Thayer Mahan played an instrumental role in shaping American imperialist policy. Mahan argued in his influential book *The Influence of Sea Power upon History, 1660-1783* (1890) that national greatness required not only the building of an efficient modern navy, but also the cultivation of foreign trade and the acquisition of outlying naval bases. Equally important in the formation of imperialism is the concept of "the white man's burden," which appealed as strongly to the naval expert Mahan as to the missionary-minded Strong. Like their British counterparts, American expansionists readily accepted the notion that the Anglo-Saxons had a special mission to extend their beneficent rule over the backward peoples of the world.

All these lines of thought found a natural point of convergence in Theodore Roosevelt. Much impressed by Mahan and other expansionists, Roosevelt argued strongly for a more militant American policy, ready to flex the national muscle in policing weak countries and in sending the American fleet around the world. Of course, not all Americans accepted the imperialist argument. William Sumner, the most respected advocator of Social Darwinism, refused to accept the argument that the acquisition of colonies advanced civilization. Another resolute anti-imperialist was William James, who wrote to the newspapers, ridiculing "the white man's burden." Respectable though the anti-imperialists were as individuals, the tendencies sweeping the United States toward greater expansion were too strong to be checked. It was significant to note that many political leaders condemned imperialism in the abstract, but served the cause of imperialism in concrete cases when they became convinced that the national interests of the United States were at stake.

1.6 *War, Prosperity, and Depression*

WWI and Its Impact

The outbreak of the European war in 1914 shocked all Americans and particularly distressed American progressives. Full of optimism for achieving a better society, American liberals regarded the resort to arms as a regression in civilization. But as time went on, the progressives became divided in their attitudes. Some of them continued to oppose any American involvement in the struggle, suspecting that this war, like all others, had resulted from the intrigues of sinister financial interests and that the only groups that stood to gain were the bankers and the munitions makers. Other progressives like Theodore Roosevelt took a very different position. They saw the war as a struggle between right and wrong. They were convinced that autocratic German had deliberately begun the conflict in order to extend its domination over Europe.

Up to the very beginning of American entry into the war, President Wilson was torn between these conflicting attitudes. Believing that involvement in war would engender his program of domestic reform, and hoping to play the role of neutral peacemaker, Wilson long clung to a policy of neutrality. Yet he believed that England and France had much the better cause, and he was particularly disturbed by the German submarine campaign, which he regarded as an inhumane violation. In this connection, when he finally decided to ask for a declaration of war, he stated American objectives in highly idealistic terms. The nation must "vindicate the principles of peace and justice" as against "selfish and autocratic power." The world, he insisted, "must be made safe for democracy." Thus, Wilson elevated the war from a sordid scramble for territory and indemnity to a crusade for international justice.

Although the active participation of the United States was brief, its influence on American life was profound. Almost five million men were enrolled in the armed services, and more than ever before, the nation's economic life was subjected to national control. The mobilization of thought was no less thorough. On the one hand, official agencies poured out a torrent of propaganda, appealing to young men to enlist and older men to buy "Liberty Bonds." On the other hand, dissenting opinion received scant tolerance. Socialists who opposed the war received long prison terms, and the radical Industrial Workers of the World was crippled through the imprisonment of its leaders. Those who spoke or wrote anything that threatened to interfere with the war were severely punished. What was more troublesome was that after Wilson succeeded in concluding the Treaty of Versailles in Paris at the end of war, the U. S. Senate rejected his work, leaving many Americans in the state of

Chapter One
Out of the Past

confusion and disillusionment. If Americans refused to be part of the League of Nations for future peace, why should have America joined and fought the war in the first place?

The Automobile Age

Economic mobilization during WWI had carried the government into business to an unprecedented degree, and transition from war to peace was tumultuous. For one thing, there was a rapid increase in consumer prices after the war was over. For another, labor unions that had refrained from striking during the war engaged in several major job actions. For still another, during the summer of 1919, several race riots occurred, reflecting apprehension over the emergence of a "New Negro." To make matters worse, the first two years of the 1920s saw a continuance of the economic recession, making people wonder when they would return to their normal way of life. By 1923, as if by divine intervention, prosperity was back, and for the next six years, the United States would enjoy the strongest economy in its history.

Of all the indicators of economic prosperity in post-war America, the amazing growth of the automobile industry stood out most conspicuously, turning the postwar era, as many people say, into the automobile age. It is true that the early development of the motor vehicle had been almost entirely the work of Europeans. But once Americans entered the field, they did it with enthusiasm and ingenuity. Henry Ford, for example, revolutionized the industry by introducing his "Model T," an awkward and uncomfortable vehicle, but affordable and practical means of transport. More significantly, Ford's low prices reflected the extraordinary organization of his production. Through simplification of design, standardization of parts, and development of assembly-line techniques, Ford speeded manufacture amazingly. However, Ford's most important discovery was the advantage of making a narrow margin of profit on a large volume of sales rather than a wide margin on a smaller volume.

The second great giant in the automobile industry was the General Motors Corporation, organized in 1908 by William C. Durant. By acquiring control of the separate companies manufacturing the Buick, the Cadillac, and Oldsmobile and several less well-known cars, Durant hoped to dominate the market for automobiles of every type and price range. The founder's Napoleonic policies soon plunged the new company dangerously into debt. New York bankers rescued the overgrown infant in 1910 and ousted Durant from the management. Thereafter, Morgan and Du Pont interests dominated the great corporation. Still, for over a decade, Ford kept well ahead of General Motors. In 1917, he produced nearly four times as many cars as his rival, and it was not until the 1920s that General Motors advanced rapidly.

The significance of Henry Ford's Model T was the car had transformed the automobile from the rich man's toy to the poor man's servant. When the new Ford—Model A—was finally exhibited in showrooms throughout the country in 1927, the event was heralded like the birth of a royal child. Model A sold well, yet Ford's preeminence in the industry was ended. If the Ford was handsome and relatively cheap, so was the Chevrolet, and so also was the Plymouth, introduced into the low-priced field by the Chrysler Corporation in 1929. The Ford, once unique as the company's car, was now only one of several. In 1929, almost 4,800,000 units were produced, and the number of passenger cars registered in the country had climbed from 8,226,000 in 1920 to 23,122,000 in 1929. Since this amounted to one automobile for every six inhabitants of the nation, it would have been possible for the entire population to have taken to the road with no more crowding than was considered normal in many family cars.

Of course, the automobile's contribution to prosperity was not confined to the industry's management and labor. In every city and village of the country, Americans found profit in selling and repairing cars, in lubricating them, and in filling their tanks with gasoline. Thousands were kept busy producing steel, glass, tires, and other products required by automobile manufacturers, and additional thousands were employed in constructing new hard-surface roads. In short, everyone, except the poor, seemed to partake of the joy and fun the automobile provides to human beings.

Clashes of Cultures

As America became increasingly modernized, tensions between rural and urban way of life grew more alarmingly. While many Americans embraced the material comforts industrialization and urbanization had brought to them, some Americans expressed their discontent with the character of modern life in the 1920s. They focused on the importance of

Chapter One
Out of the Past

family and religion in society, as an increasingly urban and secular society came into conflict with older rural tradition. Fundamentalist preachers such as Billy Sunday provided an outlet for many who yearned for a return to a simpler past. Perhaps, the most dramatic demonstration of this yearning was the religious fundamentalist crusade that pitted Biblical texts against the Darwinian theory of biological evolution. In the 1920s, bills to prohibit the teaching of evolution began appearing in Midwestern and Southern state legislatures. The issue came to a head in 1925, when a young high school teacher was prosecuted for violating a Tennessee law that forbade the teaching of evolution in the public schools. The case became a national spectacle, drawing intense news coverage. Urban sophisticates ridiculed fundamentalism, but it continued to be a powerful force in rural, small-town America.

Another example of a powerful clash of cultures—one with far greater national consequences—was Prohibition. In 1919, after almost a century of agitation, the 18th Amendment to the Constitution was enacted, prohibiting the manufacture, sale, or transportation of alcoholic beverages. Indented to eliminate the saloon and the drunkard from American society, Prohibition created thousands of illegal drinking places called "speakeasies," made intoxication fashionable, and created a new form of criminal activity — the transportation of illegal liquor, or "bootlegging." Widely observed in rural America, openly evaded in urban America, Prohibition was an emotional issue in the prosperous Twenties. When the Depression hit, it seemed increasingly irrelevant, and in 1933, the 18th Amendment was repealed.

Fundamentalism and Prohibition were aspects of a larger reaction to a modernist social and intellectual revolution in changing manners and morals that caused the decade to be called the Jazz Age, the Roaring Twenties, or the era of "flaming youth." In many ways, World War I overturned the Victorian social and moral order, and mass prosperity of the 1920s enabled an open and hedonistic life style for the young middle classes. H. L. Mencken, the decade's most important social critic, was unsparing in denouncing sham and venality in American life. Similarly, novelist F. Scott Fitzgerald captured the energy, turmoil and disillusion of the decade in his monumental work—*The Great Gatsby*. Sinclair Lewis, a Nobel Prize winner for literature, satirized mainstream America in such works as *Main Street* and *Babbitt*. In short, in this age of great transformations, social and cultural values often found themselves at odds with each other, with rural and traditional values pitting themselves against urban and modern ones.

The Great Depression

Throughout the twenties, most Americans had maintained their faith in a set of closely-related propositions. They believed that the nation's business leaders constituted a natural elite. In making available to ordinary people such marvels as automobiles, radios, washers, and vacuum cleaners, these men had distributed the benefits of material progress more widely than the most utopian governors could have planned. Seemingly, all of this had served the interests of both consumers and laborers. Wages had risen and working conditions had improved. European experience in providing old-age pensions and unemployment insurance was regarded as irrelevant to America, where individual thrift provided adequate safeguards. With the economic system functioning so well, the best policy for government was to avoid interference and limit its activities to cooperation with the business community.

In October, 1929, however, the booming stock market crashed, wiping out many investors. Although the collapse did not in itself cause the Great Depression, it reflected excessively easy credit policies that had allowed the market to get out of hand. It also aggravated fragile economies in Europe that had relied heavily on American loans. Over the next three years, an initial American recession became part of a worldwide depression, smashing to bits most of those above-mentioned comfortable assumptions. All the wisdom of the business community seemed inadequate to rescue the foundering economy. Factories closed; unemployed workers walked the streets; farmers were unable to pay their interest installment; bank depositors lost their lifetime savings. By November 1932, approximately one of every five American workers was unemployed.

Inevitably, the victims of the Depression looked to the government for help. They demanded relief and temporary jobs; they demanded protection for their savings; they demanded better prices for their crops; they demanded social security; they demanded reform of the business abuses believed to have contributed to the catastrophe. Against the backdrop of all these demands, the presidential campaign of 1932 was chiefly a debate over the possible remedies of the Great Depression.

Chapter One
Out of the Past

President Herbert Hoover had tried harder than any other president before him to deal with economic hard times. He had attempted to organize business, had sped up public works schedules, established the Reconstruction Finance Corporation to support businesses and financial institutions, and had secured from a reluctant Congress an agency to underwrite home mortgages. Nonetheless, his efforts had little impact, and he was a picture of defeat.

His Democratic opponent, Franklin D. Roosevelt, already popular as the governor of New York during the developing crisis, radiated infectious optimism. Prepared to use the federal government's authority for even bolder experimental remedies, he scored a smashing victory—receiving 22,800,000 popular votes to Hoover's 15,700,000. With FDR's victory and his New Deal programs, the United States entered a new era of economic and political change. By fixing upon the government responsibility for providing work and security for the citizens, it greatly enlarged the role of the state. By supporting agricultural prices and limiting agricultural production, it gave the farmers a protected position in the national economy. By encouraging the growth of unionism, it enabled big labor to rise to a point where it could bargain with big business on relatively more equal terms. And by passing the Social Security Act, it created a system of state-administrated welfare payments for the poor, unemployed, and disabled. In short, by doing all this, the New Deal set in motion irreversible trends in American society.

1.7 World War II and Its Impact

WWII and American Participation

Before Roosevelt's second term was well under way, his New Deal was overshadowed by the expansionist designs of totalitarian regimes in Japan, Italy, and Germany. Preoccupied with domestic problems, the American people gave only fractional attention to these antidemocratic developments on other continents. Not until the totalitarian states were guilty of repeated acts of aggression did Americans begin to feel the threat of fascist imperialism. Japan invaded China in 1931 and Italy followed by crushing Ethiopia in 1935. Germany, most dangerous of all, absorbed Austria in 1935 and Czechoslovakia the next year, finally precipitating World War II by attacking Poland in September, 1939. Thereafter,

German conquests followed in sickening succession. Poland, Denmark, Norway, Holland, Belgium, and France all fell to the Nazis before the summer of 1940.

Meanwhile, the United States, disillusioned by the failure of the crusade for democracy in World War I, announced that in no circumstances could any country involved in the conflict look to it for aid. Neutrality legislation, enacted piecemeal from 1935 to 1937, prohibited trade in arms with any warring nations, required cash for all other commodities, and forbade American flag merchant ships from carrying those goods. The objective was to prevent, at almost any cost, the involvement of the United States in a foreign war. Even though Americans favored the victims of Hitler's aggression and supported the Allied democracies, Roosevelt could only wait until public opinion regarding U.S. involvement was altered by events.

When Japanese carrier-based planes executed a devastating surprise attack against the U.S. Pacific Fleet at Pearl Harbor on the morning of December 7, 1941, American opinion was unified overnight by what President Roosevelt called "a day that will live in infamy." On December 8, U.S. Congress declared a state of war with Japan; three days later, Germany and Italy declared war on the United States. Swiftly, the United States geared itself for mobilization of its people and its entire industrial capacity, and equipped with its enormous industrial power and military might, it confidently entered the war by joining the anti-fascist forces in Europe and Asia. Altogether, over 12 million Americans served in the Second World War.

For forty-five months, Americans fought abroad to subdue the Nazi and Japanese aggressors. After military engagements against fascists in North Africa and Italy, American troops joined the dramatic crossing of the English Channel on D-Day in June 1944. The massive invasion forced the Germans to retreat through France to Germany. They finally capitulated in May 1945. In the Pacific, Americans drove the Japanese from one island after another before turning to the just-tested atomic bombs that demolished Hiroshima and Nagasaki in August and ultimately helped spur a Japanese surrender.

Among many important results of the war, the most important one was probably the more direct involvement of the United States in world politics. Before the war came to the end, Roosevelt cautiously laid down the foundations for a new world organization. Striving to avoid Wilson's

Chapter One
Out of the Past

mistakes, Roosevelt carefully selected the American delegation for the conference which was to draft the Charter of the United Nations. By the time that the San Francisco Conference actually convened in April, 1945, Roosevelt was already dead. Yet, his work had helped prepare American opinion for participation in the new world organization. When the United States Senate ratified the Charter of the United Nations, America's acceptance of its new position in the world was impressively demonstrated.

The Origins of the Cold War

After the end of WWII, economic chaos rocked Europe and Asia. Factories had been reduced to rubble, agricultural production plummeted, and displaced persons wandered around in search of food and family. How would the devastated economic world be pieced back together? America and the Soviet Union offered very different answers and models. Besides, the collapse of Germany and Japan had also created power vacuums that drew the two major powers into collision as they both sought influence in countries where the Axis had once held sway. Beyond that, the political turmoil that some nations experienced after the war also spurred Soviet-American competition.

More importantly, as empires were disintegrating, the international system became quite unstable. Financial constraints and nationalist uprising forced the European imperial states to set their colonies free. As new nations were born in the Middle East and Asia, America and Russia vied to win these Third World states as friends that might provide military bases, resources, and markets. Equally important, the shrinkage of the globe also ensured conflict. With the advent of the airplane, the world had become more compact. Faster travel brought nations closer and made them more vulnerable to surprise attack from the air. The Americans and the Soviets collided as they strove to establish defensive positions, sometimes far from home.

Driven by different ideologies and different economic and strategic needs in this volatile international climate, the United States and the Soviet Union shelved diplomacy to build their military strength and establish respective defense alliances, dividing the world into two spheres of influence. Indeed, both nations marched into the Cold War with convictions of righteousness that gave the contest an almost religious character. By now, each saw the other as the world's bully—Americans feared "Communist aggression" and Soviets feared "capitalist encirclement." With such suspicions building upon both sides, hostile rhetoric intensified. In 1946, for example, Stalin declared that international peace was impossible "under the present capitalist development of the world economy." Similarly, former British Prime Minister Winston Churchill delivered a dramatic speech in Fulton, Missouri, declaring that "from Stettin in the Baltic to Trieste in the Adriatic, an iron curtain has descended across the Continent." Thus formally began the Cold War.

One of the first Soviet-American clashes came in Poland in 1945, when the Soviets refused to admit conservative Poles from London to the Communist government, as Americans believed they had agreed to do at Yalta. Then, Soviet-American conflicts spread to other Eastern European countries, as Russia established its virtual domination over all these countries. To justify their actions, the Soviets pointed out that the United States was reviving their traditional enemy, Germany. The Soviets also protested that the United States was pursuing a double standard—intervening in the affairs of Eastern Europe but demanding that the Soviet Union stay out of Latin America and Asia. American officials called for free elections in the Soviet sphere, Moscow noted, but not in the U.S. sphere in Latin America, where several military dictatorships ruled. At any rate, with the two superpowers' mistrust escalating and animosity deepening, the Cold War was felt in virtually every corner of the world, manifesting itself sometimes in the form of containment and sometimes in the form of military conflict.

The Postwar Booms

When the postwar era began, many Americans wondered whether it would resemble the most recent postwar epoch, the Roaring Twenties. Most Americans, however, expected a replay of the 1930s. After all, it was the war that had created jobs and prosperity; surely the end of war would bring a slump. But, neither prediction was correct: in 1945, the United States entered one of its longest, steadiest periods of growth and prosperity, the keys to which were increasing production and increasing demand. Between 1945 and 1970, the American economy grew at an average annual rate of 3.5 percent. Despite occasional recessions, the

Chapter One
Out of the Past

gross national product seldom faltered, rising from just under $210 billion in 1946 to almost $1 trillion in 1970.

When the economy produced more, Americans generally brought home bigger paychecks and had more money to spend. Between 1946 and 1950, per capita real income (based on actual purchasing power) rose 6 percent — but that was only the beginning. In the 1950s, it jumped another 15 percent; in the 1960s, the increase was even greater — 32 percent. The result was a noticeable increase in the standard of living. To the vast majority of Americans, such prosperity was a vindication of the American system of free enterprise.

One of the more salient features of the postwar prosperity was the so-called baby boom. In many ways, the baby boom was both a cause and an effect of prosperity. It was natural for the birthrate to soar immediately following a war; what was unusual was that it continued to do so throughout the 1950s. During the 1950s, the annual total exceeded four million, reversing the downward trend in birthrates that had prevailed for 150 years. Births began to decline after 1961, but continued to exceed four million per year through 1964, the largest by far in America's birth history. For builders, manufacturers, and school systems, the baby boom meant business. Following the baby boom, demands for housing, schools, and automobiles all went up, and much of all this took place in suburbs, stimulating the process of suburbanization in the U.S.

While the postwar economic boom resulted mainly from construction and automobile industries, military spending equally contributed to the unprecedented economic prosperity. When the Defense Department was established in 1947, America was spending just over $10 billion a year on defense. By 1953, it was more than $50 billion; in 1970, it exceeded $80 billion. Defense spending helped stimulate rapid advances in the electronics industry. The NIAC computer, completed at the University of Pennsylvania in 1946, and the introduction of the transistor in the 1950s accelerated the computer revolution. The silicon microchip in the 1960s inaugurated even more stunning advances in electronics, facilitating the shift from heavy manufacturing to high-tech industries in fiber optics, lasers, video equipment, robotics, and genetic engineering.

Of course, the defining characteristic of the postwar affluence was a vast increase in the size of the middle classes. In describing the postwar class structure, sociologists often compare it to a diamond instead of a pyramid, with the bulge of the diamond representing the 60 percent of the population that had joined the middle classes. More impressively, a large increase in college enrollment accompanied the growth of middle-class households, with college education accessible to young people from average American families. As the 1950s ended, nearly four million young people were enrolled at more than 2,000 colleges and universities across the land. Most individual members of this large college population sought the conventional goals of family, career, and a home in the suburbs, shunning intellectual adventure and radicalism of any kind. Living and growing up in the era of prosperity, these young men and women became what observers called the "silent generation."

The Advent of Television

Americans not only fashioned an affluent society at mid-century, they also evolved a flourishing popular culture in the form of television. Americans, especially young Americans, were vigorously participating in the 1950s popular culture: they watched hours of television daily, in addition to going to movies and listening to popular music. The most remarkable aspect of television was how quickly it became a mass medium. Regularly scheduled telecast began in the United States in 1947. As late as 1948, fewer than two million households owned a television set. That year, most people watched television in bars and taverns, or perhaps stood in front of a department store window, gazing in wonderment at the new electronic marvel that broadcast pictorial imagery. But within five years, half of America's households had a television set, and by 1960, 90 percent of homes had at least one black-and-white set. No new household technology had ever spread so wide or so fast, nor acquired such a tight hold on the entire culture. By the mid-1950s, studies revealed that the average American spent more time watching than he or she spent in school or on the job.

Prime-time evening television viewing became the social focus of family life during the 1950s. It displaced listening to the radio, playing records, attending movies, reading magazines and books, playing cards and board games, and conversation. A comedian joked that after-dinner conversation in the typical television-saturated American household of the 1950s consisted of two phrases: "What's on the tube tonight?" and "Good night." 1950s' television programming relied on standard formats or genres. In addition to variety shows, popular TV genres included

Chapter One
Out of the Past

thirty-minute situation comedies (sitcoms), dramatic series, musicals, and Westerns. In the late 1950s, Westerns became the most popular television genre. At one time, there were thirty-nine Westerns on each week.

In addition to the programs produced in studios such as sitcoms, television covered many live events during the 1950s. Sporting events quickly became a staple of live television: professional wrestling, auto races, boxing, and roller derby were early favorites. Football, baseball, and basketball, all of which had been covered extensively on radio, also received television coverage. Besides, during the television's early years, many hours were devoted to live coverage of public affairs and news features. For instance, United Nations sessions and major political parties' presidential nomination conventions both received extensive live coverage. Finally, serious scandals of the late 1950s also were heavily covered by the major networks.

Television programming during the 1950s generally reinforced official values and established hierarchies of power, wealth, and status. Popular programs such as *Father Knows Best* portrayed the warm inner life of a typical, middle-class, white suburban family. It celebrated togetherness and the domestic destinies of women, functioning basically as a conservative cultural instrument. Indeed, it never challenged the powers of elite class, nor their official views. Racial minorities hardly appeared on television; when they did, they were cast in traditional servile roles and depicted as demeaning stereotypes. More significantly, as a commercial instrument or an advertising conduit, television quickly became the vital center of the consumer culture, teaching Americans about the latest styles of consumerism and creating desires to purchase the vast array of goods and services consisting of consume civilization.

1.8 Decades of Change: 1960—1980

The Civil Rights Movement

By 1960, the United States was on the verge of a major social change. While the society was still dominated primarily by old-stock, white males, groups that previously had been submerged began more forcefully and successfully to assert themselves. Among them, African

Americans played a most instrumental role.

The struggle of African Americans for equality reached its peak in the mid-1960s, becoming more committed to non-violent direct action than ever. Groups like the Southern Christian Leadership Conference, made up of African American clergy, and the Student Nonviolent Coordinating Committee, composed of younger activists, sought reform through peaceful confrontation. In 1960, African American college students sat down at a segregated Woolworth's lunch counter in North Carolina and refused to leave. Their sit-in captured media attention and led to similar demonstrations throughout the South. The next year, civil rights workers organized "freedom rides," in which African Americans and whites boarded buses heading south toward segregated terminals, where confrontations might capture media attention and lead to change.

They also organized rallies, the largest of which was the March on Washington in 1963. More than 200,000 people gathered in the nation's capital to demonstrate their commitment to equality for all. The high point of the rally came with the "I Have a Dream" speech given by Martin Luther King, Jr., in which King proclaimed that one day the sons of former slave and the sons of former slave owners will be able to sit down together at the table of brotherhood. King's passionate oratory marked the apogee of the civil rights struggle.

Immediately following the rally, King and other civil rights leaders met with President Kennedy, who was initially reluctant to press white Southerners for support on civil rights because he needed their votes on other issues. Events, driven by African Americans themselves, forced his hand, but before he could take any serious action, Kennedy was assassinated. President Lyndon Johnson, who succeeded him, was more successful, persuading Congress to enact the most comprehensive civil rights bill in American history. The Civil Rights Bill of 1964, for example, guaranteed equal access to all public accommodations such as restaurants, bars, hotels, resorts, and theaters. Additionally, the bill also strengthened federal machinery for combating discrimination in hiring and promotions, requiring corporations and trade unions to ensure equal employment to all applicants.

More importantly, the Voting Rights Act of 1965 authorized the federal government to register voters in districts where historic patterns of disfranchisement prevailed. Empowered by the new law, federal officials registered hundreds of thousands of African American and Hispanic voters in six Southern states during the next three years. The 1966 election was the first one held in the country in which most adult Southern African Americans could vote. By 1968, a million Blacks were registered in the deep South, and in the same year, Congress passed legislation banning discrimination in housing.

The Women's Movement

The social and cultural ground was being prepared during the 1950s for a rebirth of feminism. By 1960, it had become the norm for middle-class white married women to perform paid work outside of the home. By 1962, married women accounted for nearly two-thirds of the female workforce, but in 1963 the average working women earned only 63 percent of what a man made. Usually, they took mostly "women's jobs," such as nursing, clerical work, teaching, and domestic service, jobs that paid less than men's and offered few prospects for promotion. Traditional assumptions about the proper societal roles for men and women remained deeply ingrained and were continuously reinforced by all of the mass-circulation women's magazines, all of which were controlled by men.

Because women did not share a common social experience as men, they tended to view their problems as being individual rather than socially derived. It was left to the founder of the modern women's movement, Betty Friedan, author of the best-selling *The Feminine Mystique* to show middle class suburban housewives that what they had previously understood to be their individual problems were in fact women's problems. They were caused not by personal inadequacies but by deep-rooted attitudes that would have to be changed before women could achieve equality and fulfillment. Friedan, giving eloquent voice to the discontent of middle-class women, called the suburban, split-level home "a comfortable concentration camp." In particular, she called attention to the "problem which has no name": feelings of emptiness, of being incomplete, of wondering, "Who am I?"

Friedan's timely book defined and created the modern women's movement, encouraging women to seek new roles and responsibilities and to find their own personal and professional identities, rather than have them defined by a male-dominated society. However, in so doing, Friedan's focus on white middle-class suburban housewives obscured other women's realities during the 1950s and early 1960s. Millions of working and middle-class women, of various ethno-racial backgrounds, worked outside the home, often struggling to improve working conditions. They were active in civic reform movements, trade unions, peace movements, and civil rights struggle.

It was the civil rights struggle of the early 1960s that catalyzed a sense of grievance among women. Also, the civil rights movement provided a model for political activity. Women made connections between black demands for freedom, equality, and dignity and their won lives. They saw possibilities for acting for themselves and of mobilizing for group political action. Thus, drawing inspiration from the black struggle for civil rights, 28 professional women established the National Organization for Women (NOW) "to take action to bring American women into full participation in the mainstream of American society now." Other groups soon mobilized, and the women rights movement was reborn.

Basically, these women's organizations were political pressure groups that sought to mobilize public opinion and obtain litigation on behalf of their cause. In other words, they sought change from within the existing. In part, the new feminism was a species of liberal reform, calling for equal pay for equal work, and demanding that women have equal access to all professional schools and occupations. Gradually, there evolved a radical feminism out of the experiences of young women in the 1960s radical student movement. They defined the problem as "sexism," or "male chauvinism," and based on that diagnosis, they called for "women's liberation," demanding that women have control over their own bodies. Together, the liberal and radical feminists fought for empowerment of women in political, social and economic life, bringing more and more women into the feminist movement.

The Counterculture

The agitation for equal opportunities by Blacks and women sparked other forms of upheaval. Young people in particular rejected the stable patterns of middle-class life their parents had created in the decades after WWI. Some plunged into radical political activity, but many more young people who felt alienated and frustrated by the affluent liberal society of the 1960s fled from it rather than radically confronted it. Those who embraced new standards of lifestyles were called "hippies."

Chapter One
Out of the Past

    These hippies took a path previously traveled by Bohemians during the 1920s and the Beats during the 1950s. In fact, the best of the Beat poets, Allen Ginsberg, was a prominent member of the 1960s' counterculture. The hippies embraced a new youth culture that ran counter to much that was cherished by middle-class Americans—affluence, economic growth, and high technology. The discipline of parents, schools, and jobs was abandoned for a free-lowing existence expressed by the hippie motto: "Do your own thing."

    In "doing their own thing," hippies displayed many visible signs. They grew long hair and donned jeans, tank tops, and sandals. These refugees from the "upright, straight" world of parents, schools, and nine-to-five jobs flocked to havens in San Francisco and New York City's East Village. They joined communes that cropped up in both urban neighborhoods and rural retreats. The appeal of the commune movement lay in a romantic urge to return to the land: to adopt a simpler life, to regain physical and mental health, and perhaps to seek spiritual renewal.

    The counterculture repudiated science, systematic knowledge, and rationalism. It embraced a notion of organic, mystical consciousness in which the Self merged seamlessly with Community and Nature. Infinite "being" supplanted the linear boundaries of time and space, and feeling and intuition replaced thought and knowing. Nature was valued as being superior to society and technology, and for that reason, a wide array of synthetic consumer products was rejected as artificial—"plastic." Hippies prized being natural, using nature's products, and eating natural foods. In essence, hippie ideal was personal authenticity: to live a life free of conflict, exploration, and alienation; a life in harmony with nature, and one's true self.

    Equally important, hippies also repudiated the restrictive sexual practices of "Puritan" America. Although sexual behavior in the U.S. had become more liberal, hippies moved far beyond middle-class proprieties and inhibitions. The freer sexuality of the hippie lifestyle became one of its main attractions and also provoked the wrath of elders. Casual sex was often tied to countercultural music, as flocks of teenage "groupies" sought out rock musicians. English groups, especially the Beatles and Rolling Stones, expressed the central themes and ideals of the hippie world view. Bob Dylan was the main American countercultural bard. He composed and sang "The Times They Are A-Changing" and "Blowin' in the Wind," signaling exactly what hippies were trying to do in the 1960s. In many ways, drug, sex, and rock and roll music formed the vital center of the counterculture.

The counterculture lasted for about a decade, then it simply evaporated, quickly becoming only an exotic memory. Although short-lived and engaging only a fraction of young people during the 1960s, it left its marks in history. It, for instance, heightened consciousness of social suppression, called attention to the negative ecological and human consequences of technology, and forced people to confront the disparities between their professed ideals and the lives they lived. But the most enduring impact of the counterculture came in lifestyle realms—in diet, dress, decorative art, music, and sexual practices. People became more concerned with developing their inner selves, more interested in achieving their human potential than seeking the external trappings of success.

The Era of the Yuppie

Social activism did not disappear in the aftermath of the 1960s, but it diminished in intensity and shifted in focus. The heightened environmental consciousness of the early 1970s remained central as Americans expressed rising concern about air and water pollution and the peril to endangered species. However, millions of young people turned from public to private concerns in these years, prompting social critics to call this generation the "Me" generation, and this decade the "Me" decade.

The sour political climate and constricted economy of the 1970s did not inspire the kind of civic idealism that John Kennedy and Martin Luther King, Jr., had once aroused. Rather, in turning inward, most people began to embrace individualism, which easily translated into a self-centered materialism. Under such circumstances, the "campus radical" of the 1960s gave way to a new social stereotype, the "yuppie" (young urban professional), who were preoccupied with physical fitness, psychic harmony, and a consumption-oriented lifestyle. Reversing the middle-class flight from the city, many yuppies purchased run-down inner-city apartments of town houses and expensively restored them. This process, known as gentrification, often had the effect of pushing out poorer residents, including countless elderly citizens.

During the "Me" decade, physical well-being became a middle-class obsession—sometimes to good effect. Yuppies jogged and exercised with

Chapter One
Out of the Past

sweaty assiduousness. A vogue for "natural" food free of pesticide residues and chemical additives spread, and the rate of cigarette smoking declined as medical evidence linked the habit to lung cancer, heart diseases, and other maladies. Transcendental meditation and other "consciousness-raising" techniques won devoted followers in the 1970s. Literally, millions of Americans joined the consciousness revolution to seek salvation in narcissistic self-absorption, stripping away the artificial elements of personality in order to find the Real Me. Meanwhile, tens of thousands of Americans sought refuge from the stresses of secular society by joining religious cults, embracing any religious practice that seemingly provided spiritual rebirth.

A revolution in consumer electronics shaped the era as well. The TV set remained the living-room icon. Average daily viewing time in American households stood around six to six and a half in the 1970s. At the same time, the rise of cable television gave birth to a variety of new channels offering everything from business reports to rock music. Additionally, the introduction of the videocassette recorder (VCR) enabled Americans to tape TV shows for later viewing or rent movies in cassette. Instead of going out to the cinema, many families spent Saturday night at home with the VCR. More significantly, this was the era of the personal computer. A product of WWII, the computer moved into the home in the late 1970s when two young Californians developed a small-scale model. In 1977, the Apple II computer hit the market, and sales reached $118 million by 1980.

By the late 1980s, the self-absorbed materialism of the preceding two decades seemed finally in retreat, but it remained influential. In a 1987 survey of college freshmen, 76 percent identified "being very well off financially" as a top goal—nearly double the percentage that had embraced this objective in 1970. Only 39 percent ranked "developing a meaningful philosophy of life" as particularly important.

1.9 America at the Turn of the Century

The Evangelical Renaissance

A striking aspect of post-1970 American society was the high visibility of religion. In a time of unsettling or tumultuous social change, many Americans sought the assurance of a belief system that would give meaning to life and provide ethical guidance. Historically, religious faith has always loomed large in America, but after 1970 it played a more decisive cultural and political role than it had for years. Of all the religious sects, the rapid growth of evangelical Protestant denominations such as the two-million-member Assemblies of God church and the fourteen-million-strong Southern Baptist Convention, was most impressive. Though these groups differed among themselves, all believed in the Bible's verbatim truth, in "born-again" religious experience, and in an early life governed by personal piety and strict morality.

Evangelical Christians had pursued social reform before the Civil War, and many 20th-century evangelicals, particularly those of conservative type, also turned to political activity. As a California evangelical minister observed in 1985: "I always thought that churches should stay out of politics. Now it seems almost a sin not to get involved." Jerry Falwell's Moral Majority registered an estimated two million new voters in 1980 and 1984. While targeting specific issues such as abortion, pornography, and public-school prayer, evangelicals also embraced a strongly conservative anticommunist view.

Evangelicalism's rejuvenation was fueled by a network of religious bookstores, by radio stations featuring religious programs, and above all, by television evangelists. Along with Falwell's "Old Time Gospel Hour," popular broadcasts included Pat Robertson's "700 Club," Jim Bakker's "Praise and Lord" program, Oral Roberts's telecasts from Oklahoma, and Jimmy Swaggart's from Louisiana. Many of these shows aired on Robertson's CBN (Christian Broadcasting Network), the nation's fourth-largest cable network. With their endless pleas for money, the televangelists repelled many Americans, but millions of others found their spiritual message attractive and reassuring.

Born-again Christians frequently attacked what they called "secular humanism," the world view that held all truths to be relative, all moral values to be situational, and all ethical judgments to be necessarily tentative. They supported the "right to life" movement, denounced Roe v. Wade (an abortion case), and condemned abortion as murder. They opposed most feminist demands and the Equal Rights Amendment. They declared war on pornography and insisted that homosexuality was "unnatural" and sinful. Reversely, evangelical Christians sought to reintroduce school prayer and to have "creation science" taught in public

Chapter One
Out of the Past

schools as an alternative to the theory of evolution. Indeed, Falwell's Moral Majority activists even developed a "hit list" of liberal Senators and Congressmen. During the elections, they mailed out more than one billion pieces of campaign literature to selected voters gleaned from their computerized lists.

The "electronic church" suffered severe jolts after 1987. Jim Bakker resigned after acknowledging a sexual encounter with a church secretary and subsequent payoffs to buy her silence. The fiercely moralistic Jim Swaggart fell from grace when his repeated trysts with prostitutes became known. But the TV preachers' tribulations could not obscure the growing influence of evangelical religion. Confronting change on all sides, evangelicals found certitude in their faith. In the process, they profoundly influenced American life in the late twentieth century.

Culture Wars

With the rise of conservative forces in the 1980s, debate erupted in the public arena, as hitherto marginalized groups demanded cultural as well as political equality, pitting conservatism against multiculturalism. Newly empowered advocates for women, African Americans, Hispanic Americans, Asian Americans, and native Americans, gays and lesbians, and fundamentalist religious groups demanded that high schools and colleges revise their curricula. Multiculturalists challenged course reading lists that continued to privilege DWEMs (dead white European males). Literary scholars revised reading lists to include works by women, persons of color, and Third World writers. Historians hastened to rewrite textbooks to include previously neglected or excluded groups. Some professors and teachers expressed dismay at working in repressive environment in which newly empowered champions of multiculturalism and "politically correct" speech imposed a new bureaucratic orthodoxy that stifled academic freedom and encouraged an aggressively litigious culture of victimization.

The multicultural reforms provoked a backlash. For many conservatives, multiculturalism replaced Communism as America's most dangerous enemy. They insisted that these efforts at more inclusive scholarship eroded any sense of a shared national identity. Critics insisted that all of that counting by race, ethnicity, gender, sexual preference, age, and religion affiliation could lead to a balkanization of American society, leading to the disuniting of the United States of America. They worried that such a heedless rush to multiculturalism would destroy the basic unity of the most successful pluralistic society in world history.

Another dimension of the culture wars of the 1990s was the controversy over the legal recognition of marriage for same sex couples. In May 1993, the Supreme Court of Hawaii ruled that the law barring marriage between same-sex couples was unconstitutional. Responding to the court's decision, Republican Congressmen, fearing that if any state recognized same-sex marriage, all the states would be forced to recognize these marriages as legal, sponsored federal legislation that would deny recognition of these unions. In 1996, President Clinton signed the Defense of Marriage Act, which defined marriage to be a union of one woman and one man. It also specified that gay couples would be ineligible for spousal benefits. Shortly afterwards, over thirty states, including Hawaii, enacted similar legislation.

A number of voices resisted all efforts to polarize Americans into warring factions and insisted that multiculturalism's many positive contributions could be retained, while rejecting its extremist claims. In this view, the cultures carried by ethnically and racially defined communities could be appreciated without expecting individuals to define themselves narrowly as members of the descent-based community into which they were born. David Hollinger, one of America's most eminent historians, distinguished sharply between biology and culture, complaining that multiculturalists too often assumed that a person's values and tastes flowed from skin color or facial shape. In a brilliant and timely book, *Postethnic America: Beyond Multiculturalism*, Hollinger offered his cosmopolitan and inclusive vision of a dynamic, pluralistic society in the U.S., embracing all people of whatever descent: "Postethnicity prefers voluntary to prescribed affiliations, appreciate multiple identities, pushes for communities of wide scope, recognizes the constructed character of ethno-racial groups, and accepts the formation of new groups as part of the normal life of a democratic community." When that happens, according to him, America will have no more culture wars.

Ending the Cold War

While the culture wars were going on in the United States, the Cold War was coming to an end. As George H. W. Bush entered the White House in the late 1980s, his presidency witnessed some dramatic

Chapter One
Out of the Past

developments occurring in international affairs that brought about the most fundamental changes in American foreign policy since WWII. The most important of these developments was the decline of the Soviet Union, as evidenced by the disintegration of the Soviet empire in eastern Europe and then the collapse of the Soviet Union itself. The Cold War, which had been the dominant reality of international life for nearly a half century, suddenly ended.

It is impossible to know exactly what role President Ronald Reagan's hard-line policy played in the Soviet Union's downfall. Conservative spokesmen were quick to say that the rapid American military buildup in the 1980s, especially Reagan's commitment to the Strategic Defense Initiative, along with the Reagan Doctrine, brought about the demise of the Soviet Union. To many Sovietologists, it appeared that the Soviet Union imploded, meaning a kind of internal collapse happened as a result of Gorbachev's bumbling efforts to reform his country, which led to consequences that could not be foreseen by himself.

The sudden demise of the Soviet Union caught official Washington by surprise. No one appears to have seen the collapse coming, nor did any intelligence agencies have the slightest inkling that the Soviet system was on the verge of collapse until it disintegrated. At first, few Americans grasped the magnitude of the transformation overtaking the Soviet Union and the full implications for the world order they had known all their lives. As events were unfolding in Russia, Americans watched with a mixture of approval, fascination, and apprehension. Many people believe that the collapse of the Soviet empire was heralded by the fall of the Berlin Wall on November 9, 1989. Since disputes over Germany between the Soviets and Americans were the major causes of the Cold War that originated during the mid-1940s, it was historically appropriate that the reunion of Germany signaled the beginning of the end of the long conflict.

Anyway, the death of the Soviet Union was officially proclaimed on December 21, 1991, by Boris Yeltsin who announced the formation of a new federation of sovereign states. On December 26, major European powers and the United States officially recognized the Russian republic under Yeltsin's leadership as the de factor successor to the defunct Soviet Union. After the liquidation of the Soviet Union, the United States and the new Russian Federation agreed to phase out all multiple-warhead missiles over a ten-year period. The disposal of nuclear materials and the ever-present concerns of nuclear proliferation now superseded the threat of nuclear conflict between the two countries. However, while Russia's nuclear power is second only to the United States, the latter is indisputably the only superpower left after the demise of the Soviet Union.

The War on Terrorism

On the morning of September 11, 2001, at 8:45 A. M. local time, American Airlines Flight 11, a Boeing 767, ripped into the North Tower of the World Trade Center. Twenty minutes later, United Airlines Flight 175, also a Boeing 767, slammed into the South Tower. Ninety minutes later, both of the 110-story structures had collapsed into gigantic mounds of burning rubble. Located at the southern end of Manhattan, the twin towers of the World Trade Center, the financial and commercial nerve center of the global economy, had been potent symbols of America's wealth and power, and of its dominant role in international financial relations. All who saw the televised image of the second plane crashing into the tower must have felt as if they were witnessing an unimaginable horror, a nightmare from which there could be no awakening.

What made the horror worse on that dreadful day, and for many days afterward, was the fear that more attacks were imminent. How many other planes might have been turned into flying bombs? What other weapons of mass destruction would terrorists unleash on vulnerable Americans—chemical, biological, even crude nuclear weapons? Searching for historical parallels, media pundits were quick to compare the terrorist attacks with Pearl Harbor attack. But the attacks at Pearl Harbor had been carried out by Japanese Naval aviators, who attacked only U. S. military targets and personnel. The terrorist attacks of September 11 were carried out by members of a shadowy, decentralized terrorist network that represented no nation or state. If anything, the terrorists justified their attacks by espousing an extremist religious ideology that was premised on hatred of the United States foreign policy, its culture, and its people.

Probably, the 9/11 attacks were best understood as the most recent and by far the most destructive terrorist assaults on the United States. After quickly forging an alliance, the United States launched a retaliatory war against the Taliban and the al-Qaeda terrorist networks within Afghanistan, and most Americans responded positively to what many of them regarded as the defining moment of 20th-century America. Soon, a surge of old-fashioned patriotism swept across the nation. American flags

Chapter One
Out of the Past

were proudly flown from porches and vehicles. Red, white, and blue quickly became the colors of choice for patriots from eight to eighty. Tens of thousands sports fans stood in stadiums to sing the "Spangled Banner" and "America the Beautiful" with renewed pride and spirit. Strangers hugged, cried together, and vowed to respond in whatever ways they could to meet the challenges posed by the horrible events of 9/11.

Preoccupied with war on terrorism, and determined to establish an American-dominated world order, President Bush on August 21, 2002 stated publicly that the United States was considering "regime change" in Iraq. Despite protests by many countries, the U. S.-led military offensive to oust the regime of Saddam Hussein got underway on the evening of March 19, 2003, and on April 14, being vastly outnumbered, Saddam was finished and Iraq fell into the hands of U. S.-led coalition's forces. While celebrating their quick victory, American occupying troops had to face the daunting tasks of reconstruction and fighting back insurgent attacks. Furthermore, they have to rebuild a country filled with angry people, who resent the occupiers of their country who had killed thousands of their countrymen, caused serious damage to the Iraqi infrastructure, battered an economy already weakened by years of U. S. sanctions, and brought anarchic conditions in which neither life nor property is secure.

Meanwhile, public protest against the Iraq War keeps growing both in the United States and around the world, and the U. S. government is under increasing pressure to withdraw its troops from Iraq.

Meanwhile, while still embroiled in Iraqi and Afghanistan wars, America in 2008 also found itself in deep trouble on the home front. Triggered by the sub-prime loan crisis, American economy quickly tumbled, causing many financial institutions and business giants to collapse almost overnight. In the face of such a once-in-a-century economic crisis, President Barack Obama proposed a stimulus package worth of billions of dollars of taxpayers' money to curb the runaway free fall and restore the failing economy. At the same time, the new President has also decided to shift the focus of war on terrorism from Iraq to Afghanistan by reducing American troops in the former and increasing military forces in the latter. Whether President Obama can fight and win on both fronts — economic recovery at home and victory over terrorism abroad—remains to be seen. However, what is certain is that because of the current economic crisis and the two wars in Iraq and Afghanistan,

America as a world leader has been greatly weakened, both in terms of its economic power and in terms of its international credibility.

SUMMARY

(1) Before the arrival of Europeans in North American, Native Americans had lived on the continent for hundreds of thousands of years, whose life was closely tied to the land. To the Indians, humanity was only one link in the great chain of living nature, but the land-hungry Europeans believed that God had given humanity domination over nature, hence, the clashes of two civilizations.

(2) During the period of "salutary neglect," colonists developed a strong sense of self-government, which helped stiffen their resistance to the tax policies imposed upon them by the British Parliament. After the founding of the new Republic, America experienced a surge of nationalism and democracy, as the nation embarked on its century-old journey of westward movement.

(3) Due largely to the two diametrically opposed systems, one free-labor system and the other slavery, the Civil War broke out between the North and the South in the mid-19th century. With the slave system finally abolished, American capitalism was able to take off with greater energy and at a faster speed, eventually turning the country into an industrialized and urbanized society.

(4) Although an economic empire of enormous power by the late 19th century, America remained largely noninterventionist until its involvement in the two world wars in the first half of the 20th century. From then on, America has never stopped its effort to seek global leadership and domination in world affairs in virtually every area, political, military, economic, scientific, financial, and cultural.

(5) Post-war America enjoyed unprecedented economic prosperity, entering an era of "affluent society." However, in this post-industrial society, the gap between the rich and the poor, the tension between whites and the colored, and discrimination on the basis of gender, age, and sexual orientation still remained alarmingly serious, all of which eventually led to a series of social movements of the 1960s and 1970s.

ESSAY QUESTIONS

(1) In creating a new nation, the Founding Fathers were determined to establish a political system different from that of most European

Chapter One
Out of the Past

countries at the time, such as monarchy or autocracy. Instead, they wanted to build a republican democracy. Discuss the three different definitions of republicanism that the Founding Fathers were informed of in the making of the U. S. Constitution.

(2) The Civil War destroyed the peculiar institution of slavery. However, by any account, freed blacks in the South were not able to enjoy economic, political or social freedom. Indeed, it was not until the mid-20th century that the blacks gradually, and in some cases only partially, won all these rights. Explain the causes of blacks' persistent suffering in the second half of 19th-century South.

(3) America is often said to be a nation of expansion, its westward movement being the most illustrative case in point. While territorial expansion can increase the size of a country, it can also help shape the culture of a nation. It is generally believed that American national character was forged, at least partially, by the process of westward movement. Discuss the significance of frontier in the growth of American culture.

(4) In the process of great transformations from agricultural to industrial society at the turn of the 20th century, America was plagued by a cluster of problems, such as industrial monopoly, urban slums, unethical practices in business and environmental pollution. In the face of all these problems, many social reform movements sprang up to address them. Pick up one social reform movement and discuss its impact.

(5) Automobiles have played an important role not only in American economy, but also in American way of life. Ever since the invention of the car, Americans have centered their business, family, and recreational activities around it. Examine and explain how average Americans' life has been shaped by the automobile culture, paying particular attention to people's daily life and habits.

American Society and Culture
美 国 社 会 文 化

Chapter Two
The American Identity

American Society and Culture
美国社会文化

LEARNING OBJECTIVES

- Distinguish Anglo-Americans from other white ethnic Americans
- Understand the hard struggle of African Americans to win their freedom and equal rights
- Know the reasons for the rapid growth of Latinos' population in the U.S.
- Be aware of the discrimination Chinese Americans have encountered and are still encountering in the U.S.
- Learn the tragic experiences of Native Americans after the arrival of Europeans

The United States has been called "a nation of immigrants." There are two good reasons for this. First, the country was settled, built, and developed by generations of immigrants and their children. Secondly, even today America continues to take in more immigrants than any other country in the world. It is not surprising, therefore, that the United States is counted among the most heterogeneous societies in the world. Many different cultural traditions, ethnic customs, national origins, racial groups, and religious affiliations combine to make up "the new men, called Americans."

2.1 The Anglo-Saxons

The term "Anglo-Saxons" is a bit of a misnomer. It derives from northern Germanic tribes—the Saxons and Angles—that invaded England in the 5th and 6th centuries, displacing other tribes whose lives had already been disrupted by the invasions of the Celts from continental

Chapter Two
The American Identity

Europe and later the Romans. Other invaders followed, such as the Normans from France; and as a result, a considerable amount of mingling among continental and English cultures ensued. Thus, the English settlers who came to America were themselves a product of a long history of conquest and blending of ethnic subpopulations. And not only were Scots and Welsh (the remnants of the old Celts) part of the early "English" settlements, but in some areas significant numbers of Germans and Scandinavians were to follow, blending together with these "English Americans" to form the cultural core of America.

The term "Anglo-Saxon" (or one of its variants, "WASP"—White Anglo Saxon Protestant) denotes a northern European cultural and institutional complex of ethnic traditions fused with, and dominated by, the English who were the first to settle North America in large numbers and to begin the process of colonization. We use the terms "Anglo Saxon" and "WASP," therefore, to denote an ethnic complex consisting of northern European ethnic stock with light "white" skin; Protestant religious beliefs; Protestant-inspired values based on individualism, hard work, self-denial, deferment of gratification, and secular material success; and English cultural traditions (language, laws, and beliefs) and institutional structures (politics, economics, and education).

Although the early colonizers were predominantly English, there were significant numbers of Welsh and Scots. At first, the Welsh maintained their own communities, and even language traditions, but by the late 1600s, they were assimilated into the English core. Scots constituted a much larger population, coming from both the Highlands and Lowlands as well as from Ireland, where many Scots had earlier migrated. Like the Welsh, they were almost fully assimilated into English culture by the end of the 17th century. A few Irish also lived in the early settlement communities, but the flood of Irish immigrants was to come much later.

Germans constituted the largest of the non-British Isle segment of early colonists, with almost all coming from the Protestant north. Later, German immigrants were Catholics and Jews, but the early Germans were close to the English in terms of culture and institutional practices. Thus, it was not difficult for these Germans to change in ways compatible with English culture, although some distinctive German traditions remained in isolated communities. Other northern Europeans, such as Scandinavians, were not as prominent as Germans; their peak period of immigration was not to come until the late 19th century. Continental Europeans, such as the Dutch and French (who were settling in large numbers in Canada), also immigrated, but again, they did not come to the early colonies en masse.

Thus, by the close of the 18th century in the aftermath of the Revolutionary War and in the early phrases of the emergence of the United States as a nation, 60.1 percent of the free, nonslave population was English, 14.0 percent Scotch and Scot-Irish, 8.6 percent German, 3.6 percent Irish, 3.1 percent Dutch, 3.0 percent French or Swedish, and 7.6 percent other ethnic nationalities. Obviously, the English were the largest, and for the first two centuries they would continue to dominate numerically, especially if other ethnic groups from the British Isles were included. This dominant group established the cultural and institutional core of the United States. This core consisted of such cultural elements as the English language, English values and beliefs, and English legal tenets, along with mostly northern European institutional structures in economy, government, education, and religion. The core represented the environment that other ethnic groups would have to adapt to and adopt, or to live with the consequences if they did not.

2.2 White Ethnic Americans

Other than the Anglo Saxons who immigrated to North America from Europe, there were many European whites who joined the waves of immigration that occurred in the 19th and early 20th centuries. These non-Protestant white Europeans entered the United States in great numbers, with the southern Irish coming first in the early 1800s and the Catholic Italians and Poles as well as Jews following in the first two decades of the 20th century. This influx of southern and eastern Europeans not only significantly changed the demographic landscape of the United States, but also posed a threat to the Anglo-Saxon Protestant core, setting in motion the dynamics of discrimination against non-Protestant white Europeans.

The first major wave of Irish immigrants arrived in the 1700s, and the next wave began in the 1830s, owing to several factors such as the potato famine of the 1840s, persistent British persecution of poor Irish, and British encouragement of emigration as a solution to their "Irish

Chapter Two
The American Identity

problem." If the earlier wave of Irish immigrants came in search of more opportunities, many of the second-wave Irish immigrants saw themselves as banished to America by the British, which perhaps accounts for their intense loyalty to their homeland. Presently, Irish Americans constitute approximately 18 percent of the population in the United States, which makes them the third largest ethnic group behind the Germans and English.

In the early decades of the 19th century, some northern Italians began to migrate to South and North America in a steady trickle that continued for the rest of the century. The large-scale immigrants of southern Italians began in the 1860s and peaked in the first decade of the 20th century. In contrast to earlier northern Italians, who tended to be more educated, affluent, and able to enter professions and small business, the southern Italians were more likely to be poor, uneducated, and agrarian peasants. All in all, some 4 million Italian migrants poured into the United States between 1880 and 1920. Soon after entering America, they formed "Little Italys" in various cities, primarily in the Northeast. From these locations, they sought unskilled jobs in public works and similar labor-intensive sectors of the economy.

The first Jewish immigrants to the United States arrived in the 1640s to escape massacres and expulsion from Spain and Portugal. The second group of Jewish immigrants began to enter the United States in the 1840s in an effort to escape widening persecution in Europe. Most of these immigrants came from what is now Germany. The third wave of immigration, beginning in the 1880s and lasting until the 1920s, led to the significant presence of Jews in America. During WWII, some 150,000 Jews were able to enter the United States as political refugees, including Albert Einstein and Herbert Marcuse. Today, more than 6 million Jews live in America, a figure that comes close to 50 percent of the world's Jewish population. Altogether, Jewish Americans represent about 3 percent of the American population.

For a variety of reasons, all the above three white ethnic groups were heavily discriminated against when they arrived in the then WASP-dominated America. The Irish were subject to negative stereotyping largely because of their Catholicism. Also, white Protestants stereotyped the Irish as immoral and unintelligent, and Irish Catholics in particular as wicked, ignorant, and temperamental. Sometimes, stereotypes of the Irish were as vicious as against blacks, portraying them as less than human. Similarly, Italians were believed to be inferior intellectually and morally, with the media and intellectuals depicting Italians as incapable of assimilating into Anglo-Saxon society. More damagingly, Italians were portrayed as people involved with crime and having little integrity, which eventually gave rise to a more persistent "mafia" stereotype of Italians. Finally, biases against Jews had always been very strong in the United States. Although Christ was crucified by the Romans, some people believe that Jews were the culprits. In a Christian society like the United States, this belief undergirds hostility toward Jews. Also, Jews are stereotyped as shrewd, crafty, cheap, money-grubbing, materialistic, and sly. Because of these prejudices, Jews, like the Irish and Italians, experienced a considerable degree of discrimination by the Anglo-Saxons before they overcame it and moved into the mainstream society. Nevertheless, older stereotypes of Jews such as "Christ killers" and "money grubbers" still linger on, lurking below the polite surface of respect and tolerance.

2.3 African Americans

Prior to 2000, when U. S Bureau of the Census reported that Hispanics/Latinos outnumbered Blacks for the first time in American history, African Americans had been considered the largest minority group in the United States. According to the 2008 census, however, black people in 2008 represented about 12.85 percent of the total population in the U.S.A. The sheer number of African Americans in the land is quite significant, for it helps them figure prominently in present-day American political, economic, social, and cultural life.

Imported as slaves, treated as property to be bought and sold, denied citizenship rights, and considered less than human for much of American history, most African Americans have not been able to enjoy the benefits that come with living in the United States. The legacy of two hundred years of slavery, thirty years of post-Civil War oppression, and another century of systematic discrimination in housing, employment, education, and virtually every social sphere persists. Even as many of the old forms of discrimination have been dismantled since the mid-1960s, discrimination remains a central part of the African American experience.

Being black poses a problem in a white world: they stand out, and

Chapter Two
The American Identity

dramatically so. Black and white are perceived as opposite colors, and consequently a black person cannot easily "blend" into a predominantly white America. Skin color is, in the biological sense, a minor genetic trait, but in the sociological sense it is anything but minor. Identifiability makes people easy targets of discrimination. Most members of white ethnic groups look like the dominant population, and most Latinos are not physically identifiable as members of an ethnic group. Black people cannot shed their color, but commingling has occurred since the Africans were pressed into slavery, resulting in generations of individuals with various degrees of dark skin pigmentation. Interethnic marriages have increased somewhat in recent decades, further influencing the color balance of the American population. Yet, skin color, no matter what the permutation, continues to identify some as targets of discrimination.

Historically speaking, African Americans, more than any other ethnic population in the United States, have been the victims of negative beliefs and stereotypes. In the period of slavery, whites viewed Africans as "uncivilized heathens," "bestial," and "sexually aggressive," and as suffering the "curse of God" who made them black. After the Civil War, African Americans were portrayed as inferior because they had not been able to take advantage of the equal opportunities offered by Reconstruction. Even in enlightened circles, blacks were often portrayed as not having progressed as far as whites on the evolutionary scale. In the South, this state was perceived to be one of laziness, criminality, and lustfulness (especially for white women, a belief which conveniently overlooked some slaveholders' lust for black women). In the North, this state was viewed as one of childlike docility and kindness that needed to be channeled by whites. Whether vicious or benign, treatment of African Americans was based on the belief that black people were biologically inferior and must be segregated.

The post-World War II period was a dramatic shift in beliefs about African Americans. A consensus slowly emerged in more progressive circles that segregation was harmful, that blacks were not innately inferior, that the appearance of inferiority reflected cultural deprivation stemming from undesirable environments, and that improvements in schooling, job opportunities and neighborhoods were the key to making life better for African Americans. Over the last three decades, beliefs have continued to change. Many studies document that when blacks and whites have opportunities to interact and associate, prejudicial attitudes decline. But this is at the interpersonal level; at a community level, a different picture emerges. Ironically, negative beliefs about African American tend to increase as their percentage of population in a community rises. In contrast, prejudice does not increase significantly when the proportion of other minorities, such as Latinos, increase in a community. Thus, while Americans have elected a black man to be their president, prejudices and discriminations against them can still be felt, posing an enormous challenge to blacks.

2.4 Latinos/Hispanics

A Spanish language and cultural background is the inexact basis for calling people with ethnic origins in the Caribbean, Central and South America "Latinos" (or "Hispanics," according to the U.S. Census Bureau). Thus the term does not apply to people from countries in the Americas that have been influenced by other European cultures such as Brazil, Haiti or the Bahamas. Still, while the word Latino or Hispanic does not denote a unified ethnic population, Americans have been using the term to refer to American residents from such countries as Mexico, Puerto Rico, and Cuba—the three major groups in the American Latino population, though in reality it also includes immigrants from Central and South America.

Based on the census records of 1990, there were over 22 million Latinos in the United States, accounting for 9 percent of the population. This figure was undoubtedly underestimated, for a great many Latinos who entered the U.S. illegally were not counted in the federal census. Not surprisingly, when a new census was conducted in 2000, the Latino population went up to 35.3 million, replacing African Americans as the largest minority group in the United States. According to the 2008 population estimate by the U.S. Census Bureau, persons of Hispanic or Latino origin amounted to 15.1 percent of the total population in the U.S.

Like Native Americans, African Americans, and Asian Americans, Latinos have faced racial prejudice and economic discrimination in many areas. The current high number of Latino newcomers, especially illegal immigrants, has led to rising hostility against Latinos. Increasingly, Latinos are seen as a threat to some people, because of their growing numbers relative to the European-Americans. This threat, imagined or

Chapter Two
The American Identity

real, has renewed old prejudicial beliefs about Latinos and legitimated new patterns of discrimination in education, housing, politics, law enforcement, and the job market. In the southwest, for example, border patrols and local police often stop and harass Latinos on the assumption that they might be illegal aliens. Moreover, over twenty states in the United States, have declared English their official language mainly in reaction to the use of Spanish by Latinos.

Overall, Mexican Americans (Chicanos), about 65 percent of the Latino population, lag behind Puerto Ricans and Cuban Americans in educational attainment, income, and occupational status. Chicanos are thus at the bottom of the Latino population, whereas Cubans are at the top and Puerto Ricans somewhere in between. Rank in resource distribution and stratification is the result of intense and institutionalized discrimination against those of Mexican origin, somewhat less severe discrimination against those from Puerto Rico, and more favorable treatment of those early anti-Castro Cuban refugees, with growing discrimination against those who have immigrated recently.

Among Mexican Americans, the retention of the Spanish language, as well as other cultural traits, sustains their identifiability, making them easy targets of discrimination. For Puerto Ricans, who became U. S. citizens through the annexation of Puerto Rico and the Jones Act of 1917, which gave them free access to the mainland, discrimination has taken a somewhat different pattern. Puerto Ricans are visible not only because of their language and culture, but also because a significant portion of the population bears the dark skin of their African origins. As for Cuban Americans, who have been treated as desirable anti-Communist refugees of the Castro government in Cuba rather than as undesirable immigrants, discrimination has been much less intense. However, the more recent waves of poor and often ill-educated Cubans to the mainland have escalated the level of discrimination against Cubans.

Altogether, all Latinos are increasingly seen as a threat because their numbers are increasing relative to the European-American stock. This threat has reinvigorated old prejudicial beliefs against Latinos and legitimated new patterns of discrimination in schools, in the activities of law enforcement agencies, and in the job markets for low-skilled workers. Mexican-origin people suffer the most discrimination because they are the largest, fastest-growing, and hence, the most threatening of the Latino ethnic groups. Recent Cuban refugees still suffer a great deal of discrimination and prejudice within and outside the Cuban community. As for unskilled Puerto Ricans, they have a difficult struggle in the financially burdened cities of the Northeast. Taken as a whole, Latinos may rival African Americans for the dilemma they pose to the Anglo-American dominated society.

2.5 Asian Americans

"Asian American" is a convenient term that lumps together a diverse collection of immigrants and American-born population groups. It includes, for example, "boat people" who came to the United States as refugees after the Vietnam war, the most recent Asian Indians who arrived as professional immigrants, and the descendants of Chinese who were attracted to "the beautiful country" by the "Gold Rush" of the late 1840s. Obviously, the principle of continental origins is used to justify putting in one category peoples with different religions, skin colors, socio-economic backgrounds, and historical experiences.

Comparatively speaking, the Asian American population has been small in the United States, because for centuries an overwhelming majority of America's immigrants had been Europeans. As late as 1965, for example, there were only one million Asians living in the U. S. Thanks to the 1965 immigration law, Asian Americans have soared in numbers—according to the 2000 census, there were altogether over 10 million Asian Americans residing in the United States, representing about 3.6 percent of the population. It is estimated that over the past forty years or so, there have been nearly four times more Asian immigrants than during the entire span of more than a hundred years between the Gold Rush of 1849 and the passing of the new immigration law in 1965. Indeed, among the most recent immigrants, one out of every two now comes from Asia. It is projected that the Asian population could grow to 14 million by 2010, accounting for 5 percent of the nation's total.

The first Asians to arrive in the United States in significant numbers were the Chinese, who initially worked in the gold mines and, later, in building the transcontinental railroad. One-fifth of them settled in Hawaii and the rest on the West Coast, mostly in California. Between 1880 and 1908, a sizable number of Japanese arrived in the U. S. and settled in roughly equal numbers on the West Coast and in Hawaii, where they constituted the largest Asian immigrant group. Small groups of Koreans and East Indians came to the islands and west coast states from 1900 to 1930. During the same period, many Filipinos also immigrated, and about three out of every five first arrived in Hawaii. By and large, immigrants from Asia decreased dramatically in the 1920s, due primarily to a series of highly restrictive immigration laws enacted by the U. S. Congress and targeted at immigrants from Asian countries. Later, in the period after World War II, these laws were liberalized, opening the door to new waves of Asian immigrants.

Praised for their industriousness, heralded for their educational attainments, and lauded for their economic successes, Asian Americans are often viewed as the "model minority." Indeed, most Americans believe that the success of Asian Americans stems from a combination of industriousness and avoidance of discrimination. However, lurking beneath the surface of this portrayal is a revival of the old "yellow peril" stereotype in which Asians are seen by some as foreigners who take jobs, admission slots in higher education, and business opportunities away from non-Asians. For this and many reasons, Asians are still subject to discrimination from other minorities and whites. Indeed, over the past two decades, as the Asian population has increased, subtle forms of discrimination have been evident: Asians, like all minorities, including women, hit a glass ceiling, which keeps their careers in check despite good job performance and other qualifications.

Like other ethnic subpopulations in the United States, Asian Americans are victims of inaccurate perceptions by others. As the number of Asian immigrants to the U. S. increases, the perception, or rather, the misperception that all Asian Americans are foreigners increases their visibility, reinforcing negative beliefs and stereotypes about them. Over the past three decades, stereotypes of Asian Americans have shifted from those stereotypes characterizing them as sneaky, obsequious, or inscrutable to the stereotype of the model minority. According to this stereotype, all Asian Americans are hardworking, intelligent, and successful. Although this stereotype appears to be positive, it can also have negative implications, the most important of which is the perception that Asian Americans do not experience the same social and economic problems of other populations. More significantly, the model minority can easily become the "yellow peril" when Asian Americans are accused of taking jobs from white Americans, African Americans, and Latinos. In short, while anti-Asian sentiment has lessened, it still lingers on in the public mind, often targeting Asian Americans for many of the social ills and economic problems facing the country.

2.6 Native Americans

Long before Christopher Columbus' "discovery" of the American continent, people began to cross the land bridge connecting Alaska with the Asian continent, perhaps as long ago as forty thousand years. They came searching for food, hunting wild game and gathering indigenous plant life, and they settled the entire face of North, Central, and South America. As they settled in distinctive niches, diverse cultures evolved. Some developed cultures and organizational structures as sophisticated as those in other parts of the world. In what was to become the United States, however, the societies and language groups of the native people were comparatively simple. Some were hunters and gatherers, others focused on fishing, a few on herding, and some on horticulture. All constituted viable societies, but upon contact with Europeans, they were to be wholly or partially destroyed.

When Europeans arrived on the American continent, Native Americans soon found themselves the victims of their greed for gold, silver, and other treasures. Horses, steel swords, and primitive muskets gave Europeans a great advantage over the Indian inhabitants. Overwhelmed both in manpower and weaponry, Native Americans, upon their encounter with Europeans, were first driven out of their familiar land and then were either wholly or partially destroyed. In the process, Indians lost not only their land to white invaders but also their peaceful family and community life. Eventually, the overpowered Indians were compelled to move to federally designated area of land, known nowadays as "Indian Reservations." Obviously, the history of Native Americans after European contact, as with most other conquered peoples, is one of conquest and domination.

The biggest loss of the Native Americans after the arrival of Europeans is the sharp decline of their population. The first generally accepted scientific estimate of the 16th-century Native American population was about 1.2 million persons at the time of European contact. A more recent estimate puts the precontact population between 2 and

Chapter Two
The American Identity

5 million, although some still argue that the number was in fact much larger. Between 1600 and 1850, however, the Native American population decreased from around 2.5 million (a conservative estimate) to only 200,000. This decline can be viewed only as genocide, or the virtual elimination of a population. Lack of immunity to European diseases, or what some have called "ecological warfare," displacement from lands and consequent starvation, widespread killing in "war," and cold-blooded murder all account for this sudden drop. Thus, if anything is necessary to prove European cruelty towards and discrimination against Indians, a tenfold drop in the size of the population is as good as any.

Compared with other ethnic populations in the United States, Native Americans have been severely constrained in their interaction with mainstream society. This isolation is the result of the numerous treaties between the U.S. government and the Native American tribes, which marginalized and subordinated them, thereby limiting their opportunities to secure valued resources. In general, however, Native Americans have resisted assimilation, and have preferred to keep themselves separate, with their distinct way of life modified by access to electricity, television, the automobile, and recently, the Internet. It was estimated in 2007 that about 1.2 percent of American population identified themselves as Indian, about half of them living on federal reservations of varying size and prosperity. The rest have integrated with mainstream society. Most of the Indians, however, including some who live on federal reservations, take part in the dominant economy, at various levels. Many live by farming, or by making jewelry and ornaments which they sell to tourists.

U.S. federal and state governments have spent considerable amounts of money to provide Native Americans living on reservations with health, social and educational services, encouraging them to engage in various enterprises. But due to their isolation, Native Americans on the reservations remain outside the mainstream of economic development, and are often unable to make their living standards match that of other Americans. According to the recent statistics released in 2006, overall, Native Americans remain the poorest in the United States. Incomes for Native American homes, for example, remain well below the rest of the nation. Indeed, of all American ethnic groups, Native Americans have the highest unemployment, school dropout, and suicide rates. Many cases of malnutrition and mental illness as well as an exceptionally short life expectancy indicate that much remains to be done to improve the situation for Native Americans. Recently, there have occurred active movements among Native Americans to foster a pan-Indian culture. The call of pan-Indianism engages Native Americans in political and legal protest, and most importantly develops administrative expertise which can, perhaps, enhance the potential wealth of the remaining Native lands.

SUMMARY

(1) The Anglo-Saxons were the earliest settlers in the New World. WASP (White Anglo-Saxon Protestants) is used to denote an ethnic complex consisting of northern European ethnic stock with light "white" skin and Protestant religious beliefs. Culturally speaking, the term includes Protestant-inspired values based on individualism, hard work, self-denial, deferment of gratification and material success.

(2) Other than the Anglo-Saxons, there were many European whites who primarily came from Southern and Eastern Europe. Their presence completely changed the demography of America, making the once WASP-dominated nation increasingly pluralistic and complex. Among the non-Protestant white Europeans, there were a large number of Jews, who, like ethnic whites, were the targets of discrimination.

(3) African Americans were imported to America as slaves, treated as property, denied citizenship rights, and considered less than human for much of their experience in America. More than any other ethnic group, African Americans have been the victims of negative beliefs and stereotypes, suffering from discrimination in virtually every category, ranging from political, economic to social and cultural life.

(4) Of all the ethnic minorities in the United States, Latinos are the fastest-growing group, representing about 15.1 percent of the U.S. population. While the word Latino or Hispanic does not denote a unified ethnic population, Americans have been using the term to refer to American residents from Mexico, Puerto Rico, and Cuba, though in reality it also includes immigrants from Central and South America.

(5) Asian Americans made their early presence in America, particularly during the "Gold Rush" period, but their population did not grow significantly until the mid-20th century, when hundreds of thousands of Asians immigrated to the United States. Praised for their diligence, heralded for their educational attainments, lauded for their economic success, Asian Americans are often viewed as the "model minority."

Chapter Two
The American Identity

ESSAY QUESTIONS

(1) Until recently, WAPS was always believed to have been the mainline culture of the United States, helping shape and define the core values of American people. Describe and analyze the main ideas of WASP as reflected in American cultural and political beliefs, paying special attention to its role in helping promote the development of American capitalism.

(2) Non-Protestant European whites were for a long time the targets of ridicule and discrimination by Protestant whites. Apart from the fact that they basically came from Southern and Eastern Europe, there was also another important factor for their being looked down upon by Protestant whites, i.e., they were largely Catholic. Pick up one white ethnic group and explain how that group was discriminated against in America.

(3) African Americans have experienced tremendous changes over the past half a century. Trace some of the most important developments in their struggle for freedom and equality, paying particular attention to their political ideologies and strategies in fighting against racial segregation and racial discrimination. Note, too, the progress they have made in all of their endeavors.

(4) As an ethnic group with hybrid cultural heritage, Latino Americans have many characteristics of their own in their values, customs, lifestyles, behaviors, and habits. Trace the evolutionary process of this ethnic minority in its cultural development and discuss the salient traits of Latino Americans in the context of their cultural formation, noting, in particular, the diversity that exist among them as a group.

(5) Asian Americans in general, but Chinese Americans in particular, have been subject to various kinds of discrimination in many areas, such as employment, education, residence, banking, and promotion. Examine the most discriminatory acts against Asian Americans by white Americans during the 19th and 20th centuries, and discuss their impact on the first- and second-generation Asian Americans.

American Society and Culture
美 国 社 会 文 化

Chapter Three
Religion in America

American Society and Culture
美 国 社 会 文 化

LEARNING OBJECTIVES

- Understand the importance of religious belief in American life
- Know the principle of separation of church and state and its implications
- Appreciate the pervasive influence of religion in American society
- Be informed of the crucial role civil religion plays in shaping American minds
- Be aware of the intervening power of religious organizations in the policy-making process

It is almost universally acknowledged that the United States is probably the most religious country in the developed countries, not only in terms of the number of religious believers, but also in terms of church attendance. While industrialization, consumerism, materialism, hedonism, and mass culture in other countries have all significantly diminished the importance of religion in their societies, if not completely secularized it, this has not been the case in the United States, as has been attested by the religious revival of the past forty years in America. Such being the case, it can be comfortably argued that religion plays a crucial role in the shaping of American culture.

3.1 Religion in America: A Brief History

The role played by religious thought and practice is of immense importance to a full understanding of American life. In general terms, Western scholars tend to view religion as a "central part of human experience, influencing how we perceive and react to the environment in

Chapter Three
Religion in America

which we live." In specific terms, American theologian Paul Tillich insisted that religion was the soul of culture and culture was the form of religion. While this statement may sound exaggerated, several polls in recent years seem to have borne it out. One survey claimed, for example, that fully 92 percent of Americans said they believe in God. Another poll says that as high as 95 percent of American adults believe in God at various levels of belief. This was up from a 1994 survey result, when 90 percent of Americans said that they were religious. Indeed, in comparison with other Western countries, America is definitely more religious not only in terms of the number of believers in God, but also in terms of church attendance and financial commitment to church organizations. Evidently, with such a high percentage of people being religious, it is only natural for religion to play an important role in American life.

Tracing back to its beginning, one will soon find that religion enjoyed a high profile in American history. To begin with, the Catholic faith was first brought to the North American continent by the Spanish in the 1500s. For the next 300 years, Catholic missionaries and settlers from Spain and then Latin America came to what are now called California and the Southwest. In the 1600s, the European settlers began establishing colonies along the east coast of North America. Although there were some Catholics, the vast majority of these settlers were Protestants. As the nation was formed, it was the Protestant branch of the Christian faith that had the strongest effect on the development of the religious climate in the United States. Then, starting in 1836 and continuing to the Second World War, the great waves of Jewish immigrants made the United States a major centre of Judaism. From then onward, America became increasingly multi-religious, with Protestantism, Catholicism, and Judaism constituting the three most influential religious organizations in America.

Over the past forty years, the religious landscape of America has changed dramatically, transforming the country from a "Christian country" to the world's most religiously diverse nation. However, this change has been so gradual that its dimensions and scope have not been fully appreciated. It began with the "new immigration" spurred by the 1965 Immigration and Naturalization Act, as people from all over the world came to America and have become citizens. With them have come the religious traditions of the world—Islamic, Hindu, Buddhist, Sikh, African, and Afro-Caribbean. The people of these living traditions of faith have moved into American neighborhoods, tentatively at first, their altars and prayer rooms in storefronts and office buildings, basements, garages, and even recreation rooms, nearly invisible to other Americans. In the past two decades, many Americans have come to realize that they are the architectural signs of a new religious America.

Still, in terms of social and cultural influence, the most striking phenomena in contemporary American society is the resurgence of Evangelical Christianity. Mainstream Protestant denominations like the Presbyterians and Methodists have lost ground to a range of Evangelical groups including Fundamentalists and Charismatics. The most controversial and sensational popular representation of evangelicalism has been the recent growth of television preachers who have been able to reach massive new audiences through their exploitation of the electronic media, but despite their undoubted success and the attention which has been paid to them, they are not fully representative of the sheer variety of evangelicalism in practice, particularly at a grass-roots level. Evangelicalism, in other words, is a varied form of religious expression, and not all evangelicals are fundamentalists. Whatever the case, throughout the post-war era, there have been several successful evangelical movements which have sought to adapt evangelicalism more effectively to mainstream American life, rather than simply call for the restoration of the old ways.

3.2 "In God We Trust"

Anyone who has seen a U. S. banknote knows that there are four words printed on the greenback, which reads "In God We Trust," suggesting that America is very much a Christian country. As recently as July 2006, NBC television, in response to the efforts of some atheists to remove them, conducted a poll on their morning show, asking viewers if they wanted to keep the words "In God We Trust" on U. S. currency. Eighty-six percent of the respondents voted to keep the phrase, while only 14 percent said to remove it, indicating that the vast majority of Americans still believe that they ought to trust in God, both for themselves as individuals and for the nation as a whole.

Many nations have a creation myth that suggests that the beginnings of that nation were accomplished with the active assistance of the Almighty. In the case of the United States, the birth of the nation is often said to be rooted in the vision of America itself, while the fate of the country has from the very beginning been entwined with notions of

Chapter Three
Religion in America

religious destiny. In terms of vision, America was viewed as a place where good and evil would struggle in a continuing battle for supremacy. It may be that America's divine mission would ensure a victory for light over darkness, but it may also be that God could issue serious warnings about the ever-present threat of hell and eternal damnation. From the very beginning, America was compared to a "city upon a hill," with the eyes of the world upon it. Since America was expected to provide a model for the rest of the world, the Pilgrims—and their later descendants, the Puritans—presented themselves as God's Chosen People, searching for the Promised Land in the wilderness of the New World. In order to attain this goal, they tried to create a community in which life would be guided by God's will and deviations from His will in any shape or form would never be tolerated.

Of course, America did not become "the Kingdom of God," as intended by the Puritans. Indeed, by the end of the 17th century, Puritanism had already begun to lose its energy. More importantly, as America forged ahead in its industrialization drive in the second half of the 19th century, religion in general, but Protestantism in particular, no longer held the dominant influence over the souls of Americans. Still, because of its long-standing, pervasive and penetrating influence on the psyche of the nation, it has bequeathed to American culture a sense of the importance of God's purpose for America. The First Great Awakening of the 18th century, for example, provided the opportunity for a fresh reaffirmation of God's role in directing the fortunes of his chosen people. When the American Revolution broke out, it cut churches loose from government and encouraged rationalism and concepts of individual liberty. However, in the early 19th century, concern over the decline of religious belief soon sparked a fresh wave of religious revival known as the Second Great Awakening, which exerted a profound impact both on the scale of church membership and on the range of American sectarianism. In the 19th century, despite the new Republic's commitment to freedom of religion and the separation of church and state, Americans never stopped talking about the importance of religious values for their national identity. Indeed, not only was the westward movement of the nineteenth century viewed as driven by the hand of God, but the annexation of land from Mexico was seen as fulfilling America's mission as well. While such Protestant world-views gradually weakened as the nation moved into the 20th century, the idea that America had been entrusted with the mission to convert the whole world to evangelical Christianity still remained a significant force in the way many Americans thought about their country and the way they related themselves to the rest of the world.

By the end of World War II, American religion had become much more varied in its make-up. For one thing, a massive influx of fresh Christian and non-Christian beliefs served to dilute the Protestant domination of American religious culture. Catholicism, for instance, made itself a major force in American religious life through the sheer size of the Catholic population. Similarly, Judaism, through its persistent efforts against adversities of all stripes, managed to get itself well established in the major cities of the United States. For another, beginning in the 1960s, Occult and Oriental religions started to spread in the once Christian-dominated land as well, capturing the attention, indeed, winning the souls of the younger generation in particular. With Islam, Buddhism and Zenism co-existing and competing with Protestantism, Catholicism, Judaism and many other religious beliefs for spiritual attachment, American religion, just like the American population, has finally taken on its most remarkable feature, that is, religious diversity and multiformity. Yet, in spite of such multiplicity in religious beliefs, Americans, by and large, still feel that they should be God-fearing either as individuals or as a nation, and faithfully follow the long-held conviction—"In God We Trust."

3.3 Church, State and Politics

Since religion has been part and parcel of American social and cultural life from the very beginning, it has obviously played a significant role in shaping the national character of the United States, particularly with regard to the influence it could exert on American politics. According to the U. S. Constitution, church and state are separate in their roles and functions. The First Amendment of the Bill of Rights (1791) states that "Congress shall make no law respecting the establishment of religion, or prohibiting the free exercise thereof." Interpreted in plainer language, the First Amendment (1) prohibits the establishment of a national church or state-supported religion;(2) protects individuals' rights to practice their own religion and their freedom from others' religions. Religion, in other words, is a private matter, and every individual has the right to choose to

Chapter Three
Religion in America

believe, or choose not to believe.

It should be pointed out, however, that prior to the Independence War, there were officially established churches in the colonies, and Massachusetts in fact had an established church well into the 1830s. But eventually, all churches were separated from state, and all governments separated from church. Such a separation permitted a diversity of religious beliefs and practices, allowing people to choose to pursue or not to pursue any religious doctrine. Because of this separation law, there are neither church taxes nor official religious holidays in the U. S. Similarly, since no established church is supported by the Constitution, no churches receive financial or political support from state, nor is any political party affiliated to any particular denomination. Any congressional act which attempts to impose legislation in these areas will be regarded as violating the principle of separation of church and state. Since the 1960s, the U. S. Supreme Court has also forbidden government from aiding one religion over another, or even from aiding religion over non-religion.

Therefore, religious groups in the U. S. are independent organizationally and self-supporting financially. For their day-to-day operation and payment of expenses, churches depend upon their members' contributions and donations, both of which usually flow in quite readily and generously. As for their own members, churches need to reach out to the people themselves, drawing prospective believers to their religious organization in any way possible, be it religious doctrine or preaching style. As churches operate primarily at a grass-roots level, they can enjoy considerable influence in the community in which they are based. For this reason, the local religious buildings and their congregations are often said to be the real strength and centre of American religion. Apart from the religious services they offer, local churches also provide a great variety of social, cultural, and philanthropic activities, helping to forge a sense of community for the people living in the area.

However, while a wall of separation has been built between church and state, the two of them have often interacted, and sometimes even interfered, with each other. For example, states in the past restricted the free exercise of religious beliefs by prohibiting Catholics and Jews from voting or holding public offices. Additionally, laws have also been made to indirectly interfere with some minority religions that advocate or practice kinds of beliefs deemed against the public interest, such as

Mormons and Seventh-Day Adventists. Although the Supreme Court, on the whole, has stood on the side of freedom of religion by invalidating the above-mentioned restrictions, it has also occasionally restricted adherents' free practice of religion if their behavior is believed to be detrimental to the wellbeing of the public. Arguably, then, the division between church and state is not absolute; nor is the demarcation line between them easily identifiable.

Given the blurred line between church and state, and given the pervasive influence of religion in American life, it comes as no surprise that religion should influence American public and political life one way or the other. Anyone who cares to follow public debate in the United States will soon find that many of the hotly contested issues in America often have religious dimensions to them. Abortion, gay marriage, school prayer, family values and the death penalty, for example, have all pitted one religiously-based group against another. For many Americans, these issues are not merely social or political issues; they are also closely related to their religious beliefs and convictions. Therefore, their stance on them is heavily influenced by the spiritual values they hold. Fully aware of the existence of such enormous forces among their followers, church leaders of every stripe in the U. S. never hesitate to campaign on social, moral, cultural, and political issues to influence and even shape public policy on the government agenda.

More significantly, religious influence can even be felt in American national symbols and emblems, like the seal of the U. S., the currency, and in the pledge of allegiance to the American flag. Any newly elected U. S. President puts his hand on the Bible when he swears the oath of office in the inaugural ceremony. Similarly, any session of U. S. Congress commences with prayers, with chaplains sitting in both houses of Congress. Most symbolically, on most of the important occasions when Americans gather together—on national holidays, at political conventions, and especially at sports events, Americans mix patriotism with religious ideas in songs and sometime in prayers that ask for God's blessing on America. Such formal religious symbols are manifestations of the prevalent and strong influence religion holds in American life. This being the case, it is no wonder that religion should enjoy widespread popularity in the United States.

3.4 Popular Religion

Mostly, when defining religion, people tend to emphasize religions as structured social systems, institutions, or organizations. This aspect of religion can be called institutional religion, such as the Roman Catholic Church and the United Methodist Church. However, there is another aspect of religion in the United States that is at least equally significant. This is popular religion—religion that occurs outside the formal boundaries of religious institutions. The existence of widespread and flourishing popular religion in the United States indicates that what counts religion is not the sole prerogative of academics.

Most people in the United States belong to some sort of religious community—they are Protestants within particular denominations, Catholics, Jews, or Buddhists, for example. Many, however, supplement their formal membership and participation with a variety of other religious activities that do not come directly from their community of faith—revivals, watching religious television, listening to religious radio programs, and various devotional activities like private prayer and reading, chanting and meditation. These examples of "popular religion" are all present in the common culture in which most Americans participate, and are familiar enough by hearsay if not by direct experience. They are popular in two principal senses. For one thing, they have "mass appeal," i.e., they "sell." For another, they are not taught by theologians in seminaries, but rather offered to a wide variety of people of no special theological sophistication.

Theoretically speaking, popular religion is very difficult to describe, for there is no one agreed-upon definition of it. Nonetheless, there are still enough common features of it to make it distinctive. For instance, popular religion is the religious beliefs and practices of ordinary people rather than of theologians and religious leaders. Also, it exists alongside institutional religion as a complement to it. It is a supplement to participation in formal religion for some people and a substitute for it for others. More importantly, it offers people more direct access to the sacred than they have through the mediation of formal religious groups. Formal religious organizations impose order and structure on religion. Popular religion, by contrast, is distinguished by a lively sense of the supernatural without the imposition of formal structure. Finally, it draws on the core religious institutions of the culture (in the U. S., primarily Christianity) but blends this with other sources and traditions.

In the commercially oriented culture of the United States, the strength of popular religion is shown in part by how well it sells. Christian retail is a three-billion-dollar-plus industry. Some people place statues of Jesus, Mary, Saint Francis, or the Buddha in their yards, or cross symbols on their cars or trucks. Also, religiously oriented T shirts can be seen everywhere in the street or other public places. More frequently, there is religious music in any format people like. The musicals "Jesus Christ, Superstar" and "Godspell" continue to attract audiences. Beyond all this, gift items such as religiously oriented figurines, decorative items, and greeting cards sell well in religious book and supply stores and in secular stores as well. Most amazing of all, there are religious-theme computer games and educational software to help children learn about the Bible.

Although most popular religion in the United States is Christian, it is not exclusively Christian. A number of catalogs offer a variety of items for people devising their own spirituality. One such catalog has an umbrella that features the eight major symbols of Buddhism, as well as items reflecting Native American religions. In another catalog, those of Jewish faith can choose from a vast assortment of Jewish religious items such as prayer shawls, menorahs, and Passover plates. Several sources exist for Buddhists to obtain statues, meditation cushions and benches, and audiotapes or videotapes. *Hinduism Today*, a magazine for North American Hindus, routinely advertises Hindu religious articles such as deity statues, beads, and incense. Indeed, just as American religion becomes increasingly diversified, so will American popular religion become more and more pervasive and influential. Perhaps, the most notable development in popular religion at the beginning of the 21st century is the rapidly expanding presence of religion on the Internet, where ordinary people conduct "cyber-rituals" and discuss religious matters at chat rooms, making religion more informal, more accessible, and hence more popular.

3.5 *Civil Religion and Beyond*

The idea of civil religion was brought to scholarly attention and ultimately

Chapter Three
Religion in America

the American popular mind by sociologist Robert Bellah in a 1967 essay, in which he argued that, "there actually exist alongside of and rather clearly differentiated from the churches an elaborate and well-institutionalized civil religion in America... This public religious dimension is expressed in a set of beliefs, symbols, and rituals" that he called the American civil religion. As a way of illustration, Bellah cited founding documents such as the Declaration of Independence and the Constitution as well as the inaugural speeches of several presidents, along with holiday observances. Also, he included belief in God, belief in America's role in God's plan for the world, commonly accepted standards of morality and civic virtue, and routinely observed holidays among the verities of civil religion.

Bellah's essay gave religious studies scholars a new way of analyzing the roles that religion plays in the public life of the United States. It moved the study of religion beyond the study of ecclesiastical institutions and laid the groundwork for recognition of the importance of popular religion. It also provided great insight into the ways in which civic ideals and the legitimating principles of a culture are expressed powerfully in symbols that link them to divine realities. However, changes in how Americans view the culture of the United States in recent years have made Bellah's assertion that there is a common set of religious and civic convictions that underlies American life increasingly problematic. Critics point out that under the present situation the sense of national consensus that is required by Bellah's civil religion thesis flies in the face of observed reality. Instead of a single civil religion harmoniously uniting all Americans, they argue, an alternative hypothesis rooted in the pervasive sense of cultural conflict that characterizes much of America's past seems far more persuasive.

Rather than a single voice, the vision of what the United States is and ought to be has become a chorus of many voices, each vying for a hearing. Any attempt to describe a single American voice inevitably seems sectarian and exclusive. Increasing cultural pluralism has made the broadly liberal Protestant outlines of Bellah's civil religion misleading when they are used to describe an agreed-upon set of civic standards and virtues. It seems necessary now to focus on the variety of religions and cultures that are present in the United States, rather than looking for a unity that many have come to doubt. Presently, there are at least two different versions of civil religion, one more conservative and the other more liberal. Civil religion conservatives continue to understand the United States as God's chosen nation and the American political and economic order as the one most aligned with the will of God. Its advocates seek an active role for the government in promoting public and private virtue through the promotion of religion, such as school prayer. They also seek to enact laws to limit the availability of legal abortions and ban gay marriage. On foreign policy issues, they are most likely to call for U.S. military involvement to protect American interests from governments and leaders deemed "ungodly."

By contrast, civil religion liberals take the opposite approach on all these points. The privileged position of the United States in the world is understood as a call to greater responsibility and service than merely a confirmation of God's unique favor. The political and economic system of the United States is described as one among many, each with strengths and weaknesses, and none identified with the will of God. Believing that the particularities of religion can lead to disruption in the public order, liberal civil religionists want to keep them separate. Valuing diversity above conformity to a single standard, they promote individual civil liberties and call on the government to enact policies that enhance them. If they advocate military intervention, they usually try to advance American overseas interests in the name of justice and human rights, rather than in the name of the forces of good against the forces of evil.

SUMMARY

(1) Religion in the United States has a long history, dating all the way back to the early time when the Continent was settled by the Puritans from England. Ever since then, the United States has been regarded as the most religious country in the Christian world, both in terms of the number of religious organizations and in terms of the number of religious believers.

(2) Driven by their passion for religious belief and deep commitment to their self-imposed religious mission, early American settlers wanted to "build a city upon a hill" in the land of wilderness. While successful in planting the seeds of Christianity in the soil of the New World, the early settlers failed to convert the land into the "Kingdom of God," as America became increasingly multi-religious and secularized.

(3) At the very beginning, there were established churches in many colonies in early America, but after the founding of the United States, a provision was made in the Constitution that prohibits the establishment of

religion, formulating the principle of separation of church and state. Thanks to this provision, along with the principle of religious freedom, Americans have successfully built a wall between church and state.

(4) Apart from formal religion, there is popular religion which occurs outside the formal boundaries of religious organizations. The existence of widespread and flourishing popular religion in America indicates that what counts religion is not the sole prerogative of academics. In other words, popular religion is the religious beliefs and practices of ordinary people rather than of theologians and religious leaders.

(5) In America, there is also something called civil religion, which is expressed in a set of beliefs, symbols, and rituals. All of these can be found in such documents as the Declaration of Independence, the U. S. Constitution, presidential inaugural speeches, holiday observances as well as belief in God, belief in America's role in God's plan for the world and commonly accepted standards of morality and civic virtues.

ESSAY QUESTIONS

(1) Religion has played a significant role in shaping the Christian culture, American culture in particular. So influential it is that some scholars claim that religion is the content of culture and culture is the form of religion. Discuss the relationship between religion and culture in the United States, noting in particular the core Christian values as expressed in American culture.

(2) John Winthrop said that the mission of the Puritan settlers in Massachusetts was to "build a city upon a hill," meaning that the Puritans had the responsibility not only to save themselves, but also to set a good example for the rest of the world. Trace the source of this missionary concept and explain how the descendents of the Puritans tried to fulfill this mission both in the United States and around the world.

(3) The principle of separation of church and state derived partly from Protestants' persecution in Europe and partly from their experience in the New World. According to this principle, neither of the two institutions can intervene in the business of the other, thereby guaranteeing the independence of each. Discuss the importance of this principle in promoting religious freedom and diversity in the United States.

(4) Popular religion is popular in two principal senses. For one

thing, it has mass appeal; for another, it is not taught by theologians, but rather offered to a wide variety of people of no special theological sophistication. Analyze the ways popular religion exerts its influence from these two perspectives to explain the pervasiveness or persuasiveness of religion in American society.

(5) As a concept, civil religion provides a new way to analyze and understand the role that religion plays in American public life, offering insights into the ways in which civic ideals and the legitimating principles of a culture are expressed in symbols that link them to divine realities. Discuss the ways civil religion helps forge and indeed cement national consensus among Americans.

American Society and Culture
美 国 社 会 文 化

Chapter Four
American Beliefs

American Society and Culture
美 国 社 会 文 化

LEARNING OBJECTIVES

- Understand the fundamental beliefs of American people
- Distinguish the nuanced differences between American-born beliefs and immigrant beliefs
- Know the core beliefs that grew out of the frontier experience
- Learn the close links between religious and moral beliefs
- Appreciate the ways political and social beliefs relate and interact to each other

Culture, in many ways, is a set of beliefs expressed in behavior. Viewed in this light, culture is not something consciously learned; but rather it is acquired by successive generations of a people through imitating the behaviors of their elders that express certain beliefs. Defined in this way, culture can be regarded as the possession of a whole people, whose set of simple beliefs learned and validated through behavior for many generations constitutes Culture. In any society, such a culture can satisfy an ineradicable human need for a shared sense of right behavior and make it possible for human beings to live together. Once a culture has formed, it tends to persist because it meets a deeply human need. It is generally believed that every culture is the best culture to those who participate in it.

4.1 *Primary Beliefs of American Culture*

The primary American cultural beliefs derive from the initial experience of European settlers in early North America. They all relate to work, the first necessity for survival in a wilderness. It was the peculiar

Chapter Four
American Beliefs

experiences of work—what kind was done, who did it, how much it was rewarded—that began the process of distinguishing American behavior from European behavior, which led during the next eight generations to the formation of a new American culture.

Generally speaking, Americans' primary beliefs include three work-related beliefs: **Everyone must work; people must benefit from their work; and manual work is respectable.** These three beliefs began to be enculturated from the beginning of colonial settlement in America, because, firstly, in order to grow enough food to make the colonies viable, everyone had to work, including gentlemen; and, secondly, in order to motivate the colonists to work to their utmost, their labor had to benefit themselves and their loved ones in a real way; and finally since the vast majority of workers in early America were engaged in agriculture, manual work of all kinds assumed a cultural respectability.

Unlike conditions in England, small farms worked by their owners were the prevailing mode of life in America. The big landholdings that a few families acquired in Virginia or New York were exceptions to that rule. Whatever the variation in size, the small landholder constituted the major group in early America. After all, during much of early America, the opportunities to acquire land or set up a shop put "the achievement of independence within the grasp of most able-bodied, active, and enterprising free men." This being the case, not only everyone had to work for himself and his family, but everyone expected to benefit from his labor as well. More importantly, in America, the performance of physical labor made no difference in one's class standing because people of all classes, even the highest, worked with their hands, fabricating and repairing things, plowing, cultivating crops, and helping to bring in the harvest. In short, in America manual labor carried no stigma of belong to an inferior class.

Indeed, America was from the beginning, and remains to this day, a society of workers, most of whom may be said to begin life with little more than a willingness to work and an ambition to be at least self-supporting. Sooner or later, they usually earn enough wherewithal to put them in comfortable circumstances and in many cases to allow them to bequeath to their children something of value. In exempting no social class from work, in rewarding common workers to the limit of their diligence, and in making little distinction between the worth of mental and physical work, the experience of Americans began to be differentiated from that of Europe. Because of the beliefs about work that developed in American culture, a plumber in twentieth-century America may make more money than a university professor and be just as truly a member of the middle class.

The cultural beliefs that made manual work respectable, that provided workers an unusual level of benefit from their work, and that required every class of society to work, unleashed in America a focused human energy that operated with a rapidity and on a scale seldom, if ever, witnessed in human history. From two barely viable settlements in a wilderness in the first two decades of the 1600s, America had become by the first two decades of the 1900s one of the biggest, wealthiest, and most powerful nations; and is now, it is fair to say, the world's richest nation.

4.2 Immigrant Beliefs

The United States, as we know, is a nation of immigrants. More than 55 million immigrants have arrived in America in the last four centuries. This represents the largest movement of human beings to any one place in the history of humankind. And although restrictions on immigration to the United States were in place for most of the 20th century, a huge volume of migration to America never discontinued. Since historically most Americans have been either immigrants themselves or descendants of immigrants, the belief-behaviors of immigrants have had a fundamental and determining influence on the formation of American culture.

Of the beliefs immigrants to America have, three beliefs stand out most prominently. They are **improvement is possible; opportunities must be imagined; and freedom of movement is needed for success**. Regardless of their "racial" and national origins, the immigrants who have come to America during the four centuries of its history have shared the conviction that going to America would improve their lives. This conviction, *Improvement Is Possible*, is what made them potential immigrants, whatever the country of their birth. Acting on that conviction made them immigrants, and indeed, it made them Americans before they ever laid their eyes on the United States of America.

In the cultures the immigrants left behind, not everyone believed in improvement through emigration. Only a portion of those who were

Chapter Four
American Beliefs

dissatisfied with their lives in Europe acted on that dissatisfaction by leaving their homelands for America. That willingness to act on the possibility of a radical improvement in their own lives was a fundamental outlook they shared regardless of their "race" or nationality, the language they spoke, or the religion they practiced. Closely tied to their willingness to act on the possibility of improvement was their ability to "see" a better future in their mind's eye, to imagine opportunities.

In moving to the place where they hoped those imagined opportunities would be realized, they showed a conviction that freedom of movement was necessary to success. After their arrival in America, they continued to act on the belief that had compelled them to cross the ocean to a new continent: **Improvement is possible; opportunities must be imagined; freedom of movement is needed for success.** When they set foot on American soil, these beliefs gave them a nucleus of conviction with other Americans, whose immigrant ancestors had passed down to them these same beliefs through the example of their own behavior.

Because the immigrants believed they could better their lives, and because of their commitment to the pursuit of an imagined, future happiness, they were determined to succeed in America, expecting their move to America to result eventually in success. To fail meant a retreat to their native land in defeat. Such a retreat would have been an admission that their decision to emigrate had been a fool's dream. If they finally gave up all hope of success for themselves, they fell back on the hope that their offspring would succeed where they had failed, and thus justify their decision to emigrate to America.

Throughout American history, the convictions of immigrants about improvement, opportunity, and movement have periodically been refreshed by new waves of immigrants. More importantly, the behavior of the self-selected immigrants after their arrival in America has been a model for offspring to imitate in enculturating belief in improvement, opportunity, and freedom of movement. When one finds a society made up mostly of persons having such beliefs, and the descendants of such persons, one has the making of a new culture.

4.3 Frontier Beliefs

The United States, it is often said, has been a nation of expansion from the very beginning. As the nation passed from the Independence War period to continental expansion and conquest, it was clear that the ideas and doctrines of the East Coast no longer described the actual experiences of the American people in the West. As they created farms, towns and territories, the people of the West were also creating new heroes, new values, new literature, and a new culture. For instance, such American beliefs and values as **each person should rely upon himself, responsible for his own well-being; helping others helps yourself; and progress requires organization** all derived from the experiences of westward movement during the settlement of the wilderness.

Seemingly, the above-mentioned three beliefs are contradictory to each other, for how can the independence of individuals be reconciled with a fondness for forming organizations? Or how can helping others be consistent with self-reliance? In fact, the seeming contradiction in these related beliefs of American culture is more an appearance than a reality. Life in the wilderness of central North America and in the rural communities and small towns into which the wilderness was transformed required behaviors that may appear contradictory but were in fact complementary ways of accomplishing what Americans refer to as "getting ahead." "Getting ahead" has applied, and still applies, to an individual's improvement of his life; but it likewise applies to social advancement, to the development of a new civilization where before 1600 there had been only wilderness. In America, both self-reliance and cooperative social behavior were needed because the progress of individuals and the progress of society were mutually beneficial, indeed synonymous.

During the formative period of American culture, to improve one's lot in life—and at times just to survive—demanded learning by doing and forming organizations that would not only benefit the lives of individuals directly but also strengthen communities, and in that way indirectly benefit individuals. What benefited the individual in America was a measure of what benefited society; what benefited society was a measure of what benefited individuals, because improvements to the moral, economic, and political order increased the chance for self-improvement. In the wilderness, individuals in a settlement had to behave responsibly toward one another and contribute voluntarily to the general welfare of their community in order to make self-improvement and a viable community possible.

For three centuries, once the frontier of crude domestication of wild land had passed westward, land development and other forms of progress continued in the recently civilized new settlements. The advance of the frontier and subsequent improvements to post-frontier society depended on every person being responsible for his won well-being as he worked cooperatively with others to improve the economic, political, and religious institutions necessary to both society and individual lives. After all, progress that did not benefit both society and individual lives was not real progress. This identification of the good of society with the good of individuals—which in America was not a philosophical proposition but a daily reality—lay at the heart of the frontier experience and America's remarkably rapid progress from a condition of wilderness to the world's fourth-largest nation in size and the world's largest national economy.

To civilize the wilderness required every member of American society to show initiative and self-reliance. Society had no responsibility for assuring the happiness or well-being of any of its members. That could be achieved only by each member of society taking responsibility for his/her own well-being and by lending a helping hand on occasion to those in need. The exciting reality of American life was that everyone was making something of his own life and contributing to the making of a new civilization. It was that way at the beginning of colonial settlement; it is that way still. America continues to be a work in progress. After four centuries of American history, Americans still believe as a people that each person should try to "get ahead" and that American society should also be improved. The engine for getting ahead remains the willingness of individual Americans to assume responsibility for their own well-being and for helping others when self-reliance becomes, at least for a time, impossible for them.

4.4 *Religious and Moral Beliefs*

Of all the western countries in the Christian world, the United States is probably the most religious nation in the world, both in terms of the number of religious believers and in terms of the scope of religious diversity. Apparently, since religion has such deep roots in American culture, and since religion has played such an influential role in shaping American values, it has naturally found expression in the American belief system, both religiously and morally. Specifically speaking, American religious and moral beliefs include the following: **God created nature and**

human beings; God created a law of right and wrong; doing what is right is necessary for happiness; America is a chosen country; and God gave men the same birthrights.

The belief God created nature and human beings is the main cultural belief of the American people about religion. Apparently, the "big bang" theory of 20th-century science—that the earth and human beings evolved following a unique explosion of matter into a universe—has not appreciably weakened the belief among Americans in God the Creator. Multiyear polls of Americans about prayer and the Bible demonstrate that more than four of five Americans, including 71 percent of college graduates, believe the Bible is "the actual word of God to be taken literally word for word" (34 percent) or "the inspired word of God, but not everything in it can be taken literally" (46 percent). Living as they did amidst the awesome natural forces and dangers of a wilderness, Americans, through their activities as tillers of the soil and fellers of trees, gained an awareness of nature that strengthened their belief in God the Creator, who, in creating nature, had spread before them a richly endowed continent whose harvests they could gather with their labor.

As a people, Americans have also believed that **God created a law of right and wrong.** The belief in a God-created law of right and wrong for human beings incorporated the Ten Commandments, which in the spread of Christianity throughout Europe had become the moral foundation of European civilization and which were brought to the Americas to become the moral basis of new civilizations on these continents. But the moral law inherent in God's creation that Americans came to believe in was revealed in the nature of things as well in scripture. Rather than commanding resistance to specific temptations, such as worshiping false gods, committing adultery, bearing false witness, or envying the possessions of another person, this law posited that there is a right and a wrong in doing anything, whether physical or moral, and that the rightness or wrongness of an action will be revealed in its results. This belief that the Creator had revealed to humankind a law of right and wrong in the nature of things is illustrated in the writings of American statesmen, writers, clergymen, and scholars.

Since **God created a law of right and wrong**, it follows that only by doing what is right and never doing anything that is wrong can one achieve some kind of happiness, hence the belief **doing what is right is necessary for happiness.** Culturally speaking, this belief is closely linked to the Great

Chapter Four
American Beliefs

Awakening of the 1730s and 1740s, which made religion primarily a matter of personal conviction and moral conduct: an effort to please God and gain peace of mind through obedience to his moral law by "doing good to Man." While good works may not guarantee happiness or salvation, being "born again" in the spirit does require an effort to reform one's bad conduct. The spiritual revival of the early 18th century, and other revivals that have periodically appeared since, have given vitality to the religious beliefs of Americans, reinforcing the importance of conduct toward others, and further stressing the emotion of a personal commitment to Christ. In other words, since conduct is a sign of love for and thanks to God, and since true believers are all exhorted to experience the sanctifying power of Christ as their personal savior, it comes as no surprise that Americans tend to regard doing things right as necessary steps toward happiness.

Perhaps, the longest- and most tenaciously-held religious belief among Americans is their conviction that **America is a chosen country**. A Scottish historian, after a life-time living in the U. S., once observed, "deep in the American mind is a belief that his is God's Country." The United States of America is God's country in the sense that Americans for many generations have felt that their nation has been especially blessed by God, that it could never have been established and endured so successfully without God's favor and protection. The belief is also true in the sense that, as a people, Americans have believed that God has wanted to use America as part of a divine plan for the redemption of humankind as a whole—by the creation of a new nation modeled on new principles of behavior. America is also a "chosen country" in the sense that those who created it were mostly those who chose to emigrate to it and their descendants. In all three of these ways—as a country especially blessed and sanctioned by God, as a country used by God to communicate to humankind a new way of life, and as a country chosen by millions of self-selected immigrants as their preferred residence—Americans believe, whether realistically or imaginarily, **America is a chosen country**. Indeed, in creating and widely distributing unprecedented wealth, and in achieving astonishing social unity in a population of such diverse origins, the United States has seemed to generations of Americans to have God's favor and approval.

Finally, since America is a chosen country, and since God's grace is there for all true believers, Americans have all along held the belief that **God gave men** the same birthrights. One of the most distinctively American religious beliefs, "the same birthrights" argument first found expression in the Declaration of Independence: "All men are created equal" and "endowed by their Creator with certain unalienable rights." In other words, as explained later by Jefferson, "the mass of mankind has not been born with saddles on their backs, not a favored few booted and spurred, ready to ride them legitimately, by the grace of God." Although the belief initially applied only to free men, not to free women or the slaves in the American population, that fact does not diminish the culturally revolutionary development it represented. It made the consent of the governed the basis of government in the United States, demanding that government should respect those birthrights, as opposed to the right to govern of a particular class. The cultural belief of Americans that **God gave men the same birthrights** has remained unchanged since the Declaration of Independence, except that it no longer applies only to free white men of age, but rather to women and colored people alike.

4.5 Social Beliefs

Like any other society in the world, American society has also developed a set of social beliefs over the course of its social evolution. Unlike most of their European counterparts, however, Americans tend to attach far greater importance to such notions as individual success, equality of opportunity, measurable achievement, and meritocracy. Out of these notions, Americans have gradually enculturated the following social beliefs: **society is a collection of self-determining individuals; everyone is expected to succeed; success is largely measured by the amount of money or property accumulated; and finally, achievement determines a person's social rank.**

In these social beliefs of American culture, emphasis on **self-determining individuals** is probably most important and therefore stands out most saliently. As we all know, Americans are most rights-minded people, and their concept of an individual self is rooted in a philosophical tradition, which basically asserts that the biological individual is the basic unit of nature, and social systems derive from the interactions of individuals who exist prior to the social order and who are acting in their self interest. Equally important, American emphasis on self-determining individuals has its origin in the absence of feudal and aristocratic classes in

Chapter Four
American Beliefs

early America, which means that rather than relying upon family background or class privileges, individuals in America have to strike out on their own, making decisions and taking responsibility for anything they do for themselves. Only in this way, Americans believe, can they fully enjoy their rights as individuals.

As a corollary to this emphasis on individualism, most Americans are under enormous pressure to achieve success in their lifetime. While America never had anything remotely resembling a legally privileged aristocracy, it does not mean that America was or has always been a "classless" society. For a long time, the great difference between American and traditional European societies lay in how membership in the upper, middle, and lower classes was determined. If in Europe an aristocracy was supported by feudal laws, in America it was wealth rather than family or tradition that was the primary determinant of social stratification. In other words, American society has never had the kind of classes fixed by birth that one finds in Europe and other areas. Such being the case, particularly class standing being highly mobile, everyone is presumably capable of changing his/her class status, and the way to reach that goal is to blaze the path to success by him/herself. Under such circumstance, it is understandable why in America **everyone is expected to succeed**.

What needs to be pointed out is that in the American cultural context **success is largely measured by the amount of property or money accumulated**. In a society where honesty and diligent work form the best avenue to money and property, the distinction money-making and respectable citizenship is often blurred. To many Americans, property is the chief outward sign of honesty and rectitude in one's dealings with others, as well as an indication of having done something useful in his life. Accordingly, those who made greatest contribution to material improvement—a compelling requirement in a society originating in a wilderness—are respected as the most successful persons, provided that their success has been honestly achieved. Indeed, money-making and property ownership have been seen by most Americans as a means to independence and comfort. Beyond that, money and property have also been necessary to self-respect in a society in which the way to wealth is open to the great majority of persons, though men and women have been respected for reasons other than the amount of their possessions.

The almost universal interest of Americans in having things and making money reflects the need of Americans to establish themselves on their own, without reliance on their birth for social position. In American society, success requires a reputation for honest dealings and being active in doing something to improve one's life and the lives of others. Those who made greatest achievements in the form of wealth are often respected as the most deserving of higher social standing. In other words, in America **achievement determines a person's social rank**, rather than family ties or birth. The early age at which American youths leave their families to fend for themselves and the absence of support from extended families both reflect Americans' historically intense interest in making money to attain independence and self-respect. The fact that class standing is relatively mobile, and the fact that movement between classes, both up and down, is quite commonplace, have convinced many Americans that if they keep trying, they, too, can launch themselves into a social orbit higher than that of their parents. Since birth or inheritance guarantees little for anyone, individual Americans have to determine for themselves, through their own efforts, whether they will rise to a higher class, fall in social rank, or remain in the social class into which they were born.

4.6 Political Beliefs

Abraham Lincoln once said that the United States was conceived in liberty and that its government is of the people, by the people, and for the people. By that characterization of the country and government, Lincoln, in many ways, summarizes the essence of American political beliefs, that is, **the people are sovereign; the government is best when it governs least; a written constitution is essential to government**; and finally, **a majority decides.**

The belief that **the people are sovereign** took roots in America as early as the 1700s, when the sovereignty of "We the People" replaced the European belief in the sovereignty of persons of "noble" birth. In this spirit, elected representatives of the thirteen American states declared the independence of the United States "in the Name of, and by Authority of the good People of these Colonies." No other people in history had ever used this method to establish a national government. Later, the U. S. Constitution also declared the people's rights as the sovereign power, which the government was forbidden to infringe. As the servant and

Chapter Four
American Beliefs

instrument of the people, the government is limited in power, and the people as the originating source of governmental power are not limited, except as they agree to be, under law. George Washington put it best when he said to the American people in his farewell address: "The basis of our political systems is the right of the people to make and to alter their constitutions of government." Alexis Tocqueville also recognized the effects of the American belief—the people are sovereign—during his tour of the United States in 1831—1832: "The people reign in the American political world as the Deity does in the Universe." By all this, they essentially refer to the fact that the American people, by electing their own representatives, can constitute their own government and thus enjoy, in theory at least, sovereignty.

Being self-determining and self-governing, the American people are very jealous of their rights, lest their rights should be infringed upon, or taken away. Like any sovereign power, they preferred the least possible governmental restrictions. Accordingly, they have granted limited powers to those they elect to office but are not limited in their own power except by their consent. Indeed, they remain the ultimate human authority over the government they have created. Thus, from the belief that the people are sovereign comes the corollary belief that **the government is best when it governs least/the least possible government is best**. Nowhere is it more evident than in the sequence of the two national constitutions that were proposed by the elected representatives of the people for ratification, the Articles of Confederation of and the Constitution of the United States, both of which granted only limited powers to the national government. And as part of the American belief, **the government is best when it governs least**, the limited powers allotted the legislative, executive, and judicial branches of the federal government are kept separated and are balanced against one another so that each branch will keep an eye on the other two branches and restrain their actions, thus ensuring that no part of the national government becomes too powerful.

Another distinctly American belief is **a written constitution is essential to government**. As is known to all, England has never had such a single written warrant and plan for national government produced by the elected representatives of the people specifically limiting the government's powers. In America, however, an amendment to the Constitution is not approved by the same body of representatives that writes it, because patently what is written and passed by any body has its approval. Rather,

103

the functions are kept separate. If people are to retain their sovereign right to create new provisions of their nation's constitution, and not to have it altered by those "in power," they themselves must retain the ultimate authority to create constitutional law. The American people apparently developed the belief, **a written constitution is essential to government**, in imitation of the royal charters that established England's colonies on the Atlantic costal plain of North America, specifying how and by whom those colonies were to be governed. By the 18th century, the belief in a constitution as a written agreement for government was enculturated in the political thought and behavior of an overwhelming majority of Americans. This is evidenced by the willingness of Americans to take on the king's military forces if he, or Parliament, claimed a right to change the terms of the colonial charters. In other words, rather than have governmental actions take place at the whim and caprice of an individual or a special interest group, Americans expect rule by law and proper procedure guaranteed by a written constitution.

Whatever beliefs mentioned above, be it popular sovereignty, limited government or a written constitution, their ultimate purpose is the same—to ensure a government of the people, by the people, and for the people. It is exactly based on this purpose that American democracy is founded on the belief in the constituting power, or sovereignty, of people, that is, the belief in **majority rule**. The cultural belief **a majority decides** can be traced back to early American experience, when, given the absence of a class of persons whose right to govern was culturally recognized, representatives of assemblies were elected by majority vote. In other words, circumstances in America were not suitable for a governing class based on "noble" bloodlines, for every man was reduced by the circumstances of daily life to the same footing, and one-man rule, or even rule by a small group of men, was either undesirable or unacceptable. Accordingly, the exercise of governmental authority should be established on some other basis, say the will of the majority. Of course, allowing the voice of a majority to decide political matters does not necessarily make their decision any wiser than the judgment of one well-informed person. But neither is the will of a majority more likely to be in error. American experience seems to suggest that in a wilderness society made up mostly of self-determining individuals, republican government and **majority rule** were the most natural forms for government to take, for they allow the people to ultimately determine what is in their best interests.

Chapter Four
American Beliefs

4.7 Beliefs on Human Nature

From their experience on the Atlantic coastal plain of North America in the 17th and 18th centuries, the cultural ancestors of Americans derived certain fundamental beliefs regarding "human nature," a phrase that occurs frequently in the writings of the American Founding Fathers. Their isolation in a wilderness apart from the rest of the civilization, which forced them to cooperate with one another, and their common goal of improving their lives in America, which bound them together in a joint effort, brought home to them a particularly vivid sense of the ways people resemble one another. Additionally, from the experience of rapidly civilizing a continental space the size of Europe, Americans acquired a strong awareness of a basic interest that cut across individual differences. That experience unified an unusually diverse collection of human beings by giving them a common focus on one monumental task, and in the process enculturated certain beliefs about human nature, among which two stand out most saliently: **almost all human beings want to do what is right, and human beings will abuse power when they have it.**

Compared with Europe, there was too much moving around, too much need for productive workers, too many opportunities to be imagined in America for any group of immigrants to remain permanently apart from the mainstream of American society. Because of the diminished sense of ethnic and class differences among Americans, their manners became simpler and less formal than the manners of Europeans. Indeed, in America there are no strangers for very long. Even today, this propensity of Americans for affable relations with everyone nearby and for instant friendships continues to impress foreign observers as a distinctly American trait. This American characteristic can be explained by the fact that in a society historically constituted by strangers, Americans have had an acute historical need to get along. This has meant forming effective work relationships among groups of individuals thrown together by chance and common goals and needs. From this kind of experience, and the behaviors it involved, a cultural conviction of a common humanity developed among Americans. Generations of Americans afterwards have found that they are essentially not much different from one another, and that a person's individual interests can be best served in cooperation with others. Accordingly, Americans tend to look upon everyone they encounter as having the same basic nature as themselves.

American beliefs about human nature are based on historical experiences that convinced the great majority of Americans in every generation that human beings have certain wholesome interests in common. Their experience as a people also convinced them that the satisfaction of those interest required trusting other human beings and treating them as equals. The cultural belief **almost all human beings want to do what is right** differs markedly from the belief that only certain men—those of superior birth and breeding—can be trusted to act honorably and responsibly in their relations with others. That aristocratic belief, which associated virtues with a certain social class constituted by birth and superior education, did not square with the historical experience of Americans.

Another belief about human nature that developed among Americans is negative rather than positive. It is known to all that Europe's aristocratic culture concentrated governing power in the hands of a few persons who were considered to have superior bloodlines. The corollary to this outlook is that persons who do not belong to the superior class cannot be trusted with responsibility because of their inferior nature and lack of "breeding." American culture is democratic because Americans came to have a different view: that those in positions of power could not be trusted and had to be watched constantly to prevent their abuse of power. However, this skeptical view of persons in power does not apply to a category of human beings. All human beings, when they acquired power, are viewed as susceptible to the temptation to abuse it. In American thought, powerful persons have the same human nature as powerless persons; and people who are poor and those who are rich are believed to have the same human nature. Thus, in American political thought, a majority may be just as tyrannical as a minority. The belief that almost everyone can be trusted to want to do right by their fellow human beings made the institution of democracy in America possible. The belief in the inevitable abuse of power by those who have it has enabled American democracy to endure.

The belief **human beings will abuse power when they have it** holds that all men and women are capable of evil as well as good; that the freedom which is part of human nature consists of the ability to do wrong as well as good. Intrinsically, freedom itself is neither a virtue nor a vice. Whether it is a virtue depends entirely on how it is used. In trusting human nature, American culture has not attributed evil to one class of human beings, whose elimination would remove the basis of evil from human affairs. Rather, America's democratic culture has recognized a potential for the abuse of power in all human beings. In believing that **human beings will abuse power when they have it**, Americans attribute evil to a potential in themselves and other human beings that is not created by the conditions of their upbringing or the experiences of their social relations or a particular genetic inheritance. In short, in American culture, neither nurture nor nature is ultimately responsible for what human beings do. American culture requires each individual to accept his/her human nature and be responsible for whether he/she does, good or evil.

SUMMARY

(1) Primary beliefs of American culture include three-work-related beliefs: everyone must work, people must benefit from their work, and manual work is respectable, all of which derive from the initial experience of early settlers in North America, where they were compelled to work in order to survive in this new and sparsely populated world. Because of this tradition, manual work is held in respect by Americans at large.

(2) Immigrants to America may hold three beliefs more firmly than any other belief, namely, improvement is possible; opportunities must be imagined; and freedom is needed for success. This is largely due to the fact that in their own countries, they did not have opportunities to improve their lives, nor did they have freedom to achieve success. By coming to America, they believe, everything becomes possible.

(3) The American frontier experience helped create many new beliefs about what they can do in their life. They include: each person should rely upon him/herself and be responsible for his/her own well-being; helping others helps oneself; and progress requires organization. All of them, together with many others, have become part of American myth and American values, forging the character of Americans as a whole.

(4) Out of their values and social environment, Americans have developed a set of social beliefs, the most salient of which include: society is a collection of self-determining individuals; everyone is expected to succeed; success is largely measured by the amount of wealth accumulated, and achievement determines a person's social rank. These beliefs basically stress individualism and material success.

(5) From their experiences of immigration to seek opportunity and

freedom, and from their close contact with nature in the process of settling the vast stretch of the wilderness, Americans have formulated certain fundamental beliefs regarding "human nature," among which two stand out most prominently: almost all human beings want to do what is right, and human beings will abuse power when they have it.

ESSAY QUESTIONS

(1) Work ethic is one of the most important Protestant values in American culture, which, among other things, is believed to have contributed to the rapid development of American capitalism. Explore the origin of Protestant work ethics and explain its instrumental role in motivating Americans to work "like a dog" to accumulate wealth, paying particular attention to the transformation taking place among the Puritans.

(2) Throughout U. S. history, immigrants from around the world have come to the United States with all kinds of dreams. Some of these dreams are materialized, others only partially realized, but many more never fulfilled. Pick up any immigrant group from any country, examine their beliefs and dreams in their adopted country, and finally explain how and why their dreams are fulfilled or broken.

(3) There is an almost inherit paradox in American frontier belief. On the one hand, it attaches great importance to individualism, emphasizing self-reliance and self-responsibility, but on the other hand, it lays stress on community and organization, believing that helping others helps oneself. Discuss these two seemingly contradictory values in the frontier belief, and explain how they may find room for reconciliation.

(4) In American value system, an individual is expected to succeed and those who succeed are held in respect and those who fail are looked down upon. Additionally, individual worth in America is measured not so much by his/her family background as by his/her own achievement. Discuss the positive and negative impacts of these social values on American individuals as well as American society as a whole.

(5) Americans as a nation are quite optimistic, believing that human beings are perfectible, and that human beings can find certain wholesome interest in common. Nevertheless, they are also suspicious of human integrity, believing that all men and women are capable of evil as well as good. Explain how Americans accommodate these two mutually exclusive beliefs in their understanding of human nature.

American Society and Culture
美 国 社 会 文 化

Chapter Five
American Values and Assumptions

LEARNING OBJECTIVES

- Understand the importance of individualism in American core values
- Know the yardstick by which Americans assess and measure achievements
- Be aware of the tension between liberty and equality
- Learn the ways Americans behave and interact to each other
- Be aware of the contradictions inherent in a pair of two core values of Americans: individualism and cooperation

As people grow up, they learn certain values and assumptions from their parents, relatives, teachers, books, newspapers, and television programs. "Values" are ideas about what is right and wrong, desirable and undesirable, normal and abnormal, and proper and improper. "Assumptions," as the term used here, are postulates, the unquestioned givens, about people, life, and "the ways things are." In any society, people who grow up in any particular culture share certain values and assumptions. That does not mean that they all share exactly the same values and assumptions to exactly the same extent. But it does mean that most of them, most of the time, agree with each other's ideas about what is right and wrong, desirable and undesirable and so on, and agree with each other's assumptions about human nature, social relationships and so on. Values and assumptions often overlap with and support each other, guiding, if not dictating, people's behavior. In this sense, a culture can be viewed as a collection of values and assumptions that go together to shape the way a group of people perceive and relate to the world around them.

Chapter Five
American Values and Assumptions

5.1 Individualism and Privacy

The most important thing to understand about Americans is probably their devotion to "individualism." The American concept of an individual self is rooted in a philosophical tradition represented by John Locke. Locke asserted that the biological individual is the basic unit of nature, and social systems derive from the interactions of individuals who exist prior to the social order and who are acting in their self-interest. This view was influential in early American history and was best epitomized by Benjamin Franklin, who, in his writing, suggested that "God helps those who help themselves."

The American stress on the individual as a concrete point of reference begins at a very early age, which can bee seen in the way Americans treat their children. Even very young children are given opportunities to make their own choices and express their opinions. A parent, for example, will ask a one-year-old child what color balloon she wants, which candy bar she would prefer, or whether she wants to sit next to mommy or daddy. More often than not the child's preference will be accommodated. Trivial as all this seems to be, it demonstrates the encouragement of autonomy in children. In other words, as early as age one, the American child has already learned to express his/her own preferences and make his/her decisions, at least with regard to food.

In general, Americans have been trained early on in their lives to consider themselves as separate individuals who are responsible for their own situations in life and their own destinies in the future. They have not been trained to see themselves as members of a close-knit tightly interdependent family, religious groups, tribe, nation, or other collectivity. Through this process, Americans come to see themselves as separate human beings who have their own opinions and have to rely upon themselves. Along this line of thinking, American parents' objective in raising a child is to create a responsible, self-reliant individual, who, by the age of 18 or so, is ready to move out of the parents' house and make his/her own way in life. A person beyond the age of about 20 who is still living at home with his/her parents may be thought to be "immature," "tied to the mother's apron strings," or otherwise unable to lead a normal, independent life.

Americans, then, consider the ideal person to be an individualistic, self-reliant, independent person, who prefers an atmosphere of freedom,

111

where neither the government nor any other external force or agency dictates what the individual does. For this reason, Americans see as heroes those individuals who "stand out from the crowd" by doing something first, longest, most often or otherwise "best." Examples are aviators Charles Lindberg and Amelia Earhart. Similarly, Americans also admire people who have overcome adverse circumstances, for example, poverty or a physical handicap, and "succeeded" in life. Black educator Booker T. Washington is one example, and the blind and deaf author and lecturer Helen Keller is another. Certain phrases one commonly hears among Americans capture their devotion to individualism: "Do your own thing," "I did it my way," "You'll have to decide that for yourself," "You made your bed, now lie in it," "If you don't look out for yourself, no one else will," and "Look out for number one."

Closely associated with the value they place on individualism is the importance Americans assign to privacy. Americans assume that people "need some time to themselves" or "some time alone" to think about things or recover their spent psychological energy. If parents can afford it, each child will have his/her own bedroom. Having one's own bedroom, even as an infant, inculcates in a person the notion that she is entitled to a place of her own where she can be by herself and keep her possessions, like clothes, toys, and books. Americans assume that people have their "private thoughts" that might never be shared with anyone. Sometimes, Americans' attitudes about privacy can be difficult for foreigners to understand. Their houses, yards, and even offices can seem open and inviting, yet, in the Americans' minds, there are boundaries that other people are simply not supposed to cross. When the boundaries are crossed, the Americans' bodies will visibly stiffen and their manner will become cool and aloof.

5.2 Equality

Together with freedom and democracy, equality is one of the long-held key values in American culture. However, in the United States, social equality is more of a moral ideal than a fact of life, because great differences of wealth, education, opportunity, and privileges still exist, and in some cases are expanding. Nevertheless, the frontier experience and the immigration process in American history did represent a huge

Chapter Five
American Values and Assumptions

historical experiment in social leveling. American legal and institutional heritage prescribes equal rights, condemns special privileges, and demands equal opportunity and representation for every citizen. American national manners with few exceptions are standardized for nearly all adult citizens. Indeed, egalitarianism is so pervasive in American society that Americans have made a cult of the Average Man.

Although they sometimes violate the ideal in their daily lives, particularly in matters of interracial relationships, Americans have a deep faith that in some fundamental way all people (at least all American people) are of equal value, that no one is born superior to anyone else. "One man, one vote," Americans often proudly say, conveying the idea that any person's opinion is as valid and worthy of attention as any other person's opinion. Because of this sense of everyone being as good as anybody else, Americans are generally quite uncomfortable when someone treats them with obvious deference. They dislike being the subjects of open displays of respect—being bowed to, being deferred to, being treated as though they could do no wrong or make no unreasonable requests.

It is not just males who are created equal, in the American conception, but females too. While Americans often violate the idea in practice, they do generally assume that women are the equal of men, deserving of the same level of respect. Women, according to the viewpoint of the feminists who since the 1970s have been struggling to get what they consider a "fair share" for females in the society, may be different from men but are in no way inferior to them. This is not to say that Americans make no distinctions among themselves as a result of such factors as sex, age, wealth, or social position. They do, but the distinctions are acknowledged in subtle ways. Tone of voice, order of speaking, choice of words, seating arrangements—such are the means by which Americans acknowledge status differences among themselves. People of higher status are more likely to speak first, louder, and longer. They sit at the head of the table, or in the most comfortable chair. They feel free to interrupt other speakers more than others feel free to interrupt them.

To some extent, equality can be viewed as part of individualism, especially when individualism is understood politically. Here, the political aspect of individualism can refer to the single individual effort to battle for what he/she considers to be his/her rights. This can happen in one person, as in the case of Ralph Nader, who almost single-handedly pushed for a great national demand for controls on automobile design and won it. More often than not, however, it occurs when individuals sharing common interests organize themselves in a crusade for equal rights. Civil rights and women's movements of the 1960s are the best examples of this kind of individualism: seeking to enjoy those rights that have been accorded to others as citizens, and to protect those rights that have long been granted to them by the Constitutions—equality defined in a broad sense. In asserting their equal rights in the battle against discrimination, individuals, single or organized, tend to show more concern to the community interest, rather than merely their own individual interest.

5.3 Informality

Americans, more than any other nation in the world, are known for their informality. This can be explained, in part, by the great importance they attach to the notion of equality, and, in part, by the friendly character of American people in general. Such informality is displayed visibly in their general behavior and in their relationships with other people. For instance, Americans look directly into each other's eyes when talking, conveying informality, spontaneity, and equality in the exchanges of glances. When eyes shift and avoid meeting those of the other, Americans sense connivance and may even believe that there is some deception on the part of that person. In many ways, the direct spontaneous informality indicated by direct eye contact sets a better stage for Americans' friendly relations.

Because of their stress on informality, Americans readily use first names to address each other in their early relationship. Store clerks and waiters, for example, may introduce themselves by their first names and treat customers in a casual, friendly manner. American clerks, like other Americans, have been trained to believe that they are as valuable as any other people, even if they happen to be engaged at a given time in an occupation that others might consider lowly. Whereas this informal behavior can outrage foreign visitors who hold high stations in countries where it is not assumed that "all men are created equal," in America, the average person tends to regard formality, style, and protocol as somewhat pompous or arrogant.

> Chapter Five
>
> American Values and Assumptions

People from societies where general behavior is more formal than it is in America are often struck by the informality of American speech, dress, and postures. Idiomatic speech (commonly called "slang") is heavily used on most occasions, with formal speech reserved for public events and fairly formal situations. People of almost any station in life can be seen in public wearing jeans, sandals, or other informal attire. People slouch down in chairs or lean on walls or furniture when they talk, rather than maintaining an erect bearing. A brochure advertising a highly-regarded liberal-arts college contains a photograph showing the college's president, dressed in shorts and an old T-shirt, jogging past one of the classroom buildings on his campus. Americans are likely to find the photograph appealing: "Here is a college president who's just like anyone else. He does not think he is too good for us."

The superficial friendliness for which Americans are so well known is related to their informal, egalitarian approach to other people. "Hi!" they will say to just about anyone. "Howya doin?" (That is, "How are you doing?" or "How are you?") This behavior reflects less a special interest in the person addressed than a concern (not conscious) for showing that one is a "regular guy," part of normal, pleasant people—like the college president. If Americans develop a stronger than usual attachment to someone, they may experience difficulty in expressing it since exchanges from the beginning have been informal and friendly. Consequently, what at first may appear to be a personal way of treating others can ultimately become depersonalizing, because it is extended to everyone alike. Few discriminations are made among people (with the exception of blacks in history), each being kept at the same distance. Sometimes, even enemies are likely to be treated with a controlled friendliness that may not look much different from behavior directed toward cherished acquaintances.

5.4 *Achievement, Action, Work, and Materialism*

"He is a hard worker," one American might say in praise of another. Or, "She gets the job done." These expressions convey the typical American's admiration for a person who approaches a task conscientiously and persistently, seeing it through to a successful conclusion. More than that, theses expressions convey an admiration for *achievers*, people whose lives are centered around efforts to accomplish some physical, measurable thing. Social psychologists use the term "achievement motivation" to describe what appears to be the intention underlying Americans' behavior. "Affiliation" is another kind of motivation, shown by people whose main intent seems to be to establish and retain a set of relationships with other people. As a kind of value orientation, the achievement motivation predominates among Americans in their daily action and work.

Foreign visitors commonly remark that "Americans work harder than I expected them to." Perhaps, it is because foreigners have been excessively influenced by American movies and television programs, which are less likely to show people working than to show them driving around in fast cars or pursuing members of the opposite sex. While the so-called "Protestant work ethic" may have lost some of its hold on Americans, there is still a strong belief that the ideal person is a "hard worker." In the conception of Americans, a hard worker is one who "gets right to work" on the task without delay, works efficiently, and completes the task in a way that meets reasonably high standards of quality. Hard workers are admired not just on the job, but in other aspects of life as well. Housewives, students, and people volunteering their services to charitable organizations can also be "hard workers" who make "significant achievements."

More generally, Americans like *action*. They do indeed believe it is important to devote significant energy to their jobs or to other daily responsibilities. Beyond that, they tend to believe that they should be *doing* something most of the time. They are usually not content, as people from many countries are, to sit for hours, and talk with other people. They get restless and impatient, believing that they should be doing something, or at least making plans and arrangements for doing later. People without the Americans' action orientation often see Americans as frenzied, always "on the go," or "on the move," never satisfied and compulsively active. They may, beyond that, evaluate Americans negatively for being unable to relax and enjoy life's pleasures. Even recreation, for Americans, is often a matter of acquiring lavish equipment, making elaborate plans, then going somewhere to *do* something.

Generally, Americans tend to define people by the jobs they have. "Who is he?" "He is the vice president in charge of personal loans at the bank." Their family background, educational attainments, and other characteristics are considered less important in identifying people than the jobs they have. Usually, there is a close relationship between the job a person has and the level of the person's income. Americans tend to measure a person's "success" in life by referring to the amount of money he has acquired. Being a bank vice president is quite respectable, but being a bank president is more so. The president gets a higher salary, so he can buy more things—a bigger house and car, a boat, more neckties and shoes and so on.

Closely related to the job and income is the notion of materialism. As mentioned previously, for Americans, materialism is natural and proper as a way of personal pursuit. They have been taught that it is a good thing to achieve—to work hard, acquire more material badges of their success, and in the process assure a better future for themselves and their immediate families. Just like people from elsewhere, Americans do what they are taught; but unlike people in other countries, Americans do it all too seriously, and for that they are often criticized—being too materialistic and too concerned with acquiring possessions. But Americans like material possessions so much that they continue to produce and acquire them, not only taking fancy to material gadgets but also assigning a high value to them. Indeed, in American civilization, such material well-being is both the criterion and the undeniable proof of success and progress.

5.5 *Directness and Assertiveness*

Americans, as has been said before, generally consider themselves to be frank, open, and direct in their dealings with other people. "Let's lay our cards on the table," they say. Or, "Let's stop playing games and get to the point." These and many other common phrases convey the Americans' idea that people should explicitly state what they think and what they want from other people. Based on their stress on directness, Americans tend to assume that conflicts and disagreements are best settled by means of forthright discussion among the people involved. If I dislike something you are doing, I should tell you about it directly, so you will know, clearly and from me personally, how I feel about it. Bringing in other people to mediate a dispute is considered somewhat cowardly, the act of a person without enough courage to speak directly to someone else.

The word "assertive" is the adjective Americans commonly use to describe the person who plainly and directly expressed feelings and requests. Based on this understanding, Americans will often speak openly

117

and directly to others about things they dislike. They will try to do so in a manner they call "constructive," that is, a manner which the other person will not find offensive or unacceptable. If they do not speak openly about what is on their minds, they will often convey their reactions in nonverbal ways, such as facial expressions, body positions and gestures. Americans are not taught, as people in many Asian countries are, that they should mask their emotional responses. Their words, the tone of their voices, or their facial expressions will usually reveal themselves when they are feeling angry, unhappy, confused, or happy and content. They do not think it improper to display these feelings, at least within limits.

However, Americans are often less direct, open and assertive than they realize. There are in fact many restrictions on their willingness to discuss things openly. It is difficult to categorize those restrictions, and the restrictions are often not "logical" in the sense of being consistent with each other. For instance, Americans are reluctant to speak openly when the topic is in an area they consider excessively personal, such as unpleasant body or mouth odors, sexual functioning, or personal inadequacies. Similarly, Americans would say "no" to a request that has been made of them but do not want to offend or "hurt the feelings of" the person who made the request. All of this is to say that Americans, even though they see themselves as properly assertive and even though they often behave in open and direct ways, have limits on their openness. It is not unusual for them to try to avoid direct confrontation with other people when they are not confident that the confrontation can be carried out in a "constructive" way that will result in an acceptable compromise.

Despite these limitations, Americans are generally more direct and open than people from many other countries. They will not try to mask their emotions, and they are much less concerned with "face" than most Asians are. To them, being "honest" is usually more important than preserving harmony in interpersonal relationships. Still, Americans would use the words "pushy" or "aggressive" to describe a person who is excessively assertive in expressing opinions or making requests. But the line between acceptable assertiveness and unacceptable aggressiveness is difficult to draw. People from countries where forceful arguments and negotiating are common forms of interaction risk being seen as aggressive or pushy when they do so in America. In this sense, it can be argued that while Americans are direct and assertive, they do not want to be pushy or aggressive.

Chapter Five
American Values and Assumptions

5.6 Cooperation and "Fair Play"

Although competition predominates in such a free society as the United States, it occurs among Americans within the context of cooperation, for competition requires a considerable amount of coordination among individuals and groups. One of the reasons Americans can do this—and they are well known for it—is that they do not commit themselves wholeheartedly to a group or organization. They pursue their own personal goals while cooperating with others who, likewise, pursue their own. They accept the goals of the group, but if their expectations are unfulfilled, they then feel free to leave and join another group. This separation between membership in a group and personal objectives allows the individuals to adjust their goals to those of other group members if it is necessary for carrying out joint action. To Americans, this compromise is practical, allowing them to achieve a benefit they could not attain on their own. Cooperation is given for the sake of action and it does not imply that the Americans are yielding their principles. They are in fact simply following one of the dominant values in American culture, that of *doing* as discussed above. In other words, cooperating to get something done is more important than the personal relationships among the doers.

The Americans' preference for cooperative action may work against their individualism in a social setting. The necessity for compromise in cooperative action may undermine other values, principles, or objectives. To insure that they adjust or compromise no more than necessary, Americans are likely to stress the means used to reach a group decision. In formal groups, for instance, they may be preoccupied with matters of agenda and procedure, which give some formal protection to the rights of the individual. Americans believe that "due process" establishes a frame for the use of persuasion to achieve compromises which are fair to each individual. By contrast, in Latin America, people regard appeals to the agenda or to group procedures as efforts to avoid the issue. They prefer to invoke concepts such as the dignity of man, honor, or other principled beliefs as a logic for settling differences. This abstract humanism of the Latin Americans contrasts with the instrumental technicism of Americans.

The American value of fairness, indicated by their concern with procedures, is not confined to formal groups. It has widespread ramifications, often appearing as the social norm of fair play. The essence of fair play is not so much that rules ought to be followed as it is the inclusion of the other person's weakness inside the rule. Rules should be applied with knowledge of the relative strength of the opponents, so that the stronger opponent does not use the rules to beat a weaker one. This American modification of the English notion of fair play is both an arbiter of personal relations among Americans and a motivating force. Americans will stand up for their fair share, but they will also be concerned that others are dealt with fairly. If they perceive themselves to be stronger, they tend not to initiate aggressive action since they do not believe in starting a fight. It is important for Americans to be able to say, "They started it," and then of course, "but we'll finish it."

SUMMARY

(1) Individualism is probably the single most important value Americans hold in their value system. In their eyes, the ideal person is an individualistic, self-reliant, independent person, who prefers an atmosphere of freedom, where neither the government nor any other external force dictates what the individual does. Heroes are those who "stand out from the crowd" by doing something first, longest and best.

(2) Together with freedom and democracy, equality is one of the long-held key values in American culture, though social equality is more of an ideal than of a reality. American legal and institutional heritage prescribes equal rights, condemns special privileges, and demands equal opportunity for every citizen. Though there exists tension between liberty and equality, the latter can be viewed as part of individualism.

(3) Americans are known for their informality. This can be explained, in part, by the great importance they attach to equality and, in part, by the friendly character of American people in general. Such informality is displayed visibly in their general behavior and in their relationships with other people. For all these reasons, formality, style and protocol are often viewed as somewhat pompous or arrogant in America.

(4) Americans are essentially achievement-oriented. They tend to admire a person who approaches a task conscientiously and persistently, seeing it through to a successful conclusion. They also admire a person who has a clear goal in mind, concentrating his/her efforts to accomplish something ambitious and measurable. Therefore, Americans like action and tend to define a person by the job he/she holds.

Chapter Five
American Values and Assumptions

(5) Although competition predominates in American society, it does not rule out cooperation, for competition requires a considerable amount of coordination among individuals and groups. As a nation that treasures "free associations," Americans often pursue their own personal goals by cooperating with others. If they cannot accomplish their goals in one group effort, they are free to leave and join another group.

ESSAY QUESTIONS

(1) As a value growing out of their political and religious convictions as well as social and cultural beliefs, individualism has played a crucial role in the development of American civilization. While positive in many ways in American society, especially in terms of realizing a person's full potential, individualism has many negative effects. Examine and analyze the plus and minors of individualism as a value.

(2) America as a nation is committed to equality, in principle at least. However, in much of its history, many social groups, most notably women and African Americans, had been, and in some cases still are, denied equality in political, social and economic life. Explain how come a nation that believes "all men are created equal" should have denied more than half of the population their equal rights.

(3) In handling relationships between people, Americans prefer informality to formality, which is expressed in the way they address and greet to each other and the way they dress for public events. Behind these informal behaviors and expressions, there is a value issue. Discuss the possible reasons for Americans' stress on informality in communication, behavior and interpersonal relationship.

(4) Driven by the American Dream, and inspired by legendary success stories in American history, most Americans aspire for success, which, by American standards, is often measured by material achievement. Analyze the influence of achievement motivation on the average American and examine its implications for individuals and American society at large.

(5) Competition and cooperation seem to be exclusive to each other. Yet, Americans tend to look at them as the two sides of the same coin, believing that the two of them can not only accommodate each other, but also benefit each other. Discuss the way(s) these two values may be neutralized, making it possible for them to be complementary rather than exclusive to each other.

American Society and Culture
美 国 社 会 文 化

Chapter Six
Cultural Regions in America

American Society and Culture
美 国 社 会 文 化

LEARNING OBJECTIVES

- Know the contributions of New England to the development of American culture
- Understand the uniqueness of the Southern culture
- Make sense of average Americans in the context of the Midwestern culture
- Be aware of the cultural legacy of the Far West
- Appreciate the diversity of regional cultures

The United States is commonly divided into four major regions: Northeast, South, Midwest, and West. This subdivision is used by journalists, the United States Census, and polling organizations for variations in attitudes or opinions. In addition to that, there are many other common regionalizations that take off from this beginning. Several attempts have been made to regionalize the country by economic criteria, although with the declining dependence of economic location this approach has been largely limited to agricultural divisions. Recent interest in regions of America has been primarily concerned with cultural regions, that is, with regions defined by the historical experience and qualities of the people that make up their population. The following discussion is along the line of cultural division of the country.

6.1 New England

We begin with the New England cultural region, not because it is the oldest of American major cultural-geographic entities—an honor it shares with the South and perhaps the Hispanic Southwest as well, but because it was the most clearly dominant region during the century of American

Chapter Six
Cultural Regions in America

expansion following the Independence War. New England may have been strong, if not preeminent, in the fields of manufacturing, commerce, finance, and maritime activity, but it was in the sphere of higher social and cultural life that the area exercised genuine leadership, for instance in education, politics, theology, literature, science, architecture, and the more advanced forms of mechanical and social technology. Thus, if any single section must be nominated as the leading source of ideas and styles for the remainder of the nation from 1780 to 1880, New England is the logical candidate.

Relatively small though it is, the territory occupied by the six New England states may be usefully split into two subregions: the older, more densely settled, highly urbanized and industrialized southeastern segment; and the newer, rather thinly occupied northern area, taking in all of Vermont and nearly all of New Hampshire and Maine, an area colonized mostly after 1770 by settlers from the nuclear zone. It is the former tract, of course, which has been so potent as a source of people, ideas, and influences for much of North America. By virtue of location, wealth, and seniority, the Boston metropolitan area has acted as the functional hub for all of New England both culturally and economically.

Historically, New England had been established in the 1600s by deeply religious people anxious to escape the domination and corruption they found in England. By settling down in the place they called New England, they meant to turn their colonies and their communities into "a city upon a hill," that is, to set a good example for the rest of the world to follow. Driven by a strong desire for redemption and salvation, they were intensely religious, emphasizing such virtues as piety, self-denial, sense of community, and deferment of gratification. In order to make sure that their effort to create a "Holy Commonwealth" would come to fruition, this group of Puritans made stiff provisions for individual behavior, seeking not merely to worship in their own way, but also to demonstrate that theirs was the only way. In the process, they placed their doctrines on the members of the "Holy Commonwealth" strictly.

The New England Puritans derived their doctrine only in part from the great John Calvin. More immediately influential were the writings of William Ames and other English "federal" theologians who had developed the theory of the "covenant of grace." According to this, God had "contracted" with humankind that whoever should have faith in Him and follow in His way would be saved. Calvin's predestination still determined which souls would benefit by this act of grace, but covenant theology modified strict Calvinism to place greater emphasis on God's justice and to stress the obligation of the elect to obey God's law. The elect did not earn their salvation by good works, but they fulfilled their part of the covenant by faith and by sincere effort, however faltering, to follow the path of righteousness. At its best, covenant theology quieted men's anxieties and stirred them to Christian action; at its worst, it encouraged complacency. The ability to live an upright life was likely to be equated with election by God. In the opinion of Puritans, by fulfilling the obligations in the "covenant of grace," they would create an ideal state as well as an ideal church in the New World.

As part of their endeavors to build an ideal state, education, work ethics, family, community, and town meeting were central, in addition to church. While later generations strayed far from such ideals, the tradition has lasted in many ways, particularly before the 20th century, making New England very different from the rest of the country. Taken as a whole, the New England region is more tradition-oriented, emphasizing such things as public school, family values, community spirit, work ethics, and congregationalism. In essence, it is the tradition of the dissenters that is New England's greatest tradition. In the words of Henry Adams, "Resistance to something was the law of New England's nature. The boy looked out on the world with the instinct of resistance, because for generations, his predecessors had viewed the world as chiefly as a thing to be reformed, filled with the evil forces to be abolished." Today, several of the country's greatest universities and many of its finest colleges are concentrated in the region. Politics continues to be seen in highly moralistic terms, and the region responds more than others to liberal and internationalist appeals. Its elite continue to have a sense of mission, believing that they represent the idealism of the country.

6.2 The South

What is usually called the South is in reality three subregional cultures—the Deep South, the Upper South (a border strip of states), and the Southwest. The Deep South is the region where agriculture is important, and where blacks are numerous enough to exercise influence in all areas. Roughly, this area includes Georgia, Alabama, Mississippi,

Chapter Six
Cultural Regions in America

South Carolina, Louisiana, and Florida, while the Virginias, North Carolina, Kentucky, and Tennessee are in the border strip of the Upper South, and Texas, Oklahoma, and Arkansas may be seen as part of another border strip adjoining the Southwest. For most Americans, all these three areas form part of an on-going regional unity that they call "the South."

Most of the characteristic traits of the Southern mind are a heritage from the past. The old aristocracy dreamed of the South as an autonomous nation—a Greek republic rising proudly from the cotton fields, built firmly on the economic base of the plantation system and the social base of slavery. The imaginative flame of this dream burned intensely in the political theory of states rights, whose followers saw the South as a separate culture, conscious of its destiny. But the Civil War and the Reconstruction destroyed the old aristocracy and undercut the plantation system. The South paid a terrible price for the war in the whole young generation, in economic ruin, in the memory of armed occupation, and in hatred.

The "new South" that Henry Grady evoked in the 1880s was in fact turned toward the past, with a nostalgia for its lost glamour and glory, a hatred of the Northern absentee owners whom it identified with the conquering army, and a sense of guilt about slavery which is always interwoven with a fear of the growing black population. The South is the only region in America that is tied together not by its common consciousness of present and future potentials but by its past, not by what it can achieve or build, but by what it cherishes and fears. Indeed, the South has been so distinct from the non-South in almost every observable or quantifiable feature and so fiercely jealous of its peculiarities that for many years the question of whether it could maintain political and social unity with the non-South was in serious doubt. Only during the 20th century can one argue for a decisive convergence with the rest of the nation, at least in economic behavior and material culture.

In both origin and spatial structure, the South has been characterized by diffuseness. If one has to narrow the search for a nuclear hearth down to a single tract, the most plausible choice is the Chesapeake Bay area and the northeastern corner of North Carolina, the earliest area of recognizably Southern character. This was, and still is, an emphatically rural area, despite the growth of two large metropolitan districts—Baltimore and the Hampton Roads conurbations—toward either end of the

Bay. It was via this corridor and the routes running further inland from the Delaware River ports that the great bulk of the Southern territory was eventually peopled. The cities of Charleston and Savannah, which have nurtured their own quite special civilizations, dominated this subregion in every sense. Similarly, one can easily demarcate a French Louisiana that received elements of culture and population not only from the Chesapeake Bay area, but also directly from France, the French West Indies, and of course, Africa. In the south central Texas, the Teutonic influx was so heavy that a special subregion can quite properly be designated, while in the Southwest, there has developed a strong presence of Latinos, who have either lived there for centuries, or recently migrated there. Taken as a whole, then, the Southern cultural region may be understood as one consisting of a variety of elements arriving along several paths without any truly coherent structure.

If there is anything common among Southerners, particularly southern whites, it is their tenacious clutching of past enmities and ideals. In the process of reconciliation with the past in a rapidly changing society, Southerners demonstrated their creativeness in writing that placed it with the best American writing of modern times. In fact, the "Southern renaissance" parallels the Midwestern literary movement of the early 20th century and the Renaissance of the New England "Golden Day." From Ellen Glasgow through Thomas Wolfe to William Faulkner, and in Robert Penn Warren and in Tennessee Williams, Southern writers reflected the deep internal stirrings produced by regional conflict. Something of the same sort happened in the Midwest when Dreiser, Sherwood Anderson, and Sinclair Lewis expressed the heightened awareness that came from watching their world being transformed from an agrarian and small-town world into a city world of industrialism and of revolution in moral standards. But in the case of Southern writers, one feels that while they are being pushed reluctantly into the future, they are forced into a similar heightened awareness of their regional past, and of the moral and psychological transformation being wrought around them.

Partly because of its emphasis on literary tradition, partly because of its legacy of agricultural society, and partly because of its stress on family and community, the South, among American regions, has been noted for its hospitality and friendliness, and also for its relatively relaxed and unhurried way of life. Alongside these traits, there has been a southern emphasis on personal honor and valor that is not characteristically

American. For many years, the South has been a major contributor to American military forces, a tendency reinforced perhaps by the placing of so many of the country's military facilities in the South. Indeed, the military tradition—the Southern plantation owners lived almost literally on horseback—has persisted in the South alongside its literary tradition, making the region not only a land of literary elegance and grace, but also a land of social violence and sadism.

6.3 The Midland

Between New England and the South lies an area called the Midland. Together, they constitute the three principal cultural hearths along the Atlantic seaboard, whose genesis, development, and expansion, with some minor exceptions, literally draw the outline of the contemporary map of American cultural regions.

Among the above-mentioned three regions, the Midland has received the least attention, because it is the least conspicuous, either to outsiders or to its own inhabitants. This fact may reflect its centrality to the course of American development. The serious European occupation and development of the Midland began a generation or more after that of other cultural areas, and after several earlier, relatively ineffectual trials by the Dutch, Swedes, Finns, and British. But, once begun late in the 17th century by William Penn and his associates, the colonization of the area was an instant success. This was especially so in the lower Delaware, and Philadelphia, the major port of entry, also became preeminent as economic, social, and cultural capital.

It was within southeastern Pennsylvania that this cultural area first assumed its distinctive form: a prosperous agricultural society, then quite quickly a missed economy as mercantile and later industrial functions came to the fore. By the middle of the 18th century, much of the region had acquired a markedly urban character, resembling in many ways the more advanced portions of the North Sea countries. In this respect, the Midland was well ahead of neighboring areas to the north and south.

It also differed in its polyglot ethnicity. From almost the very beginning, the full range of ethnic and religious groups of the British Isles were joined by immigrants from the European mainland. This diversity has, if anything, grown through the years, and promises to persevere indefinitely. The spatial mosaic of colonial ethnic groups has persisted in much of Pennsylvania, New York, New Jersey, and Maryland, as has the remarkable variety of more recent nationalities and churches in coal fields, company towns, cities large and small, and many a rural tract. Much the same sort of ethnic heterogeneity was to be seen in New England, the Midwest, and a few other areas, but the Midland still stands out as America's most polyglot region.

If we limit our attention to Pennsylvania and the adjacent tracts of New Jersey, Delaware, and Maryland, a useful distinction can be made between an inner zone, in which the Midland culture reached its climactic development, and an outer zone, which is much more nondescript. The former is entirely inland and focused upon those sections of the upper Piedmont and the Great Valley lying to the west and northwest of Philadelphia. Within the Pennsylvania subregion, the Teutonic element has always been notably strong, accounting for more than 60 percent of the population of many townships. If it were not for the fact that the Anglo-Saxon culture finally proved supreme, one would indeed be tempted to designate the area as Pennsylvania German. Indeed, the demographic and cultural effects of the Midland and the Pennsylvania subregion are legible far down the Appalachian zone and into the South in general. The latter, that is the areas to the west and north of the two subregions, are less clearly Midland in character. Much of central and southern New Jersey, except for a zone within a few miles of Philadelphia, is difficult to classify in any way.

The northern half of the Midland Region, New York, is arguably the heart of this area. New York City and its suburbs form a "regional city" in themselves. The familiar warning that "New York is not America" is doubtlessly true, but neither is any other regional culture. The fact that this obvious observation has to be asserted is more than an index of the common hostilities to New York: it shows the extent to which New York's culture has impinged on the imagination of America and the world. Perhaps, it is sensible to think of it as a hybrid place, inheriting a double heritage —that of the old Dutch aristocracy, now replaced by the aristocracy of finance, talent, and "café society," and the intellectual heritage of western Europe toward which it faces. It has fused, adapted, and transformed that heritage, and used it as a base for a cosmopolitan culture which is nonetheless American, because it results from the enormous suction force it has exerted on the world. Its ethnically diverse

Chapter Six
Cultural Regions in America

population is drawn from every corner of the world and from every region and subregion of America. Latterly, the currents of population in and out of New York have changed its character, making it largely Catholic, Jewish, Black, and Puerto Rican. But, this is to see it residentially. As a working entity, or as a regional city, it reaches into the surrounding counties and states and retains millions who still work in it and use it as the center of their energies, although they make their homes elsewhere. What is particularly worth mentioning is around New York City, where a powerful communications industry is located, be it newspapers, books or television, feeding the nation (even the world) news, ideas, entertainment, fashion, and other forms of intellectual products. For this and many other reasons, New Yorkers tend to view themselves as living in the center of the country, or probably the center of the world.

Toward the west, the Midland, or more specifically, its Pennsylvania subregion, retains its integrity only for a short distance, certainly no further than eastern Ohio, as it extends out between the South and the extended New England region. Still, the significance of the Midland in the genesis of the Midwest or of the national culture must not be belittled. The precise details remain to be worked out, but it is probable that the Midland contribution to the overall national patterns is quite substantial, just as with the other two east-coast cultural regions. Its very success in projecting its image upon so much of the remainder of the country may have rendered the source area less visible. As both the name and location would suggest, the Midland is intermediate in character in many respects between New England and the South. Moreover, its residents are much less concerned with, or conscious of, its existence (excepting the "Pennsylvania Dutch") than what is true for other regions, and, incidentally, the Midland also happens to lack their strong political and literary traditions.

6.4 The Midwest

Unlike the Midland, there is no such self-effacement in the case of the Midwest, that large triangular region that is justifiably regarded as the most modal. More than any other region in the United States, this is the region that is most nearly representative of the national average. Everyone within or outside the Midwest knows of its existence, but no one seems sure where it begins or ends. The older apex of the eastward-pointing equilateral triangle appears to rest in the vicinity of Pittsburgh, and the two western corners melt away somewhere in the Great Plains, possibly southern Manitoba and southern Kansas, respectively.

The historical geography of the Midwest remains insufficiently studied, but one can plausibly conjecture that this cultural region must be the progeny of all three east-coast regions, and that the fertile union took place in the upper Ohio Valley. The early routes of travel all converge upon the state of Ohio. It was there that the people and cultural traits from New England, the Midland, and the South were first funneled together, from which there would be a fanlike widening westward of the new hybrid area as pioneer settlers worked their way frontierward. Like the South, the Midwest lacks a genuine focal zone or city around which both ideas and commerce were built, although an unconvincing case might be made for Chicago. A parallel to the Cotton Belt's role as a climactic zone of development is the central portion of the Corn Belt, or the Cash Grain Region, but it is plainly not a core area in any functional sense.

Two major subregions are readily discerned: the upper and lower Midwest. They are separated by a line roughly approximating the 41st Parallel, one that persists as far west as Colorado in terms of speech patterns and indicates regional differences in ethnic and religious terms as well. Much of the upper Midwest retains a faint New England literary and artistic character, although the Midland is probably equally important as a source of influences. A rich mixture of German, Scandinavian, Slavic, and other non-WASP elements has greatly diversified a stock in which the British element is usually dominant, and the range of church denominations is great and varied. The lower Midwest tends to resemble the South, except for the relative scarcity of blacks, in its predominantly Protestant and British makeup. There are, of course, many local exceptions, areas of Catholic and non-WASP strength; but on the whole the subregion is more nativistic in inclination than other parts of the nation.

While the differences between the upper and the lower Midwest are salient enough, there also exist enough similarities between them to put them together as one cultural region. The most pronounced term to characterize the region has been the phrase "Midwest isolationism." The essence of this label is that until the mid-1950s the Midwest, geographically situated in the interior of the nation, had historically displayed little interest in developing ties with foreign countries. Coupled with this isolationist mindset was the Jeffersonian "continentalism," which held that America could work out its democratic destiny on a continental scale if it were not beset by foreign troubles. While both notions have been made obsolete by the globalization forces, their legacy has by no means completely disappeared. Another striking characteristic of the Midwest is the domination of middle-class values in most of the communities there. The central argument for this characterization is that while the whole American culture is middle-class in orientation, the Midwest can be said to be the embodiment of American middle-class values. For anyone to write about the Midwest, be he novelist or socialist, it is difficult to do so without assuming that any light cast upon it would somehow light up the whole of the American character.

Primarily for this reason, the Midwest has long held a special place in the American consciousness as being more "American" than the rest of the country, and Midwesterners take great pride in the image thus created. They tend to view the East as the seat of an arrogant plutocracy, the South as caught in the nostalgia for its past grandeur, and the Far West as a still unformed fledging region. Only the Midwest is blessed with all of the best, because it is the region at once solid and hustling, carrying the best of both the conservative and progressive worlds. There may be some truth in this type of self-complimentary characterization, but the argument obviously carries a clear note of simplicity, to say the least, and a strong sense of sentimentalism and idyllic feeling, to say the most. Maybe, it is better to approach the Midwest without either idealizing it as "the heartland of America," or overreacting to it as a "hot-bed" of American middle-class bigotry. The truth is that the Midwest has been the crossroads of American experience in more than a geographic sense, and has absorbed both the strengths and weaknesses of that experience.

6.5 The Far West

The concept of an "American West" is strong in the popular imagination and is constantly reinforced by the romanticized images of the cowboy genre. It is tempting to succumb and accept the widespread Western livestock complex as somehow epitomizing the full spectrum of Western life, but this would be intellectually dishonest. The cattle industry may have accounted for more than half the active Western life, as measured in acres, but it accounts for only a relatively small fraction of the total population. And in any case, a single subculture cannot represent the total regional culture.

The Far West is so immense that one can legitimately ask if there does exist a genuine, single, grand Western cultural region. Unlike the East, where settlement is virtually continuous through space, and cultural regions and subregions abut and overlap in splendid confusion, the Far West features eight major (and many lesser) nodes of population, separated from each other by wide expanses of nearly uninhabited mountain or arid desert. The only two obvious properties all these isolated clusters have in common are the recent intermixture of several strains of culture, primarily from the East, but with additional powerful influences from Mexico and Asia, and a general modernity, having been settled in a serious way no earlier than the 1840s. If there is anything else that is shared by the people in the Far West as a whole, it can only be the Gold Rush psychology of its early days.

Generally speaking, there are three, and possibly four, major tracts in the Far West that reveal a genuine cultural identity: the upper Rio Grande region, the Mormon region, Southern California, and central California. (To this group one might also add the anomalous Texan and Oklahoman subregions, which may adhere to either the South or the "West," or both.) The term upper Rio Grande region has been coined to denote the oldest and strongest of the three sectors of Hispanic-American activity in the American southwest, the other two having been Southern California and portions of Texas. The European communities and culture have been present in strength since the late 16th century. The initial sources were Spain and Mexico, but after 1848 at least three distinct strains of Anglo-American culture have been increasingly well-represented: the Southern, Mormon, and a general undifferentiated northeastern American culture, along with a distinct Texan subcategory. But for once, all this has occurred without obliterating the aboriginal folk, whose culture endures in various stages of dilution. The general pattern is that of a mosaic, with the aboriginal, Anglo, and Hispanic constituting the main elements. Given the strong recent influx of Mexicans and Anglos and its general economic prosperity, this is one region that appears destined to wax stronger and nurture zealously its special traits.

Chapter Six
Cultural Regions in America

The Mormon region also promises to maintain its strength and cultural separateness for many years to come, for it is emphatically expansive in religion and demography, even though it has ceased to expand territorially, as it did so vigorously in the first few decades after establishment. Despite its Great Basin location and an exemplary adaptation to environmental constraints, this cultural complex still appears somewhat non-Western in spirit: The Mormons may be in the West, but they are not entirely of it. The historical derivation from the Midwest, and beyond that, from ultimate sources in New York and New England, is still apparent, along with the generous admixture of European converts. Here again, as in New England, the power of the human will and an intensely cherished abstract design have triumphed over an unfriendly habitat. Despite its relatively short history in the area, the region has functioned, since the great ingathering of the Latter-Day Saints during the 19th century, as a traditional region. The Mormons, a religiously defined tribal group, have been known mostly for their polygamy in marriage, but beyond that, their way of life is expressed in many other recognizable ways as well, for instance in the settlement landscape and economic activities. More significantly, this region is more homogeneous internally than any other cultural region in the United States.

In contrast, the almost precisely coeval Central California region has not yet gained its own strong cultural coloration, except possibly for the city of San Francisco and some of its suburbs. From the first weeks of the great Gold Rush onward, the area drew a thoroughly diverse population from Europe and Asia as well as the older portions of America. Speaking impressionistically, as one has to for most Western regions, it is not yet obvious whether the greater part of the Central California region has produced a distinctively local culture amounting to more than the averaging out of the contributions brought by in-migrants, early or late. San Francisco, the regional metropolis, may, however, have crossed the qualitative threshold. An unusually cosmopolitan outlook, including an awareness of the Orient stronger than that of any other American city, a fierce self-esteem, and a unique townscape may be symptomatic of a genuinely new, emergent local culture. In any case, the Central California region, along with the Southern California and the Upper Rio Grande, has recently acted as a creative zone for the nation as a whole, the springboard for many a fresh innovation.

American Society and Culture
美 国 社 会 文 化

The Southern California region is the most spectacular of the Western regions, not only in terms of economic and population growth, but also for the luxuriance, regional particularism, and general avante-garde character of its swiftly evolving cultural patterns. Until the coming of a direct transcontinental rail connection in 1885, Southern California was remote, rural, and largely inconsequential. Since then, the invasion by persons from virtually every corner of North America and by the foreign-born has been massive and ceaseless. Although every significant ethnic and racial group and every other American cultural area is amply represented, there is reason to suspect that a process of selection for certain kinds of people, attitudes, and personality traits may have been at work at both source and destination. Certainly, the region is aberrant from, or in the vanguard of, the remainder of the country. For this reason, one might view Southern California as the super-American region or the outpost of a rapidly approaching post-industrial future. But in any event, its cultural distinctiveness in social behavior and individual lifestyle is evident to all. Indeed, in Southern California people do not behold anything approaching tradition, but rather are enthusiastic for the largest and boldest experiment ever imaginable on earth.

SUMMARY

(1) As a cultural region, New England is important for many reasons, for instance it has been strong in the fields of manufacturing, commerce, finance and maritime activity. But more importantly, New England's significance lies in the sphere of higher social and cultural life, where the region exercised leadership in the nation, particularly in such areas as theology, education, literature, science, and architecture.

(2) The Southern region is unique in many ways. For instance, most of the characteristic traits of the Southern mind are a heritage from the past: the old semi-aristocratic class, plantation economy, slavery, agrarianism, states rights, the Civil War, Jim Crow laws, the "New South," literary legend, and the Southern Renaissance. It is exactly all these past experiences that make the South a unique region.

(3) The Midland lies between two giant neighbors: New England and the South. From almost the very beginning, the full range of ethnic and religious groups of the British Isles was joined by immigrants from the European mainland, taking on the image of mosaic earlier than any other region. Additionally, the presence of New York and Pennsylvania in the

Chapter Six
Cultural Regions in America

area has made the Midland a center of finance and culture.

(4) The Midwest is a large triangular region. More than any other region in America, the Midwest is most nearly representative of the national average. Everyone within or outside it knows of its presence, but no one seems sure where it begins or ends. The most striking characteristic of this region is the domination of middle-class values, which ensures the area as the heartland of America, both geographically and morally.

(5) The concept of an "American West" is strong in the popular imagination and is constantly reinforced by the romanticized images of the cowboy genre. In general, this region is dominated by California with its "Gold Rush" mentality of the mid-19th century, plus its recent intermixture of several strains of culture from the East, Mexico, and Asia. Its modernity is coupled with Native American and Mormon cultures.

ESSAY QUESTIONS

(1) Socially, culturally, politically, and theologically, New England has not only contributed a great deal to the development of the United States, particularly in its early stage, but also left a rich intellectual legacy to American culture. Examine some of the most important contributions New England has made to the American Mind in such areas as democracy, education, religion, morality, and work ethics.

(2) The South is an economically backward but culturally rich region. In the course of its development, there have been such culturally-loaded terms as "the Old South," "the New South," and even "No South." Examine each one of them in their historical context and explain their cultural and ideological implications at the time when they were used, noting, in particular, their differences and continuity over the years.

(3) The Midland has a distinctiveness of its own as a cultural region, characterized primarily by its ethnic, social, economic, and cultural diversity. Trace the origin of this diversity in the region's history and explain how such a diverse and complex society has helped promote cultural pluralism in the United States, rather than produce resentment or animosity among all different ethnic and cultural groups.

(4) America is largely a middle-class-based society and the Midwest is the most representative of all. It is often said that the Midwest is the

embodiment of American middle-class values, worshiping the "self-made" hero, cherishing the image of the "commoner," and believing in the democratic principle of equality. Examine the historical process in which all these values grew and developed in the Midwest.

(5) Many of the images people have about "American West" are referred to here as the Far West, exclusive of the Midwest. Of all these images about "American West," cowboys, violence, disorderliness, confusion, money-grubbing men, wild women, freaks, radicals, adventurers, and new riches tend to come to mind first. Analyze some of the images mentioned above and tell the genuine from the sham.

American Society and Culture
美 国 社 会 文 化

Chapter Seven
Education in America

LEARNING OBJECTIVES

- Know the evolutionary process of education in America
- Understand the functions of education in different periods
- Be aware of the birth of public education in America
- Make sense of the important ideas behind the establishment of modern colleges and universities
- Be informed of the characteristics of American education at all levels

As is the case in any other country in the world, education in the United States does not merely function as a vehicle to pass on knowledge to children, it also serves the purpose of instilling cultural values in the plastic minds of the young. Viewed in this light, American educational system can be best understood as a kind of social institution that reflects the basic beliefs and fundamental principles of the nation, rather than simply a kind of skill-training place where students are prepared to get a job. Evidently, as a way to probe into the cultural and social significance of education in the United States, it is far more important for us to understand the thought of Americans on education, particularly the ideals that have guided the American system of education, than to merely describe the structure of educational system itself.

7.1 Initial Efforts in Promoting Education

North America in the 17th century was colonial in culture as well as in politics. The growth of an indigenous intellectual life was retarded by many factors, such as geographical isolation and preoccupation with

Chapter Seven
Education in America

survival. In the middle and southern colonies, intellectual concerns had to take second place to practical affairs. New England, however, was different. The first-generation Puritans there addressed themselves zealously to establishing an educational system, developing an intellectual life that was vigorous, although narrowly constrained by its religious shell.

The zeal of the Puritans in the field of education manifested itself as early as 1643 in *New England First Fruits*, in which the Puritans stated: "After God had carried us safe to New England, and we had built our houses, and provided our necessaries for our livelihood... one of the next things we longed for and looked after was to advance learning and perpetuate it to our posterity." But the religious motivation was not the only one. An early law of New Haven, for example, provided for "the better training up of youth of this town," so that "through God's blessing, they may be fitted for public service hereafter, either in church or commonwealth." Clearly, education in early America was considered to be important for two principal reasons: one religiously/philosophically-oriented, and the other politically/socially-oriented.

Out of these considerations, several schools were founded in New England, for instance, the Boston Latin School in 1635 and Harvard College in 1636. At first, support of these schools came from voluntary contributions of the wealthier inhabitants, but later the towns where schools were located assumed responsibility for the support of these schools. Attendance at these schools was by no means compulsory, but parents were required to make some provisions for the instruction of their children. Although the local laws were made to assure that schools would be available to those who wanted them, not all New England parents followed them. Some villages were too poor to fulfill the letter of the schools. Besides, the schoolmasters and teachers were usually underpaid and sometimes had to supplement their incomes by doing odd jobs. Yet, despite shortcomings and evasions, enough money was scraped together in most communities to keep the schools alive. Indeed, the town school became a distinctive institution in such New England states as Massachusetts and Connecticut, and Harvard College, more than any other educational institution, stood out most remarkably. For some sixty years after its founding in 1636, it was the only degree-granting institution in British America, graduating several hundred students trained in such disciplines as Greek and Hebrew grammar, rhetoric, logic, divinity, arithmetic, geometry and Aristotelian physics.

By contrast, during the first few decades of the southern history, education received little attention from the settlers there. When they recognized the need for schools, one hopeful plan they worked out called for the building of a college in the Virginia forest to teach the classical curriculum to both whites and Indians. Funds were accumulated, a one-man faculty imported, and buildings erected on the James River. All was well in progress when a terrible white-Indian conflict liquidated the whole enterprise in 1622. Later attempts to found a college were made but proved to be less successful. More common were the "old-field schools," where several families on neighboring properties would cooperate in erecting a rude building, often in an abandoned tobacco field. Here, a master hired by the parents would teach during the months from April to September, and the government exercised no control over these schools except that it required that the teacher have a license. Most frequently, the teacher was the Anglican clergyman or lay reader of the parish attempting to augment his meager salary with tuition fees.

Education in the mid-Atlantic colonies was a different story. Initially, when the Dutch were in what later came to be called New York, they made provisions for education similar to those of New England. The first public school in New Amsterdam was established in 1638 and continued to be the official school throughout the period of Dutch rule. The conquest of New Netherlands by the English disturbed the evolution of the school system. The Dutch elementary schools survived—but not as public institutions, but rather as parochial schools. The English and other non-Dutch groups had to secure education for their children through private schools. Consequently, a limited number of children attended the charity schools, and even among the more fortunate classes education received little emphasis. In Pennsylvania, at the initiative of William Peen, the colonial assembly laid upon the council the duty of fostering education and ordered that all persons having children should make sure that their children be instructed in reading and writing. But in 1689, the public school was discontinued, and education was left to the initiative of private groups, especially the churches.

Chapter Seven
Education in America

7.2 Education as Philanthropy

As indicated above, of the three regions in early America, New England stood out most prominently in terms of the public attention it received. Summarized briefly, the New England pattern consisted of four principles: the state could require children to be educated; the state could require towns to establish schools; the civil government could supervise and control schools by direct management in the hands of public officials; and public funds could be used for the support of public school. But as the 18-century progressed, the colonial legislatures showed a slacking of effort to require compulsory education and gave greater freedom to private groups to educate children in schools of their own preference.

Most of the schools established at that time received a parcel of public land from the town authorities and were therefore under the supervision of the local government. To the extent that the schools existed by authority of the town government, that the town contributed public lands and even funds to their support, and that the town officials inspected and supervised the conduct of the schools, they were "public schools." However, they were not "public" in the sense that they were totally supported by public funds and therefore free of charge to everyone. While certain poor children could occasionally go to the schools free of charge, normally the parents who could afford to do so paid fees and tuition for their children's education. Thus, at the beginning of the 19th century, practically all schools in the United States were private institutions, controlled either by some religious denomination or by an individual schoolmaster, creating a serious problem for poor families about their children's education. American response to the situation was influenced by events in England, where Sunday schools were provided to teach poor children. But the American school soon evolved into a pattern different from its English prototype. Instead of providing poor children with general schooling, it gave religious training to Protestant children of all classes, and instruction in reading and writing was soon relinquished to other agencies.

Provision of schools for poor children without religious affiliations became a favorite charity for public-spirited citizens. To help these poor children to receive elementary education, many benevolent societies were organized in such cities as Baltimore, Philadelphia, Washington, and New

York. These charity societies maintained their schools with funds raised in part by private subscriptions and in part by grants from the city and state. Philanthropists who wanted maximum results from their gifts were much excited by news from England, where Joseph Lancaster, a Quaker schoolmaster, was demonstrating that the poor could be educated at an annual expense of only 5s a head. Lancaster-style methods were soon introduced by the New York Free School Society, and shortly afterwards became as popular in America as in England. In 1818, Lancaster himself came to America, where he spent much of the remaining twenty years of his life lecturing and demonstrating his methods.

For a span of twenty-plus years, schools organized and taught in Lancaster-style methods spread across the United States, particularly in cities. Visitors were fascinated by the organization and efficient functioning of a good Lancasterian school, where several hundred children were taught in a single room. The essence of the system was simple: The teacher taught the monitors and the monitors taught the other children. All was done with military precision. In comparison with contemporary ungraded schools, the Lancasterian schools were efficient. Many of the usual disciplinary problems disappeared in a system where pupils were kept busy and competition was keen. But the system proved ill adapted for subject matter that depended on thought and analysis rather than on drill and memory. Yet, despite their limitations, the Lancasterian schools served a useful function. In making education appear cheap, they appealed to thrifty philanthropists and won the support of public officials who were unwilling to erect complete systems of public schools.

7.3 *The Birth of Public Schools*

While philanthropic efforts in promoting education were praiseworthy, they did not provide education broad enough to benefit all the children. Subsequently, the question of public schools was raised. Originally, public schools in the U. S. were charged to educate qualified leadership for a republican government. In his first message to Congress in 1790 for example, President George Washington proposed a national university for training political leaders and creating a national culture. He wanted attendance by students from all areas of the country. Washington's proposal was criticized as elitist. Requiring a college education, some protested,

Chapter Seven
Education in America

would result in politicians being primarily recruited from the rich and national university students considering themselves superior to the general public. In this case, a hereditary aristocracy would be replaced by an aristocracy of the educated. If none but the rich had access to higher education, then the rich could use it as a means of perpetuating and supporting their social status.

To avoid the problem of elitism, Thomas Jefferson suggested using education to promote a meritocracy: an educational system that gives an equal chance to all to develop their abilities and to advance in the social hierarchy. Advancement within the educational system and society is based on the merit or achievement of the individual. Within the framework of an educational meritocracy, their success or failure in school determines their later position in society. Since Jefferson was concerned mainly with finding the best politicians, those who succeed would have the possibility of assuming political leadership. On the other hand, those who fail would be disqualified from political leadership. But both had been given an equal chance to succeed, and therefore there was no unfairness to them. In this case, the school becomes the key institution for training and sorting citizens.

The details of Jefferson's plan are not as important as the idea itself, which has become ingrained in American social thought—that schooling is the best means of identifying democratic leadership. This idea assumes that the educational system is fair in its judgments. Fairness of selection assumes that judgment is based solely on talent demonstrated in school and not on other social factors such as race, religion, social class and gender. Meritocracy fails if schools favor individuals from certain racial, religious, and economic groups. Beyond that, schools are also believed to be instrumental in educating future citizens. However, opinions are divided on how this should be accomplished. Jefferson proposed a very limited education for the general citizenry: three years of free education, providing instruction in reading, writing, and arithmetic. Jefferson did not believe that people needed to be educated to be good citizens; instead he believed in the guiding power of natural reason to lead the citizen to correct political decision.

In contrast to Jefferson, Horace Mann, the often-called father of American public education, wanted schools to instill a common political creed in all students. Mann felt that without commonly held political beliefs, society was doomed to political strife and chaos. Mann developed these ideas and his reputation as America's greatest educational leader while serving as secretary of the Massachusetts Board of Education from 1837 to 1848. Originally a lawyer, Mann became an educational leader because he believed schooling was the key to improving society. Out of this conviction, he and other educational supporters campaigned for a public school system for white children that would teach a common set of moral and political values and improve their economic opportunities. Native Americans and enslaved African Americans were excluded from this initial school system. While American schools never fully achieved Mann's dream of educating children to be morally responsible citizens, his campaigns for public schools met with strong support from the general public. By the mid-19th century, much of the North remodeled its schools along the lines advocated by Mann. In 1852, Massachusetts passed the nation's first compulsory school law, according to which parents were obligated to send their children to public schools which would be funded by taxpayers' money and supervised by public officials. With New England taking the lead in public schools, the rest of the country soon followed suit with varying degree of success.

7.4 The Emergence of the Academies

For quite some time, Boston took great pride in establishing its Latin School the earliest in the country, where boys were instructed in classical languages. Such Latin grammar schools were mainly designed to prepare boys for college and therefore only a few boys went there. Their narrow curriculum had little appeal for youths who wanted to become merchants, clerks, navigators, or surveyors, or to follow some other middle-class calling. Except in the larger New England cities, the Latin grammar schools languished, and state laws requiring their maintenance were relaxed. In their place there developed secondary schools of a different type, many of which were fashionable finishing schools maintained by private masters.

However, much sounder education was provided by the academies, which were initiated during the late colonial period, but saw the greatest expansion during the early 19th century. In Massachusetts, for example, the academies grew from 17 in 1800 to 154 in 1860. Elsewhere a similar development occurred. Most of the income of the academies came from tuition fees, but this was supplemented by endowments, gifts, and occasional state and local aid. Control rested in boards of trustees, often self-perpetuating—a system well adapted to keep the academies under the control of particular religious denominations.

Largely independent of both public-school laws and the curricular traditions that inhibited the colleges, the academies experimented with many lines of training. Priding themselves on being "poor men's colleges," they taught any subject for which there was demand. Some academies could offer as many as sixty different subjects, ranging from architecture, Biblical antiquities and embroidery to speaking and Hebrew language. However exotic these course offerings may seem, the general pattern is clear. To the Latin, Greek, and mathematics, the academies invariably added courses in English composition and literature, the modern languages, natural science, and practical business subjects.

Although many of the academies were for boys only, this exclusiveness was by no means universal. Before the end of the 18th century, at least two Massachusetts academies admitted both sexes, and after 1800 such coeducational institutions became more and more common. In addition, there were an increasing number of "female seminaries," serving a useful function in providing higher education for women in a day when the doors of most colleges were closed against them. Also, although the tuition rates of the academies were low by present-day standards, they were high enough to exclude a majority of the population. In states where public elementary schools had become thoroughly established, the next democratic demand was for tax-supported secondary schools. The pioneer institution of this type was founded at Boston in 1821, and was followed in other states soon. This new trend was recognized in a Massachusetts law of 1827 requiring that each town of 500 families or over maintain a high school. Taxpayers in many places rebelled against the idea of paying for education beyond the elementary level and it was not until 1857 that relevant legislation was passed to make the provisions of the earlier act fully operative.

A demand for free instruction at the secondary level swept New York during the 1840s and 1850s. Since the academies received substantial aid from the state and sometimes local public aid as well, there was pressure, oftentimes successful, to secure free tuitions for scholars from the towns where the institutions were located. Meanwhile, new "free academies" were established in New York. At first, these were under the direction of special trustees rather the local school boards, but eventually they were brought under exclusively public control. Still, despite the rise of the public school in Massachusetts, New York, Ohio, and a number of other states, there were only some three hundred such institutions in the United States. Secondary education was still dominated by some six thousand private schools and academies.

7.5 Colleges: Private and Public

At the level of higher education, private institutions were equally well entrenched. The nine colleges founded before the Independence War were incorporated under charters which gave almost unlimited power to their trustees. Since these boards were self-perpetuating bodies in which vacancies caused by death or resignation were filled by the surviving members, control could be tightly held by the denominations which had promoted the enterprise in the first place. Such monopoly of higher education did not go without criticism, of course. Critics demanded, for example, that institutions of higher learning less aristocratic and conservative be established, and the establishment of the first state universities in Georgia, North Carolina, Ohio, and South Carolina was largely in response to it. However, these institutions proved to be only quasi-public in character, because in most of them the state's control was exercised indirectly through boards of overseers, while large powers were vested in the trustees. More significantly, the state's financial support was fickle, leaving the infant institutions to support themselves largely through private endowments, gifts, and tuition fees.

Even less successful were attempts to enlarge state control over already established institutions. In Virginia, where Thomas Jefferson struggled for years to reorganize William and Mary, conservative opposition proved too strong and the college continued under Episcopal control. Harvard and Yale preserved their independence by timely compromise, according to which no effective public control was provided for either of them. The College of Philadelphia underwent various vicissitudes before it evolved into the University of Pennsylvania in 1791, but control was eventually vested in a board of trustees with little public representation. Similarly, King's College in New York, renamed Columbia, retained the status of a private institution under the nominal control of the newly created Regents of the University of the State of New York. However, the proponents of increased public control suffered their most disastrous defeat at the hands of the Supreme Court in the Dartmouth College case of 1819, when the Chief Justice declared that the College was not a public institution, but a private one, "incorporated for the purpose of perpetuating the application of the bounty of the donors to the specified objectives of that bounty." Its charter was a contract the obligation of which might not be impaired by subsequent action of the state.

The decision by the Supreme Court was hailed with enthusiasm by private college interests throughout the country. It strengthened the position of existing institutions and encouraged the establishment of new ones. To the 9 colleges of 1780 there were added during the next 80 years 173 colleges. Only a few of these were public institutions; the rest were funded in the interest of some particular denomination. The Presbyterians with their emphasis on a well-educated clergy were particularly active. Forty-nine Presbyterian colleges dotted the country from Princeton in the East to Pacific University in the West. The Congregationalist with similar traditions supported 21 colleges, mostly located in New England and the Midwest. The Methodists and Baptists at first manifested some prejudice against higher education, but quickly embraced it. By 1860, 34 Methodist and 25 Baptists colleges were founded. Active also were the Catholics, who founded 14 institutions, and the Episcopalians, who founded 11.

Meanwhile, the rival ideal of the state university had achieved limited success. Defeated in his attempt to extend public control over William and Mary, Thomas Jefferson obtained legislative support for the creation of the University of Virginia in 1819. The new institution was given a character unique in the America of its day, emphasizing more on modern languages, political economy, and science than on theological subjects. However, the most successful of the pre-Civil War state institutions was the University of Michigan. In 1837, when Michigan was admitted to statehood, the legislature granted a charter for a university completely under the public control. Like the University of Virginia, the University of Michigan also laid stress on extensive course offerings and freedom of election. Partly encouraged by what these two universities were doing, and partly prompted by the growing demands of the Industrial Revolution, other colleges also became more practically oriented. Harvard and Yale, for example, established "scientific schools" in the 1840s and added laboratories in the 1850s. Also in the 1850s, Yale and the University of Michigan established civil engineering programs. In the same decade, the Michigan State College of Agriculture (now Michigan State University) was founded.

However, the greatest boost to the state university came in 1862, when a big step was taken by the Republicans in Congress to bring higher education within the reach of the common people. Officially called the Morrill Land Grant Act, the law gave to the states proceeds of public lands to fund the establishment of universities emphasizing "such branches of learning as are related to agriculture and mechanic arts." As states were promised aid (including a grant of land) if they established institutions to train students in agriculture and mechanical arts, the colleges that were established under the Morrill Act were henceforth referred to as the land-grant colleges. This act resulted in the creation of the Universities of California, Illinois, Texas, and many others, mainly in the Midwest and West. Some states, such as Wisconsin and North Carolina, awarded their grants to existing colleges so that they could expand into universities. Massachusetts used part of its grant to aid the growth of the new Massachusetts Institute of Technology. Both Purdue and Cornell were created from a combination of land-grant and private funds. In short, the Morrill Act spurred the growth of large state universities to counterbalance private colleges.

7.6 The Arrival of the University

Today, three conditions are usually present when an institution calls itself a university. First, it offers "graduate" degrees—at least a Master of Arts/Science, but probably the Doctor of Philosophy. Second, its faculty is expected to do research and to publish. Finally, it has more than one undergraduate program. Most universities today will have colleges of business administration and engineering as well as the traditional arts and sciences college.

None of the above definitions would have fit Harvard College, the first American institution of higher learning, at its founding in 1636. The colleges established during the early days followed the Oxford and Cambridge models, emphasizing classical studies. Admission depended on a knowledge of certain traditional subjects, particularly Latin or Greek,

Chapter Seven
Education in America

rather than on previous schooling. Thus, a 12-year-old boy and 30-year-old man might be classmates. Evidently, the early colleges cannot be called "post-secondary." Additionally, since most of the students were preparing to be clergymen, religious training was more highly valued than the spread of learning itself. To facilitate that kind of training, strict discipline was provided, including beating, making the early colleges more like secret societies than institutions of learning.

Beginning about 1816, American scholars discovered the virtues of the German university and decided to follow its model. American educators were excited by several qualities in the German university. First, it was a post-secondary institution (its students had to finish secondary school before they could enroll). Second, the students were free to choose their own field of study, and even to transfer from one university to another. The third, the faculty was free to teach what it wished and to do pure research, often in the sciences. In addition, German universities had extensive libraries, physical education programs, and other characteristics that seemed right for American education. In comparison with the German model, the American college was apparently too narrowly focused, when it took college education merely as a matter of studying Latin, Greek, Hebrew, mathematics, and moral philosophy.

Inspired by the "discovery" of the German university, American scholars began to come up with their conception of a university. Essentially, a university should offer post-secondary education. This idea does not distinguish "university" from "college" today, but 175 years ago, a university was superior to a college, because it would offer more than one field of study, and as a result, it would be larger than a college. Also, universities should encourage pure research and academic freedom, just as German universities did. However, when modern subjects like science were introduced into the curriculum, some of the older Eastern colleges resisted: Yale changed slowly, and Princeton maintained its traditional education throughout the 19th century.

With the conception of the university achieved, American universities not only started allowing students to choose their own courses of study, but also began offering courses that represented both traditional and modern curricula. Science had found its place in higher education, so had the practical arts. The emphasis was no longer only on forming students' character, but on helping them learn. The faculty still lacked academic freedom, but at least they might be chosen for their intelligence and training, not simply for their good moral character. To develop American universities into modern ones, only two more steps remained, and they followed quickly. The first was to establish admission requirements—that is, to make the university clearly post-secondary. Until 1870, colleges and universities in the U.S. had both engaged in preparatory training to complete the secondary education of their students. The second was to certify public secondary schools which met the students' preparatory needs. It gave the secondary schools a focus on university preparation and freed the colleges and universities from remedial instruction. From then on, universities were truly "post-secondary" institutions, and the modern higher education finally took shape. Later on, some more changes were made to the university, like providing graduate education, hiring faculty solely on the basis of excellence, emphasizing pure scientific inquiry, requiring publication of scholarly papers, and finally expanding the size of the university itself.

7.7 *Progressivism in Education*

Like anything else, education never remains unchanged. Under the influence of the Progressive Movement at the turn of the 20th century, American education also experienced significant reforms, producing the first formal school of American educational philosophy known as Progressivism. Broadly speaking, Progressivism brought together all those qualities for which American culture was becoming known: democracy, equality, optimism, practicality, and industry. The Progressives believed that the school was an extension of the community, and education an extension of experience. All living experience, in their view, was educational. Formal education was a part of life and, therefore, an end in and of itself, not simply preparation for life.

John Dewey, the chief representative of Progressivism, stated his pedagogical creed most succinctly when he summarized his educational philosophy in five basic principles: (1) all education proceeds by the participation of the individual in the social consciousness of the race; (2) the school is primarily a social institution; (3) the social life of the child is the basis of concentration in all his training or growth; (4) the question of method depends on the order of development of the child's powers and interests; (5) education is the fundamental method of social progress and reform. In other words, the schools would maintain and improve society. They would do so by

Chapter Seven
Education in America

helping students organize and integrate their experience at the students' natural pace. Like life, the curriculum should be broad and integrated rather than narrowly-focused and divided into formal subjects. After all, work was as educational as study, and so was play.

The Progressives encouraged the idea that the school must help children develop all of their abilities and interests. A school garden was educational; woodworking was educational; and for small children, cutting cardboard figures was educational, too. Children helping their parents with household tasks were educating themselves, as were teenagers organizing game. Dewey stated emphatically that education should not be dull, but enjoyable, relevant, and practical. By arguing in this way, Dewey not only affirmed Americans' desires for practical and vocational education, but also stimulated the growth of extracurricular activities. Here, American education moved far away from schooling in other countries: The schools were to provide special learning experiences which had more to do with general living than with textbooks and examinations. Under the influence of Progressivism, the school changed from a teacher-centered-or subject-centered-institution to a child-centered one. The Progressives endorsed the idea of the importance of the child's self-esteem in successful learning, believing that young people should make some of their own decisions, thus promoting the trend to electives for high school and college students.

Most significantly, the Progressives' concern with the whole person led them to new ideas of teaching methodology. Children were people; they had the right to ask questions and to respond to the teacher's ideas. Accordingly, the teacher should interact with them, not simply speak while they sat in total silence. Here, Progressivism made perhaps its most profound contribution to American education, because traditionally, the learning matter was often a series of moralistic rights and wrongs. Whatever the subject, the teachers always had the truth—the only right answer. The children said little and their way of learning was by rote memorization. Moreover, the traditional curriculum had been influenced by theology, and some of the accepted "facts" might be simply moral beliefs. The Progressives, on the other hand, subscribed to Darwinism. They wanted ideas submitted to scientific testing. Their position was that truth was relative, and so facts could and should be challenged.

Progressive innovations had varying degrees of success. First, the idea of integrating the disciplines did not fully succeed in elementary schools, and a few universities, such as Columbia, maintained a "core curriculum"—a set of broad-based, interdisciplinary courses. Second, their attempt to replace moral platitudes with scientific relativism was only partially successful. Third, interactive teaching, on the other hand, became the norm throughout the American educational establishment. The most enduring legacy of Progressivism in education is threefold. First, passive learning is not really learning at all. Second, courses of study should be made as broad as possible. Third, and most important of all, the aim of education is to help the student to become the whole person, that is, the development of the individual toward self-fulfillment.

SUMMARY

(1) Initial efforts in promoting education in colonial America came from the Puritans of New England, who, out of religious as well as political concerns, argued for the establishment of schools to train youngsters in theology and government. By contrast, the mid-Atlantic colonies were slow to develop public schools, and the Southern colonies simply failed to give much attention to education in the first place.

(2) At their early stage, schools were not completely "public," because they were not totally supported by public funds, and parents sending children to school had to pay. Subsequently, many charity organizations stepped in to run their schools, literally turning education from "public" to "philanthropic." It was not until the mid-19 century that America saw the birth of public schools in the real sense of the word.

(3) Along with Latin Schools, there gradually developed a new type of schools in early 19th-century America, called the Academy, the former instructing boys in classical languages while the latter focusing on practical skills like architecture and embroidery. Called "poor men's colleges," the Academy offered any subject for which there was demand. More importantly, academies sometimes admitted both sexes.

(4) Prior to the Civil War, colleges in America had been primarily private. Of the 173 colleges in 1860, only a few were public. Initiated by Thomas Jefferson for the founding of the University of Virginia, efforts to establish state universities gradually yielded results, the most successful of which was the establishment of the University of Michigan. These efforts were crowned with the passage of the Morrill Act in 1862.

(5) In the early 20th century, American educational philosophy changed significantly, producing the first school of American education, known as Progressivism. Believing that the school was the education of

Chapter Seven
Education in America

the community, and education an extension of experience, it brought together all those qualities for which American culture became known: democracy, equality, optimism, practicality, and industry.

ESSAY QUESTIONS

(1) The earliest schools in America were almost all religiously affiliated, suggesting that Christian churches, particularly New England Protestant churches, took great interest in education. Indeed, the Puritans deemed education essential to an individual's efforts in seeking salvation. Discuss the importance of education in New England in relation to Puritans' understanding of individual responsibility for his/her redemption.

(2) The purposes of public schools changed significantly from the late 18th to the mid-19th centuries in America. Trace these changes from George Washington to Thomas Jefferson, and finally to Horace Mann, singling out their main thoughts on public schools and discussing their significance in training national political leaders and morally responsible citizens.

(3) The academies rose in reaction to the shortage of schools on the one hand, and to the narrow curriculum they provided on the other hand. Designed to teach any practical subject, the academies had a strong appeal to youths who wanted to become merchants, navigators, clerks, surveyors or businessmen. Discuss the important role the academies played in making education both more practical and more accessible.

(4) As with any other country in the world, colleges and universities in America also evolved over the time. At the beginning, only private colleges existed; then, state colleges were established; and finally modern universities emerged. Trace the development of American higher education from colonial period to modern times and discuss their contributions to the growth of the country.

(5) As a kind of philosophy on education, Progressivism exerted enormous influence on American education in the first half of the 20th century, in both teaching method and teaching concept. Of all the Progressives, no one was more important than John Dewey, an education reform architect who restructured and reoriented American education. Examine and analyze his key propositions for education reform.

American Society and Culture
美 国 社 会 文 化

Chapter Eight
The American Family

American Society and Culture
美 国 社 会 文 化

LEARNING OBJECTIVES

- Know the differences between traditional and modern American families
- Be aware of American family values
- Be informed of the changes the American family has gone through from colonial period to modern times
- Understand the characteristics of contemporary American family structure
- Distinguish between upper-and middle-class families and working-class families

Like many other aspects of American life, families are changing. Many observers attribute the principal changes evident in the contemporary American society to the feminist movement of the 1960s. Others argue that the difficult economic times are responsible, because people nowadays all live under enormous pressure, from higher education to job security, from mortgage loan to health care. Whatever the reason, the traditional father-dominated family is becoming less and less common. Instead, there are more and more households in which both parents work, and in which the males have taken on household responsibilities that used to be left to females. Also, the number of single-parent keeps growing. It is increasingly common to find unmarried couples living together, unmarried women having children, and "blended families" that are composed of a man, a woman, and both of their children from previous marriages. Strictly speaking, then, there is no "the American family," but rather there are only "American families."

Chapter Eight

The American Family

8.1 European Origins of the American Family

The cultural roots of the dominant American notions of family patterns lie in England and northwestern Europe, a region in which family practices have been more individualistic and "modern" than those of other cultural traditions. According to the demographer J. Hajnal, there was a distinct Western European marriage pattern, dating at least from the 16th-century Reformation. Found in England, Scotland, the Netherlands, and northern France, its two central features were a late average age of marriage for both sexes (often twenty-five years or more for women) and a sizable proportion of adults who never married—especially women, as many as 15 percent of whom stayed single.

The Western pattern of marriage was selective in two senses: one could choose whether as well as whom to marry, although the parents' consent was needed for the marriage partner. The relative freedom of choice has been linked to a tendency toward less gender inequality in Western societies. Additionally, the Western pattern also featured separate unclear family households, with fairly weak links with kin except for those in the three-generation nuclear family of grandparents, parents, children, aunts, and uncles.

Thus, the widespread notion that the coming of modern industrial society broke up the three-generation extended family and led to the rise of the isolated nuclear family is mistaken. In 1963, William J. Goode anticipated the recent findings when he argued that "the classical family of Western nostalgia"—the large household of parents, grandparents, and kids living happily together—had never existed as a typical family pattern. More recent research on the family has confirmed this contention. Furthermore, far from breaking up extended families, the coming of industrial society seems to have, until recent decades, fostered the tendency for kin to live together and to cooperate economically.

The history of the American family before the 18th century generally coincided with the pre-modern pattern described above, although it had been shaped by unique circumstances: the frontier, economic opportunity, and immigration. Generally speaking, the family was "a little commonwealth—a lively representation" of the whole. The father was head of the family, just as the king was head of the state—indeed, "the principle of fatherhood lay right at the heart of most political thinking during this period." The father was also the economic head of the family, because at that time the vast majority of Americans were farmers and other businesses were also family enterprises. Under such circumstances, authority, not affection, was the guiding principle in the family.

Another difference between the premodern and modern family was that in past times, death was omnipresent in everyday family life. Childbirth, for example, was lethal for mother and child. Almost half of all children died before reaching adulthood, most in early childhood. Half of those who survived died before reaching fifty. Since many parents of minor children died, orphans were a constant problem for the community. Furthermore, only a third of marriages lasted more than ten years. But what was more striking about the early family was that the boundaries between public and private were very blurred. Early Americans had far less awareness of the family as a distinctive entity than would later generations of Americans. Mostly, family life was enmeshed with community, where neighbors and servants as well as community authorities were expected to oversee and intervene in the intimate affairs of individuals and families.

Like other premodern societies, early America lacked an elaborate concept of childhood. Moreover, in Puritan America, children were seen as inherently corrupt beings, having come into the world with original sin. A central task for parents was to "break the will" of their children and vanquish their naturally evil propensities. Physical punishment and humiliation were considered legitimate expressions of parental authority. Children were expected to submit, not understand, and therefore obedience was believed to be absolutely essential to proper family government. Similarly, since the father was head of the family, he held sway over other family members as well, including the mother of the family. Although early Americans believed in the ideal of companionate marriage, social order and family stability counted far more. The authorities did not allow the individual autonomy or privacy that the companionate ideal implies, nor did they weigh individual happiness or unhappiness in making their decisions.

Separate Spheres and the Birth of the Modern American Family

Between the founding of the United States and the beginning of the

Chapter Eight
The American Family

American industrial revolution in 1820, a complex of social, economic, and demographic changes took place as the country shifted from a largely rural, agricultural society to an urban, industrial one. These changes led to a profound alteration in the function and cultural meaning of family life, as well as in the relations between family and society. They separated home and work, and transformed men's, women's, and children's roles both inside and outside the family. Instead of an economic enterprise, in which the family worked side by side with hired hands, servants, or apprentices, the family came to be defined as a man who went out to work and a woman who stayed home to keep house and care for the children.

In the decades before the Civil War, the new household functions and the new roles within the family were elaborated in a compelling and pervasive belief system known as the ideology of "separate spheres," or the "cult of domesticity." The glorification of motherhood and the notion that "women's place is in the home"—ideas that influence thinking about family life to this day—were born in this era. With men leaving home to go to work, the contrast between home and the outside world came to be seen as a contrast between Woman and Man. Domestic tasks became spiritualized and romanticized—they were no longer work but woman's God-given mission. Clergymen, fiction writers, and journalists developed a "cult of true womanhood," celebrating women's purity, piety, submissiveness, and domesticity. Home—women's sphere—was an emotional and spiritual refuge, a place where True Woman would comfort, educate, and civilize men and children. The man's sphere of work and public life was defined in opposition to woman's —a place of greed, cutthroat competition, and moral corruption. These conceptions of family and gender relations served to reverse some of the liberalizing trends of the 18th century. A more restrictive and repressive ideology of gender roles and sexuality was grafted onto the companionate ideal. As a result, patriarchal notions remerged and the notions of child rearing swung back to sterner discipline.

With women's role defined as moral guardians, and home as a tranquil harbor from the corrupting world, both women and home were viewed as separate from the public sphere—society. Being the custodians of femininity and domesticity, women, excluded from the materialistic, competitive world outside the home, were supposed to uphold the softer values banished from that world. Such an opposition between home and society at large was one of the most significant aspects of Victorian culture. Instead of the community regulating and repairing moral defects in families, now it was the burden of the family to compensate for the moral defects of the larger society. This shift had profound implications: it encouraged the belief that the perfection of the society could be realized through perfection in the home. Equally significant, the separation of home and work undid the economic foundations of family cohesiveness, yet increased its psychological importance as the only place where emotional security and release could be found. The home came to be seen as both the mainstay of the social order and a precarious enterprise in need of constant shoring up, and women were held hostage to values that men both cherished and violated in their daily lives.

Needless to say, the image of the true woman contrasted with the reality of women's lives. Ironically, the glorification of the home undermined the economic significance of women's work there. Running a middle-class household in the 19th century was hard work, but it was not recognized as such. Nor was the fact that many housewives inside and outside the middle class took part in their husbands' enterprises. Since the home was described in spiritual terms, women's household tasks were seen as a moral responsibility, rather than as an economic contribution to the family. Thus, with work split into paid job for men and unpaid one for women, and with the home separated from work and the community, but above all, with women idolized as providers of moral values and emotional support for their husband and children, the modern American family finally took shape, where love would be more emphasized as the basis of marriage and children the center of parental care and attention.

However, it should be pointed out that this ideology of separate spheres for men and women primarily applied to the white middle-class women. A considerable number of poor white women, immigrant women, black women and rural women had to work for wages outside the home in the early 19th century. These women not only had to work outside the home to supplement the family income, but also work inside the home to take care of household chores. To them, living in a "separate sphere" was nothing less than a luxury, and they had to join the middle class first before they could truly separate home from work. Anyway, the cult of domesticity sharpened class differences and at the same time encouraged working-class men and women to aspire to the ideal of the woman as full-time homemaker. Indeed, over the course of the 19th century, lower-class families preferred to send children, rather than wives, out to work to help with the family budget. By 1890, only about 2 percent of married women were gainfully employed outside the home. Not until the mid-20th century did the situation begin to change, when the majority of American women, spurred by the second feminist movement, demanded for work outside the home.

8.3 Private Lives and Paradoxes of Perfection

The elaborate façade of middle-class Victorian ideology did not actually reflect the reality of middle-class lives. Although Victorian originally referred to English culture during the reign of Queen Victoria (1837-1901), the term is also applied to American middle-class life in the 19th century. Constrained Victorian notions of gender and sexuality might undoubtedly have fit the lives of many people in the 19th century, for others, they were goals to strive for that might seem forever out of reach. According to the historian Carl Degler, Victorian bourgeois culture was more complex, ambivalent, and diverse than people generally realize. Victorian sexuality, for example, was marked not by consensus and moral certainty about traditional values but by battles over conflicting values and behavior and a spectacular gap between publicly pronounced virtues and privately practiced vices.

Scholars who have studied 19th-century marriage portray it differently. Some have found evidence that the companionate ideal of marriage was widespread, and that many married couples were indeed deeply loving companions. Some argue that married women's closest emotional bonds were with other women, not their husbands. Some stress that patriarchy and the doctrine of separate spheres undercut the possibilities of companionate marriage as well as women's equality in public life. But others argue that although the idea of companionate marriage promised women a kind of equality in the home, the crippling legal and economic disabilities of women made the idea of companionate marriage virtually impossible. It seems likely that rather than being mutually exclusive, patriarchy and marital companionship could coexist, as they do today. In other words, despite women's legal disabilities and the ideology of gender difference, a variety of historical evidence suggests that many 19th-century couples did share profoundly intimate emotional relationships with each other, especially during courtship. Patriarchy may have undermined companionate marriage, but the experience of romantic love during courtship, and the empathy and merging of selves it encouraged, may well have played a role in undermining patriarchal attitudes. Over time, companionate aspects of the family ideal came to be increasingly important, not just in the decision to marry but within marriage itself as well.

However, to many middle-class women, the 19th century in the history of the American family was a time of troubles, if not tragedy. The price paid for ideas of femininity, masculinity, virtue, and domestic perfection was often a heavy burden of failure, guilt, and even neurosis. To be sure, many middle-class men and women did find the happiness they sought in domestic life. Yet, the failure of family life to live up to idealized images and extravagant expectations contributed to the sense of family crisis that has taken a variety of forms and haunted American culture ever since. In many ways, the domestic ideology of the 19th century portrayed the family as a utopian institution, where the themes of retreat, conscious design, and perfectionism were greatly emphasized. Furthermore, the perfection of the home was also linked to the redemption of the larger society, where moral values were either losing ground or completely eroded. Defined in such an extravagant fashion, the idea of family—the key to both personal happiness and the improvement of the larger society—became too heavy a burden for the majority of middle-class families, and, as can be imagined, the makings of a crisis of the family were at hand.

By the late 19th century, critics were complaining about divorce, desertion, male drunkenness, and women's restlessness as homemakers. Additionally, while there were both rewards and costs to male and female roles as they were defined during the Victorian era, women's roles were beset by a number of strains and contradictions. For one thing, women were caught between social and economic pressure to marry and their high expectations for companionship and love. Stripped to its bare economic essentials, the job description for a wife was disturbing: in return for sharing a man's income, she had to devote herself to running his home and take care of his and their children's needs. Since divorce was a rarity at that time, this was not a job she could easily quit. For another, Victorian notions of domesticity and gender subjected married women to contradictory demands. On the one hand, it was the responsibility of the morally upright woman to create the perfect home that would reform and redeem the larger society; but on the other hand, the morally superior, strong Mother was also expected to be the weak, dependent, intellectually inferior Wife and Lady who submitted to male authority. The evidence suggests that these conflicting demands exacted a high toll on these women.

By the same token, the advent of urban industrial society also made male roles problematic. The shift of work out of the home, the erosion of early patterns of patriarchy, and the emergence of new concepts of womanhood raised questions about what it meant to be man. The father/husband was no longer the boss of the family enterprise but a breadwinner who carried the burden of supporting the entire family. His success or failure determined the family's economic well-being and its standing in the community. By relying on work to validate their manliness, men found themselves treading on psychically dangerous ground, for the ups and downs of industrial economies could not provide any economic security. Also, sexuality for Victorian men was marked by contradiction. On the one hand, aggressive sexuality was seen as the core of manliness, and yet on the other hand the middle-class Christian man was expected to exercise control over sex, both before and after marriage. Nevertheless, most people conceded that male sexuality could be not contained within the prescribed limits. Subsequently, a double standard was tacitly accepted and prostitution flourished, enabling middle-class men to indulge their sexual appetites with lower-class women, thus preserving "civilized morality."

8.4 *The Contemporary American Family*

Presently, the American family system is technically monogamous, though it has sometimes been called "serial monogamy," since every year several hundred thousand people divorce and soon remarry, and a small percentage of these people may have a succession of spouses over their lifetimes. Nevertheless, the structure of daily marital living is very different from a system in which one man is married to several wives. Also, the American family is based on the independent family unit, in which a married couple and their children are expected to live physically separated from their kin and from their parents. In most instances, even older parents prefer to live alone if they have the financial means to do so.

Because of the American emphasis upon the independence of the family unit, and because of the increasing pressure of modern life upon the young generation, the age at which Americans marry has been growing steadily. The estimated median age at first marriage (MAFM) in the United States for 2000—2003, for example, was 27 and 25 years old for men and women respectively, whereas in 1890, the average age of American males at first marriage was slightly over 26 years and the median age for females in 1890 was 22 years. In comparison with men, the average age at marriage for females is higher now than at any time in American history. Men who marry young typically have jobs that pay low wages, while men who marry late are usually better off and have more secure jobs. As for women, most want or have to work both before and after marriage.

Although the American family system is still patronymic, since the name of the family line comes from the male side, it is neither a patrilineal nor matrilineal society, but a bilateral one in which kinship is equally traced through both male and female parents. All of the major civilizations that we know of have been patrilineal in that the lineage is traced primarily through the male line. In partilineal societies, moreover, far more authority is given to the male and in some societies, to the eldest living male ancestors. In the American system, the husband does indeed have more authority than the wife, especially in major decisions, but not only do many women manage to achieve considerable influence in all family relations, but the modern movement in favor of liberating women continues to press for still greater decision-making power for wives. This marks a difference from most other major societies in the past, and of course represents a substantial departure from America's own historical pattern, because for years wives in the United States were not permitted to make contracts on their own.

Another characteristic of the American family is its kinship system has been one of equal inheritance, as contrasted with those traditional systems in which all of the family estate went to a single male hair. In the United States, the allocation of inheritance is largely a problem of the more affluent social strata, and indeed American social patterns place less and less importance on the notion of "building an estate for the children." More significantly, the American kinship system emphasizes "free courtship," which places more stress upon romance than on other factors.

Chapter Eight
The American Family

In actual practice, American system permits early dating, great freedom of physical movement, privacy, and almost no chaperonage whatsoever. Also, there is no sharp line between dating and courtship: the social assumption is that people who go together are merely dating unless they announce that they are serious about their future plans. Another assumption of American courtship is that people date one another on the basis of personal attractions, though most people do not date across broad caste, religious, class, or age lines. When people do cross these lines successfully, they, for the most part, do so only when they have already lost some of the traits that are associated with their particular caste, ethnic group, or class.

As with many other Western countries, the American family system exhibits a high rate of instability. For technical reasons, it is difficult to calculate the rate of instability with any exactitude. Nevertheless, various estimates suggest that 50% of all marriages in the America end in divorce. However, such an estimate hides all the details about distribution. The following chart, for example, shows divorce rate among different age groups in America. In other words, divorce rate varies from one age group to another. Indeed, not only does age matter in divorce rate, but the number of times in marriage also has a bearing on divorce. According to one study, 50% of first marriages in America end in divorce, but the divorce rate for second and third marriages increase to 67% and 74%, respectively. Another study concludes the divorce rate in America for second and third marriages stand around 60% and 73% respectively. Whatever the case, ample evidence indicates that the American family is in a state of instability, with more than half of the married couples feeling unsatisfied with it.

Age at marriage for those who divorce in America

Age	Women	Men
Under 20 years old	27.6%	11.7%
20 to 24 years old	36.6%	38.8%
25 to 29 years old	16.4%	22.3%
30 to 34 years old	8.5%	11.6%
35 to 39 years old	5.1%	6.5%

(http//www.divorcerate.org)

Why are there so many divorces and unhappy marriages in American society? First, many people enter marriage with unrealistic expectations. Second, many marry the wrong person for the wrong reasons. Third, marriage is a challenging type of relationship, even if one chooses a partner wisely. Fourth, little time or effort is put into developing the relationship skills needed to maintain a strong marriage. Fifth, social disapproval of divorce in America has dropped significantly over the past several decades. Sixth, men can obtain most of the services their wives provide by simply buying them, and wives in turn can support themselves by getting jobs on their own. Last but not least, too much emphasis Americans place upon "happiness through love" turns marriages into a heavy emotional burden, making divorce seem a desirable escape valve for all the tensions of a highly intimate and oftentimes emotionally overloaded relationship.

8.5 Upper, Middle, and Working-Class Families

Generally speaking, members of the upper class in America receive a distinctive education from infancy through young adulthood—beginning in private school and ending with matriculation at one of a small number of heavily endowed private universities such as Harvard and Yale. Such a separate educational system supports the distinctiveness of the mentality and lifestyle of the upper class, and gives them an edge over others in a land where "equality of opportunity" is supposed to reign. More importantly, upper-class families tend to be endogamous, that is, children are encouraged to marry someone of their own social class. To them, marriage is, first and foremost, a marriage within one's class, and consequently families in the upper class tend to be concerned with who they are rather than what they do. Almost as a rule, they keep themselves away from those they refer to as "anybodies." Still, while social activities play an important role in the lives of upper-class families, the most frequent preoccupations of men of the upper class are business and finance. Typically, finance, business and law are the occupations of upper-class males, who either control large corporations or own big law firms. The upper-class women tend to be people of both power and domesticity—playing decision-making roles in various cultural and civic organizations while fulfilling essential roles at home. Since upper-class

Chapter Eight
The American Family

families are at the top of the social hierarchy, they do not aspire to be upwardly mobile—they are "already there," representing a small proportion of the total population in the country. Generally speaking, they do not typically rub shoulders with members of other social strata, but within itself distinctions are sometimes made between the upper-class family and the lower-upper-class family. The former has "old money" (inherited wealth), while the latter has "new money" (money they have acquired themselves). Still, despite this distinction, upper-class families as a whole place more emphasis than middle-class families on relationships with members of the larger kin group. For upper-class, it is important to keep in close contact with the extended family.

People in middle-class families in the United States tend to work in service occupations with other people. Whereas most working-class occupations focus on the manipulation of objects, most middle-class occupations focus on the manipulation of ideas and symbols that require creativity. People from middle-class families generally work for a salary or fee, while people from working-class families are usually paid on an hourly wage. On the whole, the middle-class people are characterized as being very ambitious status seekers. They have long-range goals, making plans for the future rather than taking one day at a time. As is the case in most middle-class families, parents have a strong desire for their children to have a better life than they have experienced. Consequently, they emphasize education as the means for upward social mobility. Indeed, parents in the middle-class families often endeavor to instill particular values in their children, including work ethics, responsibility, respect for property, good manners, status achievement, constructive activity, and refraining from physical violence. Driven by all these values, middle-class families, unlike the upper-class people who tend to stay in the same geographic area for generations, are geographically mobile, seeking better opportunities and better occupations whenever and wherever possible. With higher geographical mobility, middle-class families establish fewer geographic roots, and often get removed from extended families. Having a stable resource base, middle-class families can afford some amount of luxury and discretionary spending. Although lifestyles of middle-class families in America vary considerably, they are usually characterized by the possession of a common set of goods—what some call the "standard American package" of a home in suburbia, two cars in the garage, a white picket, and crabgrass in the yard. In part due to their economic independence, and in part due to their great mobility, middle-class families may replace kin with friends in seeking emotional and social support. More often than not, they refrain from sharing with extended kin and maintain friendships that do not include sharing resources. Thus, the wealth that each relatively independent middle-class household is able to accumulate is invested lineally, that is, between parents and children, rather than laterally among extended family. Over the past few decades, as a growing number of middle-class-family women work outside the home, more and more middle-class women are committing themselves to advancing women's equal rights. They not only demand for equal pay for equal job at workplace, but also ask for a more egalitarian ideology in the family.

Different from both upper- and middle-class families, the working-class families in the United States are characterized by their dependence on hourly wages. Stable working-class families participate in production, reproduction, and consumption by sending out their labor power in exchange for wages. How much labor power needs to be sent out is determined by the cost of maintaining the household, the earning power of individual members, and individuals' availability to work outside the home. The work done in the household by women is simply about raising kids, making them dependent on others for access to commodities brought with wages. When women work outside the home, their primary definition as housewife contributes to their working in the lowest-paid sectors of the labor market. Like middle-class families, working-class families are usually nuclear. But when it comes to marriage, many studies seem to indicate that working-class couples may marry for love, not for money. Upper-class couples may also marry for love, but their commitment to love is sometimes comprised by the recognition of their marriage as a way to preserve their class identity. By the same token, middle-class couples may also marry for love, but the overriding task of middle-class families is also an economic one, that is, to enhance the earning power of the breadwinner. Needless to say, working-class people are also affected by the economic realities of their lives, but their economic tasks are less a part of their dreams about marriage than they are a part of the reality of their married life. Indeed, to many working-class couples, love provides a way to escape from the difficulties of their parents' home and start their own family life. After all, establishing a family, not a career, constitutes the most important ingredient of their personal gratification and life fulfillment. Partly due to lack of education, and partly due to lack of motivation, the great majority of working-class families have limited choices

Chapter Eight
The American Family

about the kinds of work available to them, which often range from blue-collar jobs to low-paid service work. More typically, working-class families tend to hold to the traditional notions of gender in marital roles, according to which the husband's world revolves around the provider role, while the wife has the primary responsibility for the home and children in addition to working outside the home. Quite often, sex segregation of this type is accompanied by a lack of communication between the spouses. Unlike middle-class couples, who highly value partner companionship, working-class couples are less likely to rely on each other for companionship and friendship. Wives have a tendency to maintain close ties with relatives, and husbands to continue premarital peer associations.

SUMMARY

(1) The cultural roots of American family patterns lie in England and northwestern Europe, where family practices have been more individualistic and "modern" than those of other cultural traditions. However, while influenced by European ideas about the family, the American family had been shaped by unique circumstances: the frontier, economic opportunity, ethnic diversity, and immigration.

(2) As America became increasingly industrialized and urbanized, the modern American family began to emerge. Instead of an economic enterprise, home was separated from work and the family was defined as a man who went out to work and a woman who stayed home to keep house and care for the children. The roles of husband and wife became clear: one was the breadwinner, the other the housewife.

(3) Along with functional changes of the family, marriage and family took on new meanings in 19th-century America. Companionate marriage as well as close family bonds became the goals of many middle-class women, who put increasing emphasis on privacy and emotion. Those who failed to achieve these goals often felt despaired and would even seek divorce. Still, many women did find happiness in domestic life.

(4) Technically, the American family system is still monogamous, though a person may marry several times in his/her life. Additionally, Americans are now putting increasing premium on the independent family unit, insisting that a married couple and their children live physically separated from their kin and from their parents. Due to life pressures and high expectations, many American marriages end in divorce.

(5) Generally speaking, American families are divided into upper, middle, and working-class families. The upper-class families tend to be

endogamous and their children often hold prestigious jobs in finance, business, and law. The middle-class families are more mobile and often take jobs in service industries of various kinds. The working-class families are characterized by their dependence on hourly wages.

ESSAY QUESTIONS

(1) The dominant American notions of family patterns derive in part from European traditions, and in part from domestic experiences. Trace the roots or origins of American family patterns and discuss how the two sources combined to produce the typical American family pattern, noting, in particular, the transformations the American family has gone through over the past half a century.

(2) In the pre-industrial society, each household was an economic unit, with all the family members participating in the family-based economic activity. With the arrival of factories, home and work became separated from each other. As a result, family functions altered as well. Analyze the economic and social forces that brought about the changes in family function in early 19th-century America.

(3) With the family function changed from economic activity to private life, the focus of family attention took a dramatic shift. Not only did marriage take on a new dimension, but the role of women became more confined to the home as well, eventually giving rise to the concept of domesticity. Discuss how industrialization minimized women's role in social and public life.

(4) The contemporary American family comes in many forms and shapes. Some people argue that it is an erosion of family values, others insist that it is an indication of family vitality, still others suggest that it is in conformity with the concept of cultural pluralism. Examine the changes the American family has experienced in recent years and analyze the causes of all these changes.

(5) In a country that claims to be "a land of opportunity," class-based families do not necessarily enjoy the same degree of equality in education, resulting in growing gaps between different socioeconomic groups. When such a practice is allowed to persist, different class-based families are likely to perpetuate, hardening the class line between them. Discuss the implications of class division for different families.

American Society and Culture
美 国 社 会 文 化

Chapter Nine
Mass Media

American Society and Culture
美国社会文化

LEARNING OBJECTIVES

- Be informed of the different forms of mass media
- Understand the role mass media play in shaping public opinion
- Be aware of the various functions mass media play in modern life
- Know the importance of television in popular culture
- Appreciate the democratic dimension of the Internet in digital age

In some ways it seems pointless to talk about mass media in America, because American magazines, television programs, motion pictures, records and tapes are available in all but the most remote parts of the world. Not only are American actors, actresses, and singers familiar figures almost everywhere, but the American public's appetite for glamorous and exciting movies and TV shows seems to be widely shared around the world as well. More importantly, there is no authoritative answer to the question of what makes the American mass media distinctively American, for different people always have different opinions on the matter. Still, since mass media, particularly such media as movies and TV shows, mirror the values and assumptions to which most Americans adhere, it is not only necessary but also imperative for us to probe into it in order to fully understand American culture and society.

9.1 Books

The book is the least "mass" of the mass media in audience reach and in the magnitude of the industry itself, and this fact shapes the nature of the relationship between medium and audience. Publishing houses, both large and small, produce narrowly or broadly aimed titles for readers,

Chapter Nine
Mass Media

who buy and carry away individual units. This more direct relationship between publishers and readers renders books more fundamentally different from other mass media. Moreover, as the medium least dependent on advertisers' support, books can be aimed at extremely small groups of readers, challenging them and their imaginations in ways that many sponsors would find unacceptable in advertising-based mass media. Because books are produced and sold as individual units, as opposed to a single television program simultaneously distributed to millions of viewers, more "voices" can enter and survive in the industry.

However, the book industry is bound by many of the same financial and industrial pressures that constrain other media, though more than the others, books are in a position to transcend those constraints. It is precisely their difference from other mass media that makes books unique in American culture. For instance, although all media serve cultural functions to some degree, books traditionally have been seen as a powerful cultural force for the following reasons: (1) Books are agents of social and cultural change. As they are free of the need to generate mass circulation for advertisers, offbeat, controversial, even revolutionary ideas can reach the public. (2) Books are an important cultural repository. Whenever we want to know something for sure, we turn to books for certainty. (3) Books are important sources of personal development. The obvious examples are self-help and personal improvement volumes. (4) Books are wonderful sources of entertainment, escape, and personal reflection. Highly entertaining and imaginative novels as well as reflective and thought-provoking books are all cases in point.

It is estimated that each year there are 120,000 new and reprinted titles are issued in the United States, and each American spends, on average, $97.69 a year buying them. The contemporary book industry in America is characterized by several important economic and structural factors. Among the most important are convergence, conglomeration, hyper-commercialization and demand for profits, the growth of small presses, restructuring of retailing, and changes in readership. Convergence in publishing is altering almost all aspects of the book industry, and its relationship with its readers. Most obviously, the Internet is changing the way books are distributed and sold, which, in the form of e-publishing, offers a new way for writers' ideas to be published. More significantly, the book industry is now dominated by a few giants, such as Hearst Books, the Penguin Group, Time Warner Publishing,

Bantam Doubleday Dell, HarperCollins, and Simon & Schuster, whereas in the past publishing houses were staffed by fewer than 20 people, the large majority by fewer than 10. Such a tendency toward conglomeration puts an increasing emphasis on the bottom line—profitability at all costs, or hyper-commercialization. Consequently, the industry becomes overwhelmed by a blockbuster mentality—lust for the biggest selling authors and titles possible, oftentimes with little consideration for literary merit. Recently, over-commercialization of the book industry is mitigated somewhat by the rise in the number of smaller publishing houses. However, although these smaller operations are large in number, they account for a very small proportion of books sold (the 18,000 houses sell no more than 4 titles annually), and therefore they cannot compete in the blockbuster world. More often than not, they specialize in specific areas such as the environment, feminism, gay issues, and how-to.

There are approximately 20,000 bookstores in the United States, but the number is dwindling as small independent operations find it increasingly difficult to compete with such chains as Bookstop, Barnes & Noble, Borders, and Books-A-Million. These larger operations are typically located in malls that have heavy pedestrian traffic. Their size enables them to purchase inventory cheaply and then offer discounts to shoppers. Because their location attracts shoppers, they can also profitably stock non-book merchandise such as audio- and videotapes, CDs, computer games, calendars, magazines, and greeting cards for the drop-in trade. But high-volume, high-traffic operations tend to deal in high-volume books. To book traditionalists, this only encourages the industry's blockbuster mentality. When the largest bookstores order only the biggest sellers, the small books get lost. More worrisomely, when floor space is given over to Garfield coffee mugs and pop star calendars, there is even less room for small but potentially interesting books. Still, while their share of total U. S. retail sales keeps falling, many independent bookstores continue to prosper by resorting to expert and personalized service provided by a reading-loving staff, coffee and snack bars, cushioned chairs for slow browsing, and intimate readings by favorite authors. Another alternative to the big mall chain stores for independent bookstores is buying books online. Amazon of Seattle is the best known of the online book sale services. Thorough, fast and well-stocked, Amazon boasts low overhead and better prices for readers. In addition, its Web site offers book buyers large amounts of potentially valuable information, such as synopses, reviews and comments.

9.2 Newspapers

Newspapers have a long history in the United States, from the colonial period of the 17th century to the present day of the 21st century. They were at the center of Americans' drive for independence, and have long been viewed as the people's medium for political expression. Also, the newspaper was the first mass medium to rely on advertising for financial support, changing the relationship between audience and media from then on. Indeed, before the invention of radio and television, newspapers were the main source of information about both news and merchandises. With the arrival of the digital age, especially the age of the Internet, newspapers are working hard to secure new identities for themselves in an increasingly crowded media environment. As a medium and as an industry, newspapers are poised at the edge of a significant change in their role and operation.

Today, there are approximately 9,800 newspapers operating in the United States. Of these about 17% are dailies, 77% weeklies, and 6% semiweekly. The dailies have a combined circulation of about 55 million, the weeklies more than 70 million, and the average weekly just over 9,000. However, these categories actually include many different types of papers. For instance, there are three national daily newspapers in the United States that enjoy large circulations and significant social and political impact. The oldest and most respected is the *Wall Street Journal*, whose focus is on the world of business, though the definition of business is broad. Following that is the *Christian Science Monitor*, which continues to hold its founding principle as a paper of serious journalism. After it is *USA Today*, a self-styled "Nation's Newspaper," but derided by critics as "McPaper" for its lack of depth. Equally influential are large metropolitan dailies, such as the *New York Times*, the *Chicago Daily News*, the *Washington Post*, and the *Philadelphia Bulletin*. These dailies not only sell newspapers in the metropolitan areas, but also publish zone edition—suburban versions of the paper to attract readers and to combat competition for advertising dollars from the suburban papers. On top of all this, there are suburban and small town dailies as well as weeklies and semiweeklies, which usually have their own specific targeted readers.

American Society and Culture
美国社会文化

The reason Americans have such a great number and variety of newspapers is that readers value them. When newspapers prosper financially, it is because advertisers recognize their worth as an ad medium. Newspapers account for more than 55% of all advertising spending in the United States. That is more than $50 billion a year, more than all other media combined. The biggest newspaper advertisers are retail stores and telecommunications, auto, computer and entertainment brands. Why do so many advertisers choose newspapers? The first reason is their reach, because six out of ten Americans read a paper a day, 85% in a week. The second is good demographics, for newspaper readers tend to be better educated, better off financially, and have more disposable income than the audiences of other media. Third, newspapers are the most trusted, credible ad medium when readers are looking to make a specific product purchase. Finally, newspapers are local in nature, and therefore supermarkets, local car dealers, department stores, movie theaters and other local merchants who want to offer a coupon turn automatically to the paper.

Much of the 35% of the newspapers that is not advertising space is filled with content provided by outside sources, specifically the wire and feature services. Wire services collect news and distribute it to their members by computer network or satellite. In the past, they distributed by telephone wire, hence the name wire service. Unlike the early days of the wire services, today's member is three times more likely to be a broadcast outlet than a newspaper. These radio and television stations receive voice and video, as well as written copy. In all cases, members receive a choice of material, most commonly national and international news, state and regional news, sports, business news, farm and weather reports, and human interest and consumer material. The feature services, called feature syndicates, do not gather and distribute news. Instead, they operate as clearinghouses for the work of columnists, essayists, cartoonists, and other creative individuals. Among the material provided are opinion pieces such as commentaries; horoscope, chess, and bridge columns; editorial cartoons; and comics, the most common and popular form of syndicated material. Among the major syndicates, the best known are *The New York Times* News Services, King Features, and the *Washington Post* News Services.

During recent years, however, newspapers have encountered many problems, such as loss of competition and hyper-commercialization.

Chapter Nine
Mass Media

Regarding loss of competition, it has taken two forms: loss of competing papers and concentration of ownership. In 1923, 502 American cities had two or more competing (having different ownerships) dailies. Today, only 20 have separate competing papers. The trend toward newspaper concentration is more troubling. Currently, the nation's 126 newspaper chains control 82% of daily newspaper circulation, own the biggest circulation papers in the country, and own 1,200 of the nation's 1,600 dailies. Another serious problem with newspapers concerns hyper-commercialization. As in other media, conglomeration has led to increased pressure on newspapers to turn to a profit, sometimes at the expense of their journalist mission. Many papers, such as *USA Today*, the *Orange Country Register*, and the *Oakland Press*, have begun selling their space on the front page, once the exclusive province of the news. Some papers now even permit and charge for the placement of pet obituaries alongside those of deceased humans. But the greatest fear expressed by critics of concentration and hyper-commercialization is the eroding of the firewall between newspapers' editorial and advertising mission.

As is the case with other forms of media, newspapers have also felt technology as being both an ally and an enemy. Once, television forced newspapers to change the way they did business and served their readers; now, online computer networks pose the greatest challenge to this medium. Online job hunting and auto sales services are already cutting into classified advertizing profits of newspapers. The Internet and the World Wide Web provide readers with more information and more depth, and with greater speed. As a result, the traditional newspaper is reinventing itself by converging with these very same technologies. The marriage of newspapers to the Web has not yet proved financially successful for the older medium, but there are encouraging signs. In fact, the newspaper industry has already recognized that it must accept economic losses while it is building online readers' trust, acceptance, and above all regular and frequent use.

9.3 *Magazines*

In the mid-1700s, magazines were a favorite medium of the British elite, and two prominent colonial printers hoped to duplicate that success in the New World. In 1741 in Philadelphia, Andrew Bradford published *American*

Magazine, followed by Benjamin Franklin's *General Magazine*. Composed largely of reprinted British material, these publications were expensive and aimed at the small number of literate colonists. Lacking an organized postal system, distribution was difficult, and neither magazine was successful. *American Magazine* produced 3 issues, *General Magazine* 6. Yet, between 1741 and 1794, 45 new magazines appeared, although no more than 3 were published in the same period. Entrepreneurial printers hoped to attract educated, cultured, moneyed gentlemen by copying the successful London magazines. Even after the Revolutionary War, U.S. magazines remained clones of their British forerunners.

In 1821, the *Saturday Evening Post* appeared. Among other successful early magazines were *Harper's* (1850) and *Atlantic Monthly* (1857). Cheaper printing and growing literacy fueled expansion of the magazine as they had the book. But an additional factor in the success of the early magazines was the spread of social movements such as abolitionism and labor reform. These issues provided compelling content, and a boom in magazine publishing began. In 1825, there were 100 magazines; by 1885, the number rose to 3,300. Thus began the modern era of magazines, which normally can be divided into two parts, one, mass circulation, the other, specialization. As said previously, mass circulation popular magazines began to prosper in the post-Civil War years. The reasons for their phenomenal growth were manifold. As with books, widespread literacy was one reason. But the Postal Act of 1879, which permitted mailing magazines at cheap second-class postage rates, and the spread of the railroad, which carried people and publications westward from the East Coast, were two others. A fourth was the reduction in cost, from 35 cents apiece to 10 and 15 cents. When advertising agencies started looking around for forms of medium to spread their messages, magazines became their perfect outlet. Finally, urbanization and industrialization provided people with more leisure time and higher personal income, facilitating the process of mass circulation.

However, with the advent of television, the fate of mass circulation magazines became dubious. No matter how large their circulation, magazines could not match the reach of television. For one thing, magazines did not have moving pictures or visual and oral storytelling. For another, magazines could not match television's timeliness, as the former were mostly weekly, whereas the latter were always continuous. For still another, magazines could not match television's novelty. In the beginning, everything on television was of interest to viewers, and subsequently, magazines began to lose advertisers to television. Meanwhile, the audience changed as well. If magazines could afford to be general in their orientation in the past, starting from the television age, they had to be specific in their readership target. In other words, when consumers have a great variety of interests, magazines have to cater to different tastes and needs, resulting in the specialization of magazines, each having its own particular group of loyalists.

Exactly who are the audiences for magazines? Magazine industry research indicates that among people with at least some college education, 94% read at least one magazine and average more than 11 different issues a month. Nearly the same figures apply for households with annual incomes of over $40,000 and for people in professional and managerial careers, regardless of educational attainment. The typical magazine reader is at least a high school graduate, married, owns his or her own house, employed full time, and has an annual household income of just under $40,000. Advertisers find magazine readers an attractive, upscale audience for their pitches. Equally interesting is that people read magazines as much for the ads as for the content. For various reasons, people keep magazines available for up to four months, and oftentimes pass them along to an average of four similar adults. Most importantly, readers tend to develop loyalty to the magazine(s) they or their families traditionally subscribe to, to the delight of magazines and advertisers alike.

Recently, Webzines, or online magazines, have emerged, made possible by convergence of magazines and the Internet. Many magazines, among them *Time* and *Mother Jones*, now produce online editions, offering special interactive features not available to their hard copy readers. In addition, several strictly online magazines have been attempted, though financially they have yet to succeed. Those produced by existing paper magazine publishers serve primarily as an additional outlet for existing material, a way to extend the reach of the parent publication. Exclusive online magazines have yet to produce a profit, and many industry analysts think it will be a long time before they do. There are several hurdles specific to purely online magazines. First, Web users have become accustomed to free access to sites, and therefore websites have to find a successful means of charging for subscriptions. Second, as opposed to Webzines produced by paper magazines, purely online magazines must generate original content, an expensive and formidable undertaking for anyone in the media industry. Beyond that, purely online magazines must also compete with all other Web sites on the Internet, for they are but one of an infinite number of choices for potential readers and advertisers.

While online magazines are still charting their terrain in the media world, several new types of magazines have emerged in recent years. The first is called the brand magazine, a consumer magazine, complete with a variety of general interest and features, published by a retail or other business for readers having demographic characteristics similar to those of consumers with whom it typically does business. The second is called the magalogue, a designer catalogue produced to look like a consumer magazine. Many fashion designers produce catalogues in which models wearing the for-sale designer clothes "frolic along sketchily drawn plotlines." A third new form, the synergistic magazine, may or may not take hold. These are magazines designed explicitly to generate stories that will become movies, television programs, or content for other media. Examples of this kind of magazines include *Talk*, *Outside*, and *Vanity Fair*. More importantly, in order to meet competition from television and the Internet, magazines are resorting to new measures, such as internationalization, which expands a magazine's reach, thereby generating additional ad revenues for the content already produced, and computer and satellite high-tech, which allows instant distribution of copy from editor's desk to printing plants around the world. Most recently, magazines have been trying to attract additional advertizing by offering advertorials, ads that appear to be editorial content. Together with editorials, advertorials help shape the meaning of all content, causing a lot of controversy over this technique in magazines.

9.4 Films

The movies are American dream factories; they are bigger than life. Along with books, they are the only mass medium that is not dependent upon advertising for their financial support. That means that they must satisfy audience; otherwise nobody will buy the tickets. It also means that the relationship between medium and audience is different from those that exist in other media.

Chapter Nine
Mass Media

Unlike newspapers which were developed by businessmen and patriots for a small, politically involved elite that could read, the early movie industry was built largely by entrepreneurs who wanted to make money entertaining everyone. Unlike television, whose birth and growth were predetermined and guided by the already well-established radio industry, there were no precedents, no rules, and no expectations for movies. Nevertheless, since the Lumière brothers showed the first film in Paris in 1895, the movies have caught on around the world, leaving few people illiterate in the grammar of film. In the United States, the movies have developed into a cultural industry, not only making huge profits, but also producing numerous romances and dreams.

In 1908, Thomas Edison, foreseeing the huge amounts of money that could be made from movies, founded the Motion Picture Patents Company (MPPC), often called simply the Trust. This group of 10 companies under Edison's control, holding patents to virtually all existing filmmaking and exhibition equipment, ran the production and distribution of film in the United States with an iron fist. Anyone who wanted to make or exhibit a movie needed Trust permission, which was not forthcoming. In addition, MPPC had rules about the look of the movies it would permit: they must be one reel, approximately 12 minutes long. Many independent film companies sprang up in defiance of the Trust. To avoid MPPC scrutiny and reprisal, these companies moved to California. This westward migration had other benefits. Better weather meant longer shooting seasons. More importantly, free of MPPC standards, they could now explore the potential of film in longer than 12-minute bits and with imaginative use of the camera. The new studio, with its more elaborate film and big-name stars, was born, and it controlled the movie industry from California. By the mid-1920s, there were more than 20,000 movie theaters in the United States, and more than 350,000 people were making their living in film production.

The industry prospered not just because of its artistry, drive, and innovation, but because it used these to meet the needs of a growing audience. At the beginning of the 20th century, urbanization picked up its pace in the United States, with people from foreign countries and rural areas crowding to the cities. These new city dwellers had money and the need for leisure activities. Movies were a nickel, offering glamorous stars and wonderful stories from faraway places. Since they were still silent, they required no ability to read or to understand English. The first sound film was produced by Warner Brothers, either in 1926, or in 1927. By then, the American film industry had firmly established itself as the world leader. Because of its size and power, not even during the Great Depression did the movie business have a hard time. With this system of operation (called vertical integration), studios produced their own films, distributed them through their own outlets, and exhibited them in their own theaters. In fact, the big studios controlled a movie from shooting to screening, guaranteeing distribution and an audience regardless of quality.

In 1948, vertical integration was illegal, as was block booking, the practice of requiring exhibitors to rent groups of movies, often inferior, to secure a better one. Such big studios as Warner Brothers, MGM, Paramount, RKO, and 20th Century Fox were forced to sell off their exhibition businesses (the theaters). Before the ruling, the five major studios owned 75% of the first-run movie houses in the United States; after it, they owned none. Not only did they no longer have guaranteed exhibition, but other filmmakers now had access to the theaters, producing even greater competition for the dwindling number of movie patrons as television began to make itself felt in the market. In the face of competition from television, the film industry worked mightily to recapture audiences from television by using both technical and content innovations. These include more attention to special effects, greater dependence on and improvements in color. Innovation in content included spectaculars with which the small screen could not compete. More importantly, now that television was catering to the mass audience, movies were free to present challenging fare for more sophisticated audiences. In short, the movies as an industry had changed, but as a medium of social commentary and cultural impact, they may have grown up.

Needless to say, when talking about the movies in the United States, one cannot avoid mentioning Hollywood, for it is not only the "dream factory," but also the maker of "movie magic." Americans want their lives and loves to be "just like in the movies." The movies are larger than life, and movie stars are much more glamorous than television stars. In other words, movies hold a very special place in American culture, a culturally special and important medium. For better or worse, today's movie audience is increasingly a young one. The typical movie goer in the United States is a teenager or young adult. These teens and 20-something, although making up less than 20% of the total population, represent more than 30% of the tickets bought. It is no surprise, then, that new screens sprout at malls, where teens and even younger people

Chapter Nine
Mass Media

can be dropped off for a day of safe entertainment. Take a look at the top 10 domestic grossing movies of all time, and one will soon find that with the exception of *Titanic* (1997) and *Forrest Gump* (1994), all are fantastic adventure films that appeal to younger audiences. Thus, the question asked by serious observers of the relationship between film and culture is whether the medium is increasingly dominated by the wants, tastes, and needs of what amounts to an audience of children. If that is the case, what becomes of film as an important medium, one with something to say, and one that challenges people?

Studios are at the heart of the movie business and increasingly are regaining control of the three component systems of the industry—production, distribution, and exhibition. There are major, minimajor, and independent studios. The majors, who finance their films primarily through the profits of their own business, include Warner Brothers, Columbia, Paramount, 20th Century Fox, Universal, MGM/UA, and Disney. Minimajors include Miramax, Artisan, Cannon, Lorimar, and New Line. These companies combine their own money with outside financing to make movies. Together, majors and minimajors account for 80% to 90% of annual U.S. movie revenue. As for independents, although they provide the majority of American movies, they contribute only about 10% of the box office revenue. Independent studios find the money to make their movies from outside sources, and they tend to have smaller budget. If they are successful, much of their funding can come from the major studios. More often, however, funding is obtained from a distribution company, a bank, or other outside sources. Whatever the case, the modern film industry in the U.S. as a whole is experiencing the same trend toward conglomeration and industrialization, and the content is greatly influenced by that fact. A blockbuster mentality leads to reliance on concept film (movies that can be described in one line, like *Twister* and *The Lost World*), franchise films (movies that are produced with the full intention of producing several sequels, like *Star Wars*, *Harry Potter*, and *The Matrix*), and television, comic book and videogame remakes (movies that are adapted from television shows and comic books and videogames). Together, they help the film industry remain competitive in the media world.

9.5 *Radio and Sound Recording*

Radio was the first electronic mass medium as well as the first national broadcast medium in the United States. It produced the networks, program genres, and stars that made this electronic medium an instant success. But for many years, radio and records were young people's media, giving voice to a generation. As such, they may be the most personally significant mass media.

 It is generally believed that radio in America has gone through three developmental stages—the "pioneer" period from the 1890s through the mid-1920s, the "golden age" of network programs in the 1930s and 1940s, and the "television age" which began in the late 1940s and is still in progress. From the viewpoint of the "old-time-radio" fans, this pattern is almost tragic, for it represents periods of adventurous youth, glorious maturity, and senile decay. From a less partisan position, however, the pattern looks better, because it shows a medium that went through a period of early technological and commercial development, then through a boom period of unstable and rapid growth, and finally achieved a stable place in the structure of American business and culture.

 Almost at the same time when radio began its "pioneer" age, sound recording found its voice heard in the late 1880s, when Thomas Edison patented his "talking machine," a device for duplicating sound that used a hand-cranked grooved cylinder and a needle. The mechanical movement caused by the needle passing along the groove of the rotating cylinder and hitting bumps was converted into electrical energy that activated a diaphragm in a loudspeaker and produced sound. After some improvements by other people, sound recordings came along in the form of two-sided disc. Public acceptance of the new medium was enhanced by development of electromagnetic recording in 1924. By then, something epoch-making was going to happen, for the parallel development and diffusion of radio and sound recording was going to change the way of life for many Americans. For the first time in history, radio allowed people to hear the words and music of others who were not in their presence. On recordings they could hear words and music that may have been created days, months, or even years before.

 The idea of broadcasting predated the development of radio. Alexander Graham Bell's telephone company had a subscription music service in major cities in the late 1800s, delivering music to homes and businesses by telephone wires. The introduction of broadcasting to a mass audience was delayed by patent fights and lawsuits. In a series of developments that would be duplicated for television at the time of World

Chapter Nine
Mass Media

War II, radio was transformed into an entertainment and commercial giant. Later, concerned that the medium would be wasted and fearful that a foreign company would control this vital resource, the U.S. government forced the combatants to merge. Consequently, American Marconi, General Electric, American Telephone & Telegraph, and Westinghouse—each in control of a vital piece of technology—joined to create the Radio Corporation of America (RCA). RCA was a government-sanctioned monopoly, but its creation avoided direct government control of the new medium.

The formation of RCA ensured that radio would be a commercial, profit-based system. The industry supported itself, first, through the sale of receivers, and then advertising, which soon led to establishment of the national radio networks. Groups of stations, or affiliates, could deliver large audiences, realizing greater advertising revenues, which would allow them to hire bigger stars and produce better programming, which would attract larger audiences and could be sold for ever greater fees to advertisers. Soon, such big networks as the National Broadcasting Company (NBC), the Columbia Broadcasting System (CBS), and the American Broadcasting Company (ABC) were founded respectively in the first half of the 20th century, setting the fundamental basis of broadcasting in the United States: (1) radio broadcasters were private, commercially owned enterprises; (2) governmental regulation was based on the public interest; (3) stations were licensed to serve specific localities, but national networks programmed the most lucrative hours with the largest audiences; (4) entertainment and information were the basic broadcast content; and (5) advertising formed the basis of financial support for broadcasting.

The networks ushered in radio's golden age. During WWII, radio was used to sell war bonds, and much content was aimed at boosting the nation's morale. The war increased the desire for news, especially from abroad. Similarly, sound recording benefited from the war as well. American soldiers brought a new technology from occupied Germany, a tape recorder that used an easily handled plastic on a reel, that boosted recording industry tremendously. However, just when radio was enjoying its heyday, television arrived. Network affiliation dropped from 97% in 1945 to 50% by the mid-1950s, as stations "went local" in the face of television's national dominance. By the same token, national radio advertising income dipped to $35 million in 1960, the year that television found its way into 90% of U. S. homes. Clearly, if radio were to survive, it would have to find new functions.

Radio, of course, has more than survived; it has prospered in the past fifty years by changing the nature of its relationship with its audiences, and by applying new technology to its operation. If the pre-television radio was nationally oriented, broadcasting an array of recognizable entertainment program formats, populated by well-known stars and personalities, post-television radio is local, fragmented, specialized, personal, and mobile. Also, if pre-television radio was characterized by the big national networks, today's radio is dominated by formats, a particular sound characteristic of a local station. By offering FM, AM, and non-commercial programs, the radio industry has been able to attract a large population as its loyal audiences. According to the recent statistics, there are 13,012 radio stations operating in the United States today: 4,727 commercial AM stations; 6,051 commercial FM stations; and 2,234 non-commercial FM stations. In an average week, more than 200 million people, 95% of all Americans aged 12 and above, will listen to the radio. Between the weekday hours of 6:00 and 10:00 a. m., 81% of all 12-year-olds and older will turn in. The majority of Americans, 60%, get their first news of the day from radio, and the large majority of all listening, 83%, occurs in cars on the road.

While DJs and formats saved radio in the 1950s, they also changed for all time popular music and, by extension, the recording industry. Today, more than 5,000 U. S. companies are annually selling more than 1 billion discs of recorded music on more than 2,600 labels. More than 60,000 stores sell recorded music, and U. S. customers annually buy one-third of the world's recorded music. Currently, five major recording companies control nearly 90% of the recorded music market in the United States. Each is part of a larger conglomeration of medial and other businesses, and all but one are foreign owned: Sony (Japan), BMG (Germany), Universal Music Group (Canada/France), Warner Brothers Music Group (USA), and EMI Records (England). Critics have voiced concern over conglomeration and internationalization in the music business, a concern that centers on the traditional cultural value of music, especially for young people. Some worry about cultural homogenization, an outcome of virtually all the world's influential recording being controlled by a few profit-oriented giants. Others worry about the dominance of profit over artistry, where potentially more innovative artists are

Chapter Nine
Mass Media

marginalized. Still others point out that nowadays promotion overshadows the music, with the result artists who do not come across well on MTV often are not signed.

Both radio and the recording industry have prospered due to technological advances. Television gave radio its new personality and, through MTV, reinvigorated the music business. Satellite delivery of music directly to radio stations, homes, and cars has made possible the proliferation of radio networks. More significantly, convergence of radio and the Internet promises to bring further change to the radio and recording industries. In fact, it promises to completely reinvent the recording business. The large audience for shock jocks (outrageous, rude, crude radio personalities) poses a dilemma for media literate listeners who must remain aware of the impact of the media and what the content of shock jock shows says about the life and culture of humankind.

9.6 Television

After the printing press, the most important invention in communication technology to date has been television. Television has changed the way teachers teach, governments govern, religious leaders preach, and the way people organize the furniture in their homes. Additionally, television has also changed the nature, operation, and relationship to their audiences of books, magazines, movies, and radio. The computer, with its networking abilities, may overtake television as a medium of mass communication. But television defines over its future. For instance, will the promise of the Web be drowned in a sea of commercials? Can online information services deliver faster and better information than television? Indeed, even the computer screens we use look like television screens, and people are now waiting for better Internet video, Web-TV, online video conferencing, and the new and improved computer video game.

Technically television is in its sixties, but culturally it is in its thirties. In the year 1926, for example, there were practical demonstrations of living scenes viewed the instant they took place by audiences removed from the events. Depression, war, and technical difficulties combined to deter the development of television. By 1951, the commercial television networks had established their hegemony and were developing means of transmitting signals from coast to coast. By 1952, 108 stations had been set up, broadcasting programs to 17 million homes. By the end of the decade, there were 559 stations, and nearly 90% of U.S. households had television, making the decade the "golden age" of television. By then, the content and character of the medium were comfortably set. For example, television genres, as with the radio networks, included variety shows, situation comedies, dramas, soap operas, and quiz shows. Additionally, two new formats appeared: feature films and talk shows, both of which attracted a large audience. More importantly, television news and documentary remade broadcast journalism as a powerful force in its own right. Its coverage of the major political events, particularly party conventions and presidential campaigns, demonstrated the power of television to report news and history in the making.

The 1960s saw the immense social and political power of the new medium to force profound alterations in the country's consciousness and behavior. Particularly influential were the Nixon-Kennedy presidential debates, broadcasts of the aftermath of Kennedy's assassination and funeral in 1963, the 1969 transmission of Neil Armstrong's walk on the moon, and the use of television at the end of the decade by civil rights and anti-Vietnam War leaders. Because of a huge audience television could attract at the same time in the evening, television is often described as providing Americans no more than a "vast wasteland." However, whether one agrees to this assessment or not, there is no doubt that audiences continue to watch. It is estimated that there are now more than 100 million television households in the United States, in which a television is on for an average of 7.5 hours a day. The average male watches 4 hours 11 minutes a day; the average female 4 hours 46 minutes; the average teen 3 hours 4 minutes; and the average child 3 hours 7 minutes.

Today, as it has been from the beginning, the business of television is dominated by a few centralized production, distribution, and decision-making organizations. The networks link affiliates for the purpose of delivering and selling viewers to advertisers. The large majority of the 1,309 commercial stations in the United States are affiliated with a national broadcasting network: ABE, NBC, and CBS each have over 200 affiliates and Fox has close to that number. Many more stations are affiliated with UPN, the WB, and Pax, often referred to as "weblets." Although cable has introduced dozens of new "cable networks"—ESPN, MTV, Comedy Central, and A&E, to name a few, most programs that come to mind when people think of television in the United States were either conceived, approved, funded, produced, or distributed by the broadcast networks. Indeed, networks control what appears on the vast majority of local television stations, but they also control what appears on the non-network television. In addition, they influence what appears on independent stations and on cable channels. This non-network material not only tends to be network-type programming but most often is programming that originally aired on the networks themselves, called off-network programs.

On average, the national broadcast networks look at about 4,000 proposals a year for new television series. Many, if not most, are submitted at the networks' invitation. Of the 4,000, about 100 will be filmed as pilots, or trial programs. Perhaps, 20 to 30 will make it onto the air. Only half of these will last a full broadcast season. In a particularly good year, at most 3 or 4 will succeed well enough to be called hits. For this reason, the networks prefer to see ideas from producers with established track records and financial and organizational stability. Therefore, a producer must attract the interest of a network with an idea that is salable on the network's schedule, while incurring years of financial loss in hopes of having content that will be of interest to syndication viewers some years later. There is little incentive to gamble with characters or story lines; there is little profit in pushing the aesthetic boundaries of the medium. Many critics of television argue that it is this production system that keeps the quality of content lower than it might otherwise.

With the development of technology in receiving signals from distant locales, the age of cable television arrived, which has significantly reshaped the face of modern television. Today, about 70% of all U. S. television homes are wired. The pre-cable television audience had very few choices—three commercial networks, public television, and an independent station. Today's cable audience has 100 or more channel options. These new outlets provide channels for innovative, first-run series. With the increased diffusion of fiber optic cable, 500-channel cable systems are becoming technologically feasible. By its mere existence, cable offers alternatives that were not available on broadcast networks. These powerful delivery systems have helped equalize the size of the audience for independent and affiliated stations. Equally significant in reshaping the face of modern television is the introduction of VCR and DVD. Viewing rented and purchased videos and DVD at home with family members or friends has become many Americans' favorite pastime, further eroding the audience for traditional over-the-air television.

Most recently, digital television and the Internet on television have been the focus of many people's attention. Digitalization of video signals reduces their size, and therefore more information can be carried over telephone wires belonging to either a cable or phone company. The traditional television broadcasters see digitalization of television signals as their salvation, because it allows them to carry multiple forms of content on the spectrum space currently used to carry their one broadcast signal. As of now, all stations in the U.S. have converted to digital broadcasting, although the unavailability of digital receivers, disagreement over a technical standard, and cable's willingness to convert are slowing digital television's full rollout. Relatively, the convergence of television and the Internet, under way for not too long, seems to hold the potential to reinvent both media, particularly because of the promise of fuller interactivity. Although American Online, @Home, and Yahoo! all announced plans to begin offering the Internet over home television, the most aggressive advocate for accessing the Net on the home screen is Microsoft's WebTV, which turns a television set into a computer screen, permitting access to the Internet. As such, it provides not only access to the Web, but also several sites of its own, offering at the same time several features that allow the Internet to enhance television viewing itself. Apparently, television is faced with both challenges and opportunities for its future development.

9.7 The Internet and the World Wide Web

It is not an overstatement to say that the Internet and the World Wide Web have changed the world, not to mention all the other mass media. In addition to being powerful communication media themselves, the Net and the Web sit at the center of virtually all the media convergence we see around us. Aided by electronic technology, people around the world are now able to enjoy increased contacts and increased involvement with one another, making Marshall McLuhan's global village truer than ever before.

There are conflicting versions about the origin of the Internet. The more common story is that the Net is a product of the Cold War. In this version, the U.S. Air Force, in order to maintain the military's ability to transfer information around the country even if a given area was destroyed

Chapter Nine
Mass Media

in an enemy attack, in 1926 commissioned leading computer scientists to develop the means to do so. According to the second version, as early as 1956 psychologist Joseph Licklider foresaw linked computers creating a country of citizens "informed about, and interested in, and involved in, the process of government." In what many technologists now consider to be the seminal essay on the potential and promise of computer networks, *Man-Computer Symbiosis*, Licklider wrote in 1960: "The hope is that in not too many years, human brains and computing machines will be coupled... tightly, and the resulting partnership will think as no human brain has ever thought and process data in a way not approached by the information handling machines we know today." Scores of computer experts, enthused by Licklider's vision, joined the rush toward the development of what we know today as the Internet.

A crucial part of the story of the Internet is the development and diffusion of personal computers. IMB was fantastically successful at exciting businesses, schools and universities, and other organizations about computers. But IBM's and other companies' mainframe and minicomputers employed terminals, and these stations at which users worked were connected to larger, centralized machines. As a result, the Internet at first was the province of the people who worked in those settings. When the semiconductor replaced the vacuum tube as the essential information processor in computers, its tiny size, absence of heat, and low cost made possible the design and production of small, affordable personal or microcomputers (PCs). This opened the Net to anyone, anywhere. However, what is interesting to note is that with the development of the Internet, it is no exaggeration at all to say that computers are rarely used for computing anymore because the Net has given the computer more versatility, like e-mail and Usenet.

Another way of accessing information files is on the Internet via the World Wide Web. The Web is not a physical place, nor a set of files, nor even a network of computers. The heart of the Web lies in the protocols that define its use. The World Wide Web uses hypertext transfer protocols (HTTP) to transport files from one place to another. What makes the World Wide Web unique is the striking appearance of the information when it gets to our computer. In addition to text, the Web presents color, images, sounds, and video. This, combined with its ease of use, makes the Web the most popular aspect of the Internet for the large majority of people. What is interesting is that for people who access a medium, we call them audience members, but for people accessing the Internet, we call them users. At any time, or even at the same time, a person may be both *reading* Internet content and *creating* content. E-mail and chat rooms are obvious examples of online users being both audience and creators at the same time. More importantly, we can now access the Web with ease, linking from site to site and page to page, and even building our own sites.

By its very nature, the Internet raises a number of important issues of freedom of expression. There is no central location, no on-and-off button for the Internet, making it difficult to control for those who want to do so. For free expression advocates, this freedom from control is the medium's primary strength. The anonymity of its users provides their expression—even the most radical, profane, and vulgar—great protection, giving voice to those who would otherwise be silenced. But to advocates of Internet control, this anonymity is a breeding ground for abuse, when freedom is coupled with responsibility. Thus, Internet freedom of expression issues fall into two broad categories. The first is the Net's potential to make the First Amendment's freedom of the press guarantee a reality for greater numbers of people. The second is the problem of setting boundaries of control. Given the justifiable arguments of each side, such a double-edge issue is unlikely to be solved soon. Consequently, the major free expression battles in cyberspace in the U. S. have revolved around containing online pornography, protecting children from inappropriate content, protecting privacy and personal information, and finally protecting copyright. None of them is easy, but improved technology may provide some solutions.

Most recently, the Internet in the U. S. has been trumpeted as the newest and best tool for increased democratic involvement and participation. Presidential candidate Ross Perot used the promise of an "electronic town hall" as a centerpiece of his 1992 campaign. Vice President Al Gore conducted history's first interactive, computer network conference on January 13, 1994. In 2008, Barack Obama utilized the Internet to the fullest extent to date for his presidential campaign, making the virtual technology an effective tool to inform voters, to rally people behind him, and to get young people interested in politics. Just as proponents of virtual democracy are jubilant about the Internet being a vehicle for self-governance, critics argue that the Internet will be no more of an asset to democracy than have been radio and television because the

Chapter Nine
Mass Media

same economic and commercial forces that have shaped the content and operation of those more traditional media will constrain just as rigidly the new. For one thing, there is the technology gap, the widening disparity between the communication technology haves and have-nots. For another, there is the information gap fed by the technology gap, making those without the requisite technology unable to enjoy full access to information necessary to exercise voting rights. Clearly, if the computer technology gap creates an even wider information gap than already exists between voters, democracy will surely suffer, rather than benefit. At any rate, the rapid changes that characterize today's communication technologies and mass communication they foster demand that America solve the economic and technology gap to make the Internet really a tool for democracy.

SUMMARY

(1) The book is the least "mass" of the mass media in audience reach and in the magnitude of the industry itself, and this fact shapes the nature of the relationship between medium and audience. Although the book industry is bound by many of the same financial and industrial pressures that constrain other media, the book is in a position to transcend those constraints, making it unique in American culture.

(2) Newspapers have a long history in America from the colonial period of the 17th century to the present day of the 21st century. Before the invention of radio and television, newspapers were the main source of information about both news and merchandises. With the arrival of the Internet, newspapers are under enormous pressure to secure new identities for themselves, redefining their role and operation.

(3) Magazines have a long history in America, first reprinting British material, and then publishing material uniquely American. With the advent of television, magazines found themselves unable to match the reach of television. In order to cater to different tastes and needs of readers, magazines have to be specialized, targeting their own particular group of loyalists. Recently, Webzines/online magazines have emerged.

(4) The movies are American dream factories, larger than life. Since the Lumière brothers showed the first film in Paris in 1895, the movies have caught on around the world, America in particular. There, the movies have developed into a cultural industry, not only making huge profits, but also producing numerous romances and dreams. Hollywood is

both the "dream factory" and the maker of "movie magic."

(5) Radio was the first electronic mass medium as well as America's first national broadcast medium. It produced the networks, programs genres, and stars that made this electronic medium an instant success. Along with radio, sound recording found its voice heard in the late 1880s. Soon, such big networks as NBC, CBS, and NBC were founded in the first half of the 20th century, setting the stage for broadcasting industry.

(6) After the printing press, the most important invention in communication technology to date has been television. Television has changed the way teachers teach, governments govern, religious leaders preach, and the way people organize their lives. Today, the business of television is dominated by a few centralized production, distribution, and decision-making organizations, such as ABC, CBS, NBC, and Fox.

(7) The arrival of the Internet has changed virtually everything in the world. In addition to being a powerful medium itself, the Net sits at the center of all the media convergence we see around. By its very nature, the Internet raises a number of important issues of freedom of expression. Most recently, the Net in America has been trumpeted as the newest and best tool for increased democratic participation.

ESSAY QUESTIONS

(1) As a medium least dependent on advertisers' support, books can be aimed at extremely small groups of readers, challenging them and their imagination in ways that many sponsors would find unacceptable in advertising-based mass media. Make distinctions between books and other forms of mass media to explain the way(s) books appeal to their audiences, noting, in particular, their relative independence.

(2) At their initial stage, both newspapers and magazines in America duplicated or imitated their counterparts in Great Britain. With the development of American economy, but particularly with the maturity of American culture, they became more American in both content and style. Trace the evolutionary process of these two mass media to illustrate their American characteristics in both concept and practice.

(3) Hollywood is often viewed as the "dream factory" in America and around the world. While everybody knows that the movies are larger than life, most Americans, if not all, want their lives and loves to be "just like in the movies." Discuss how the "dream factory" has been making dreams to fantasize American audiences, and how and why American movie-goers

Chapter Nine
Mass Media

are so credulous about all these dreams.

(4) Radio, sound recording, and television had been the major forms of mass media in America until the advent of the Internet. Even so, they still play a significant role in Americans' way of life, providing news, music, information, and various forms of entertainment. Examine the way(s) they shape people's opinion, influence people's taste, and dictate people's everyday life.

(5) It is no exaggeration at all to assert that the Internet has dramatically changed our world, the world of the young people in particular. The way we obtain information, the way we communicate to each other, the way we access the government, and the way we organize our life have all changed significantly. Discuss the way(s) Americans rely upon the Internet for their political, social, and cultural life.

American Society and Culture
美 国 社 会 文 化

Chapter Ten
Popular Culture

American Society and Culture
美 国 社 会 文 化

LEARNING OBJECTIVES

- Be informed of the various forms of popular culture
- Understand the almost universal popularity of comic arts
- Learn the ways(s) advertising functions as a hidden persuader
- Be aware of the new lifestyle the automobile culture has brought about
- Know dance, music and sports as forms of popular entertainment

At first glance, popular culture seems to be exclusively modern. If the idea brings anything to mind, it is probably images of popular music, popular movies, popular fictions, and popular arts. Such appearances may be deceiving. In truth, there has always been a popular culture. Something is popular, after all, if it succeeds in reaching and pleasing as many people as possible. In a way, popular culture attempts precisely that, no more and no less. As a way of definition, popular culture, at its simplest, is the culture of mass appeal. A creation is popular when it is created to respond to the experiences and values of the majority, when it is produced in such a way that the majority of the people have easy access to it, and when it can be understood and interpreted by that majority without the aid of special knowledge or experience. Every human society at every stage of human history has had artists and craftsmen who have produced such materials that we now call popular culture.

10.1 Comic Art

The daily and Sunday comic strips, and comic books, are part of the reading habits of millions of people at all educational and social levels in

Chapter Ten
Popular Culture

the United States. While the roots of comic art may be partly European, the comics as they are known today are a distinctly American art form that has contributed heavily to the culture of the world, from Picasso to the pop art movement. They derive from popular patterns, themes, and concepts of world culture—just as Dick Tracy was inspired by Sherlock Holmes, Superman draw on the heroic tradition to which Beowulf and Paul Bunyan belong. The comics also serve as revealing reflectors of popular attitudes, tastes, and they speak directly to human desires, needs, and emotions.

Some historians trace the comic strip to prehistoric cave drawings, the medieval tapestry, the 18th-century printings, the illustrated European broadsheet, the 19th-century illustrated novels and children's books, the American comic strip as we know it may have been influenced by all of these antecedents, yet it remains a distinct form of expression unto itself and primarily is an American creation. It may be defined as an open-ended dramatic narrative about a recurring set of characters, told with a balance between narrative text and visual action, often including dialogue in balloons, and published serially in newspapers. The comic strips shares with drama the use of such conventions as dialogue, scene, stage devices, gestures, and compressed time, and it anticipated such film techniques as montage, angle shots, panning, close-ups, cutting, and framing. Unlike the play or the film, however, the comic strip is usually the product of one artist (or an artist and a writer) who must be a combined producer-scriptwriter-director-scene designer at once and bring his characters to life on the flat space of a printed page, with respect for the requirements of a daily episode that takes less than a minute's reading time. It is these challenges that make fine comic art difficult to achieve and contribute to its distinct qualities

Identifying the first comic strip is not easy. Some would suggest James Swinnerstone's 1895 feature for the *San Francisco Examiner*, *Little Bears and Tykes*, in which bear cubs, who had been used in sport illustrations for the newspaper since 1893, adopted the human postures of small children. Others more commonly suggest Richard Outcault's *The Yellow Kid*, who first appeared in the May 5, 1895 issue of the *New York World*, a street urchin in the middle of riotous activities set in the low-class immigrant sections of the city. Unlike Swinnerston, Outcault developed a central character in his use of the *Kid*, always clad in a yellow shift on which his dialogue was printed, and by 1890 had moved from a single panel cartoon to the format of a progressive series of panels with balloon dialogue, which would become the definitive form of the comic strip. Most of the popular strips that came on the heels of the *Kid* in the following three decades used humor and fantasy as their major modes, such as Rudolph Dirks' *The Katzenjammer Kids*, the longest running comic strip in existence, Frederick Opper's several wacky creations *Happy Hooligan*, and Winsor McCay's *Little Nemo in Slumberland*, the most technically accomplished and aesthetically beautiful Sunday page ever drawn.

Although some adventurous continuity and suspense had been used in the comic strip, it was not until the late 1920s that the adventure strip was well established as a fully developed genre. The 1930s and 1940s were to be dominated by adventure titles in the comic strip. Related by the use of the same devices of mystery and suspense and also developed during these years were the soap opera strips. By the 1950s, satire had flourished in the comics. As early as 1930, Chic Young's *Blondie* had gently satirized at first the flappers and playboys of the jazz and later the institution of marriage. Soon, the comics would become a significant forum for illustrating the hypocrisies and absurdities of the larger social and political trends of the nation. Just as Capp used the hillbilly life as his main vehicle for satire, his successors would use other and often more imaginative vehicles, such as the fantasy world of children, the ancient form of the animal fable, and the fanciful world of a medieval kingdom. The most recent entries in this tradition reveal two radical trends for the 1970s, with Russel Myers' *Broomhilda* moving toward a totally abstract world and Garry Trudeaus' *Doonesbury* moving into the realistic world of the radical student generation of the 1970s.

While the comic art enjoys great popularity in the United States, for a long time, it did not win recognition by the mainstream artistic community. Indeed, as late as the early 1980s, fine arts students still had to hide their interest in cartoon drawings from teachers, because any art form associated with comic books and comic strips was not considered college material. People grew up with comics, hardly realizing how much work and time went into them. In recent years, this unappreciated state of comics has begun to change. A lot of the credit goes to the emergence in the 1980s of graphic novels, offering more complex and complete story lines for more mature audiences. They typically are more durably bound and longer than the floppy comic magazines that told the tales of Superman or the antics of small-town teenagers. Even traditional superheroes gradually have shown a darker, more personal side, appealing to older readers. Many of those series have been collected into more colorful book formats and marketed as graphic novels. The graphic novel's increased critical acclaim and greater visibility in mainstream bookstores and libraries have contributed to the growing respect for comic art.

With growing acceptance of the comic art by the established culture in the United States, not only have high schools and colleges begun to offer comic art course along with other disciplines, but galleries and museums have also opened their doors to comic and cartoon art, as educational institutions and art venues have increasingly recognized its artistic and literary value. Take New York as an example, the number of freshmen in the cartooning major at the School of Visual Arts in New York more than doubled from 2002 to 2007. The Savannah College of Art and Design offered comics art in 1992 as an elective to a handful of students. The school now has nearly 300 undergraduates and 50 graduate students pursuing bachelor's and master's degrees in sequential art, also known as comics art. Similarly, more high schools and even grade schools are seeking advice on ways to foster student interest in cartooning. Over the past two decades, schools have seen dramatic increases in the number of female students, attributed largely to manga and graphic novel themes that include romance, historical drama, autobiography, fantasy and mystery. By the same token, comics, such as those that have brought Americans popular characters like Superman and Batman, have been getting more attention from mainstream art venues. Prominent museums including the Whitney in New York and London's Institute of Contemporary Art have dedicated exhibits to comic art several times. In 1986, Spiegelman's graphic novel *Maus*, depicting his family's ordeal through the Holocaust, received the prestigious Pulitzer Prize. All this indicates that the comic art is now recognized not only for its artistic value, but also for its literary value.

People within the comic industry have always viewed them as a serious high art form that just were not given the appropriate recognition. With a bias against comics, many people tend to think of it as superheroes and other juvenile things. Now, a growing consensus is being built up, believing that comics as an art form can be used to tell all sorts of different stories, not necessarily just what they might remember about their childhood. Indeed, for many comic enthusiasts, comics are just the means for delivering a story that can be about anything, and comic art can be used to express all sorts of different stories, like prose, poetry, fiction, nonfiction. In short, it's a medium, not a genre. For instance—comics have tremendous appeal for those seeking to convey religious messages. Religious comics—comics using religious stories—are big right now. Naturally, these sorts of epics are full of great stories, and full of action and adventure. In the same vein, blockbuster movies based on comics like *Spiderman* and *Superman* have spurred renewed interest in comics and propelled the medium to new heights of popularity. The characters that come out of the comics are very strong. Such figures as Charlie Brown and Snoopy in the newspaper comics and certainly the superheroes like Spiderman and Batman and Superman are now iconic figures in world culture today. Apparently, the newfound respect that comics have gained recently will likely continue. It is influencing films, books, and much of other printed and visual culture.

10.2 *Advertising*

Advertising has been described as an institution, a business, an industry, a discipline, a profession, a science, an art, and a talent. Additionally, it has been defined as news, salesmanship in print, and mass communication. Some of the best minds in the business, outside the business, and on the fringes of the business have attempted to define and deal with this elusive subject. Scholars and advertising men themselves have examined the political, economic, social, historical, and religious aspects of advertising. Each of them has told us what advertising is, how it works, how it should work, and why it does not work; each has also told us that advertising either deceives, informs, pleases, or frightens us.

Advertising has been attacked and defended by almost every segment of society. When it is advantageous, someone will admit to having used or even liked advertising. When it is not, the vindictiveness against advertising flies, even from public relations, marketing, and retailing specialists. To a great extent, to look at the advertising of a nation is essentially to view most aspects of its existence, for advertising is the story of a nation's people. Although advertising did not originate in America, this country has probably done more than any other nation to use and foster advertising. Indeed, foreign politicians and businessmen are said to have observed American advertisements as a gauge for

Chapter Ten
Popular Culture

measuring and understanding America's tastes and values. In this sense, advertising is probably the most pervasive form of popular culture in the United States.

Although the origins of advertising have been traced back to several sources, no one is exactly sure when the trade began. However, several evidences of written advertisements have been discovered and offered as the first recorded efforts in selling. The ones most often suggested are Babylonian clay tablet announcing the services of an ointment dealer, scribe, and shoemaker, and a piece of papyrus from the ruins of Thebes offering a reward for the return of runaway slaves. Advertising in America, which grew in conjunction with the expanding colonial economy, found its greatest impetus in newspapers, once the press had won its right to exist. As early as the 1760s, *The Boston Newsletter* carried advertisements for the return of some men's clothing and for the reward and capture of a thief. Although American advertising had reached a considerable sophistication and circulation, it was Benjamin Franklin who has earned—along with his other credits—the title of father of American advertising, because he made important improvements in advertising methods, particularly in the style and format of advertisements.

Most of the advertisements of the shopkeepers of the late 18th century were directed toward the upper classes. Long notices informed the wealthy readers of the latest imported goods from England, Holland, and the Far East. Newspaper growth matched the increasing American population and income and by 1820, some five hundred newspapers were serving more than nine million Americans. By then, newspapers prided themselves on the number, not the quality, of the ads that appeared in their pages, and American reading public readily accepted the inundation of advertisements. Technological advances in the 19th century created many kinds of changes in the format and production of newspapers, making it possible to reduce the price of newspapers while at the same time creating more space for advertisements. In the ensuing years, as competition became increasingly fierce among newspapers for advertising, demands were made to provide some sort of order for the chaotic advertising business. Subsequently, there arose in the form of a middle man, the advertising agent, whose job was to inform the advertiser about the newspapers, rates, and options available to him, and to help the newspaperman keep his pages filled with advertisements. The creation of the advertising agent greatly facilitated the advertising business in the newspapers.

With the arrival of television, advertising soon took a new direction. As television commercials could let consumers see and hear the product in action, television soon became the primary advertising medium. Indeed, the ability to demonstrate the product—to smoothly shave sandpaper with Gillette Foamy, for instance—led to the unique selling proposition (USP), that is, highlighting the aspect of a product that sets it apart from other brands in the same product category. Once an advertiser discovered a product's USP, it could drive it home in repeated demonstration commercials. Because a number of commercials in an individual program or on a given night of television were selling the same or similar products, and because many of these products were essentially the same in quality and cost, the USP became even more important, as did the need to boost brand awareness—identification of a product with a particular manufacturers. Oftentimes, brand identification was achieved through slogans and jingles: "You'll wonder where the yellow went when you brush your teeth with Pepsodent (a toothpaste's brand-name)."

In television's early days, commercials were highly product-oriented. But as the number of commercial spots grew, the number of commercial minutes allowed on television rose as well. In 1967, for example, there were an estimated 100,000 number of commercial minutes aired on the networks. Less than 8 years later, there were 105,622 commercial minutes on the three commercial networks alone. As the number of spots grew and their length shrank, commercials became less about the products—there was too little time to give any relevant information—and more about the people who use them. Image advertising came to television. Today, the price of commercial time continues to rise, production costs for programming continue to increase, the number of commercials on the air continues to grow, the air time available for advertising continues to expand, and as a result, the length of commercial spots continues to shrink. Fifteen- and ten-second spots are now common. One-second spots, called blink ads, now appear on some stations and networks. More and more spots crammed into a commercial break produce a lot of clutter. How does an advertiser get heard and seen above the clutter? The answer for many contemporary television advertisers is to give even less information about the product and place greater emphasis on style, image, graphics, and look. Today's television ads can cost as much as $1 million a minute to produce.

It is estimated that the typical individual living in the United States spends more than one year of his or her life just watching television commercials. It is a rare moment when Americans are not in the audience of some ad or commercial. Because of its pervasiveness, criticisms have been made about the negative impact advertisings have produced upon the public. Some critics fault advertising for its intrusiveness; other critics argue that advertising is inherently deceptive in promoting its products; still other critics accuse advertising of exploiting children by taking advantage of their intellectual immaturity. Most common of all, critics believe that irresponsible, vulgar and distasteful advertising tends to corrupt culture, because by creating a consumer culture, it tries to convince the people that personal worth and identity reside not in themselves as human beings but in the products with which they surround themselves. However, despite all these perceptive and sharp criticisms, advertising has not been slightly shaken, nor has been limited in its function. Indeed, in this money-oriented consumer society, advertising is not only going to be around in virtually every aspect of American life, but also enjoy greater influence and more power in all possible ways in the future. Indeed, in this Information Age, nothing can escape the influence of advertising.

10.3 Automobile Culture

Although man had dreamt of a self-propelled vehicle for centuries, it was not until the end of the 19th century that a practical road machine capable of sustained distances emerged for general use. Historians disagree on the actual inventor of the first American automobile, but it is widely known that several people were constructing and testing gasoline engine vehicles in the last two decades of the 19th century. However, it was not until the first decade of the 20th century that the automobile emerged as a commercially practical business and industrial venture. From an inauspicious beginning in 1901, the automobile industry grew to become a giant that has influenced American physical, intellectual, and moral lives in a way that is unequalled in modern times. By the mid-20th century, nearly fifty million automobiles were registered in the United States. There are indeed few Americans who can truthfully claim that the motorcar has had no place in their lives.

However, few people know that when the automobile first appeared, it was treated as a curiosity, a plaything for the rich and a tinkering project for the inventors or the hapless blacksmith who might be called upon to aid a motorist who by some malfunction had suddenly become a pedestrian. But the automobile quickly took hold, capturing people's minds as well as their imagination. Born into an America that had virtually no road system, it soon began to shrink the size of the vast continent, providing means for people to enjoy cross-country expeditions. After the automobile emerged from its novelty stage, its influence on American life became markedly greater. The mass production of Henry Ford's Model T, which began in 1908, ushered in a new era of attitudes and convictions about the motorcar. Although sudden death might lurk around the next curve and the neighborhood horses might be terrified, there was a new sense of freedom across the land. Urban dwellers could escape to the country for a day; isolated rural residents could visit each other and the nearby towns and cities more easily; lovers had a ready-made mobile bedroom; and businessmen could move more quickly in their daily routines.

As the automobile became a way of life in America, American life had to adjust to accommodate it. While the motorcar was shrinking the size of the continent, it was also altering both its physical and moral landscape. Service stations, garages, and parts warehouses popped up around the country at the same time that legislators and judges were pondering complex problems about how the use of the automobile should be governed. Also, both culturally and socially other changes were taking place. Society took a negative attitude to women driving automobiles, for example, steering wheels sometimes carrying a warning sign that read "Men and Boys Only." Clothes styles were altered to be more in keeping with what the motorist would need. Hotels began giving way to the more modern motel, and city dwellers found that they could live outside urban areas and motor to work, thus creating America's vast and sprawling suburbs.

In the decade of the 1920s, important social distinctions began to be made between owners and drivers of the myriad cars available in the country. Ford's Model T had been superseded by the more manageable and sleeker Model A. Meanwhile, the owners of expansive cars such as Cadillacs, Buicks, Chryslers, and Packards set them aside from those who drove the more plebian Fords and Chevrolets. Also, the female driver came into her own, with such automobile manufacturers as, for

Chapter Ten
Popular Culture

example, Jordan, actually making a sales pitch to women. The liberated woman, so the ads implied, should choose a Jordan, and advertising pictures of this sleek car would often show a woman driving, with a man sitting beside her on their way to the club, tennis, or golf. Indeed, throughout the 1920s and 1930s, the automobile continued to be the great emancipator of middle-class America. It was not until the belt-tightening occasioned by WWII that serious thoughts about the longevity of the automobile began to be considered. "Is this trip necessary?" became the question of radio newscasters and politicians alike.

Emerging victorious from WWII, the American "sacrificed his life as a whole to the motorcar." Freeways and interstates took the place of the prewar highways, which now became relegated to secondary road status. Drive-in movies, drive-in restaurants, drive-in banks, drive-in churches, and even drive-in funeral parlors made their appearance across America. By then, it could be comfortably argued that America was the car and the car was America. Before long, however, something happened. In the early 1970s, Americans began to face the reality that fossilized fuels might indeed be depleted in the foreseeable future. Moreover, the motorcar, long suspected as a serious atmospheric pollutant, came under the study of scientists who proved such to be the case. Adding to the already major problems the one of safety, the automobile thus became a political issue, and Detroit car manufacturers found themselves dictated to more by Washington than by their own boards of directors. Suddenly, the automobile became in many people's minds the great enemy. As gas prices skyrocketed, Americans stopped buying the inefficient gas-guzzlers that Detroit had marketed for years, and instead they developed their preference for smaller but more fuel-efficient cars imported from overseas.

Still, despite oil crises, traffic jams, air pollution, parking problems, and the growing traffic accident rate, Americans are not willing to stop their love affair with the automobile. Like electrical appliances, the A-U-T-O has reached into the lives of ordinary Americans, making them dependent upon it for daily routines. Family vacations, group outings, grocery shopping, hospital visitations, church attendance, courting couple dating, to name just a few, all depend on the magic power of the automobile. People applaud it for the freedom it offers, and welcome it for the conveniences it provides. Because of its virtual universal popularity, the automobile has not only become the symbol of modern America, but also accelerated the standardization process of American life. Everyday in the United States, from the East Coast to the West Coast, from the Southern rural villages to the Northern urban areas, millions of Americans chug around in their motor vehicles of every type and every shape, moving somewhere to function as an individual.

10.4 Dance

Dance at its most popular level in America has served as a form of social, participational recreation. Country or folk dancing and city or social dancing together describe the major patterns. In early America, as in all lands, dance initially played a purely ceremonial role as part of religious observances. Ritualistic Indian circle dances constituted the only form of dance European settlers in the New World encountered. The Puritans themselves brought no dance tradition with them and were, in fact, strongly discouraged from engaging in couple dancing. Other English, French, and Spanish colonists, however, brought rich native traditions of folk dancing which included hornpipes and jigs in addition to stately court dances such as the minuet and gavotte. Therefore, despite the railings of Puritan ecclesiastics, dancing was part of colonial American life. By 1716, for example, Boston claimed two rival dancing masters, one of whom was forced to move to New York, when rivalry for authority and for students became too keen. In Philadelphia, the first ball was held in 1748, establishing a tradition of a yearly social gathering with dancing as the main activity.

In the late 18th century, French entertainers and dancing masters came to America to escape the terrors of the French Revolution, and their performance greatly influenced the course of theatre as well as social dancing in America. Having the greatest influence in high society circles of Newport, New Hampshire, New York and Philadelphia, the French dancing masters brought sophisticated versions of country dances to American dance enthusiasts. So widespread was the French influence, that the French quadrille, a slowed down version of the minuet, became the forerunner of the American square dance. Also quite important was the effect French and all dancing masters in America had well into the late 19th century upon improvising and complicating the country dance steps, and upon standardizing their execution as well as developing dance rules of etiquette. In the late 18th and 19th centuries, anti-British sentiment in

Chapter Ten
Popular Culture

America fostered general preference for the French quadrille over English contra dances, although rural areas of New England kept alive the English folk dancing tradition. In the Southern Appalachian mountains of Kentucky, West Virginia, North Carolina and Tennessee, the Scottish and Irish settlers and their descendants continued to jig and clog which eventually became the trademark of Southern country dancing.

In the city, social dancing became increasingly refined and adapted rules of etiquette under the dancing masters. Hundreds of manuals were published during the 19th century, dictating correct placement and deportment. Couple dancing had been popularized in the first half of the 19th century by waltz and the polka of the day. Initially considered scandalous because of the close contact of the couple, the waltz grew so popular that the dancing masters were forced to accept a refined version of it. By the early 1900s, the waltz, the polka and the schottische were the favorite social dances. Not only was "correct" dancing fully accepted as a cultivated activity for high society, but social dancing was also established as a fixed feature of American social life at all levels. Around this time, however, the rich musical and dance traditions of Southern Blacks which had been nurtured in New Orleans was being heard more frequently and was to permanently change the face of social dance in America by introducing a new sense of rhythm. New Orleans saloon music known as "ragtime," with its "ragged" or syncopated rhythm, gave rise to the Turkey Trot, Grizzly Bear, Bunny Hug, and the Kangaroo Dip. So popular did these dances become that they set off a dance craze that lasted well into the late 1920s. Far more daring than the tame waltz had been, these new dances allowed couples to hang on to each other and dance cheek-to-cheek.

The decade of the 1930s is perhaps best known as the classic period of the Broadway musical and the Hollywood film, both of which featured dancing. Many performing artists not only performed routines, but also contributed toward making dancing the center of stage and film entertainment during the decade. Young people were increasingly becoming the biggest followers of dance fads, particularly when the big dance bands and swing music along with jitterbugging became popular. In the 1940s, jitterbugging quickly became the favorite dance of American servicemen and their dance partners in entertainment centers and army canteens. The second feature of social dance during this period was the rage for Latin music and dances. Samba, rumba, conga, and mambo were performed for an American dance public who diligently tried to learn the syncopated rhythm and hip movements. But with the decade of the 1950s came Elvis Presley and rock-and-roll music and dancing, providing an arena for teenagers to dance to the new music, though adults still preferred the fox trot and the cha-cha and vocal hits. In the early 1960s, the Twist, a dance that both adults and teenagers found easy to perform, dominated the rock-and-roll dance scene. However, the period also produced such fads as the Mashed Potatoes and the Jerk, which, like the Twist, separated the dancing couple and stressed the ingenuity of individual styles and movements. More significantly, black music and dance came into vogue during the 1960s, producing a host of "Motown" celebrities. ("Motown" is the record label under which much of the music was produced.) As the Beatles began to revolutionize rock music, social dancing waned in the mid- and late 1960s. Subsequently, the rock concert replaced dancing as the popular social entertainment pastime.

In the 1970s, a return to dancing brought back the discos and a new, updated version of "American Bandstand" (the old version of it was developed as a TV program in 1956). The 1971 show "Soul Train" featured black dances, demonstrating again black dance's emphasis upon complicated rhythm and timing. The Hustle, a dance originating in Hispanic community of New York City, was at the center of the dance craze in the 1970s and is credited with bringing back technique to social dancing. In addition, the 1977 movie *Saturday Night Fever* gave the dance craze of the 1970s new life. Studios and instructors once again became popular, and television came up with programs such as "Dance Fever" where dancing couples from across the country competed for prize money. The period also witnessed a nostalgic yearning for the good old days of dancing, and afternoon tea dances, held at hotels and clubs, featured programs of music from the 1930s and 1940s while couples glided across dance floors.

In more recent times, the popularity of New Wave and Punk Rock music of the 1980s attested to a new breed of dancers. Sporting Mohawk hairdos dyed pink, purple or blue, and wearing leather clothing, these newest dancers reject stylized movement. Their dancing is often performed in New York City and other urban area street corners and parks and may consist of repetitious, ritualistic-like jumping up and down while shivering and shaking the body. The contemporary cult of both Punk Rock and New Wave music provides the latest evidence that popular music and dancing are so closely connected that one inevitably influences and shapes the direction of the other. Over the past two decades, audience response to modern dance concerts have been mostly positive, and the number of people attending these dance concerts has increased significantly. Among the young people in the United States today, the most popular dances are popping and locking, leaning and rocking, and hip hop dancing. In short, while the number of Americans attending a ballet performance has been declining over the past few decades, those participating in modern, folk and tap dances have grown steadily.

10.5 Music

While thoughtful attention to popular music is relatively new, the music itself has been vigorously alive in the United States for a long time. Some of the music brought to the New World by the colonists was serious academic music; some was what we now call folk music, belonging to the community, passed down through generations by tradition. Some, however, was popular music, printed and sold in broadsides and song books or performed by professional entertainers to paying audiences. The source of this popular music was the mother countries of the new Americans, chiefly England. The same ballads sold in the streets of London were sold in the colonial American cities and towns; the same ballad operas and other musical entertainments were heard in English and American theaters.

In fact, English music remained in the American marketplace throughout the 19th century. Gradually, it became mixed with, then edged by, popular music that is distinctly American. Although it cannot be said for certain as to where this genuine American popular music really began, a sign of the beginning can be located in 1827. Among the few scattered relics of the music sold or professionally performed one hundred and seventy years ago that were known to be hits of the day, two songs suggest in retrospect that that year marks a turning point. In *Variety Music Cavalcade* 1620-1969, Julius Mattfeld lists four prominent songs for 1827, and of the four, two, "My Long-Tail Blue" and "The Coal-Black Rose" were popularized by the minstrel singer George Washington Dixon, a white man performing in blackface. He is believed to represent with these two hits an emblem of the course of American popular music—

American Society and Culture
美国社会文化

the native American note was struck in the meeting of African American and Euro-American styles.

Most popular songs in the years after 1827 continued to be the work of English writers or indistinguishable from English work. Similarly, tunes continued to be borrowed, as the tunes of "Yankee Doodle" and "The Star-Spangled Banner" had been borrowed, from English songs. However, a new way had been opened. The music that black slaves brought with them from west Africa evolved into an African American folk music and then evolved into a variety of styles of professional performances for black audiences. In themselves these styles are an American popular music, but throughout their history, in all their forms, they have also exerted an influence on the shaping of the rest of American popular music. Still, the first truly native American popular songs, according to some scholars, are those a generation after George Washington Dixon, at the next stage of interactions between black and white music. The disruption of the Civil and Reconstruction in the lives and culture of black men and women kept black music away from the ears of white Americans and popular music entered a recession that ended in the 1890s when the sounds of ragtime played by young black pianists began to be heard by white public. The distinctively American feeling that derived from ragtime rhythm enters the mainstream of those major songwriters of the 20th century.

At the opening of the 20th century, the decisive influence of the ragtime pianists fell on white audiences tiring of the minstrel show and willing to pay to hear black performers. At the same time, the American band was being heard everywhere. Both phenomena would modulate into dance bands playing vigorous dance music. Burgeoning displays of sheet music in neighborhood stores, often music calling itself rag, attracted a diverse public, much of which never heard the concerts of the creators of ragtime. A boom in social dancing began in the second decade of the twentieth, along with the first recognition of music called jazz. It was estimated that in the mid-1920s, there were 60,000 dance bands playing on the dance floors of jazz age America. Beginning in 1920, radio broadcasting brought recorded and live music into homes. During the Depression and WWII, a significant economic struggle surfaced in musical entertainment, with one music company pitting itself against another. When the war ended, the entertainment industry responded to the ready money of a new public, more urbanized but less in touch with sophisticated music, targeting the young families that were preparing themselves to be the next generation of popular music consumers. This generation was raised with unprecedented pocket money and leisure time and with unsuspected susceptibility to the energies of rock and roll they would first hear in the 1950s and the 1960s.

Rock and roll jarred the music industry into new patterns, new companies, new small-group recording economics, new audience definitions, and new relationships to radio broadcasting. Some of the story can be told in terms of technical innovations. Television as the surging home entertainment medium turned radio stations toward the disc jockey format of record programming. New sizes, speeds, and materials for the records themselves may have had wide implications. Some scholar makes an interesting analysis of the cultural meaning of the shift from 78 to 45 rpm records, as streamlining the experience of recorded music toward casualness, especially for the young audiences. The relationship of popular culture to ideology in the 1960s and the 1970s has become of interest to academic sociology, particularly the relationship between rock and roll and drug, called the "acid rock." However, the history of popular music suggests that it is very unlikely that musical entertainment itself can induce new behavior. Nevertheless, as rock has evolved in the last half a century and brought, among other things, self-consciousness to popular music, it has prompted an immense volume of reportage and analysis, much of which empty but some perceptive and judicious. Indeed, the attention that rock, rap, and other forms of rebellious music have demanded has occasioned the first widespread critical attention to the popular arts in general, music in particular.

Following the turbulent political, social and musical changes of the 1960s and early 1970s, rock music diversified. What was formerly known as rock and roll, a reasonably discrete style of music, had evolved into a catchall category called simply rock music, an umbrella term which would eventually include diverse styles like heavy metal music, punk rock and, sometimes even hip hop music. During the '70s, however, most of these styles were not part of mainstream music, and were evolving in the underground music scene. In the 1980s, rhythm and blues, which had been replaced by the term soul music in the 1960s to describe popular African American music, came back into use, most often in the form of R&B, a usage that has continued to the present. Contemporary R&B arose when sultry funk singers like Prince became very popular, alongside dance-oriented pop stars like Michael Jackson and female vocalists like Whitney Houston. By the end of the 1980s, pop-rock largely consisted of the radio-friendly glam metal bands, who used images derived from the British glam movement with macho lyrics and attitudes, accompanied by hard rock music and heavy metal virtuosic soloing.

Perhaps the most important change in the 1990s in American popular music was the rise of alternative rock through the popularity of grunge. This was previously an explicitly anti-mainstream grouping of genres that rose to great fame beginning in the early 1990s. Grunge became commercially successful in the early 1990s, peaking between 1991 and 1994. Bands from cities in the U. S. Pacific Northwest, especially Seattle, Washington, were responsible for creating grunge and later made it popular with mainstream audiences. The supposed Generation X, who had just reached adulthood as grunge's popularity peaked, were closely associated with grunge, the sound which helped "define the desperation of that generation." By the end of the decade and into the early 2000s, pop music consisted mostly of a combination of pop-hip hop and R&B-tinged pop, including a number of boy bands and female divas. Like Hollywood movies, American popular music enjoys worldwide popularity. Rock, hip hop, jazz, country and other styles have fans across the globe.

10.6 Sports

What is sport? It is a term not easy to define, but the word "sport" is often equated to "play." Both of them have in common the idea of being cut off from the workaday world. According to some scholars, "play" is free, separate, uncertain, unproductive, and governed by both rules and make-belief, while "sport" means to disport, that is, to divert and amuse. In this sense, "sport" can be regarded as that aspect of culture by which people divert themselves from labor as opposed to work.

To such questions as "What is play?" or "What is sport?" the Puritans would have had far less difficulty answering. For them, any effort not devoted to the good of the colony was to be eschewed, and sport did not seem to lend itself to the general welfare. In 1621, Governor Bradford rebuked the young men he found in the street at play. Indeed, the Puritan hostility to games took the form of official prohibition and even punishment, and their attitude toward fun and games can perhaps be

Chapter Ten
Popular Culture

best illustrated by a minister's remark: such games as bear-baiting were stopped not because they gave pain to the animals involved, but because they provided pleasure to the spectators. In other words, given their emphasis on hard-working spirit and self-denial discipline, the Puritans did not approve of games/sports because of their detestation of idleness, which, in fact, found expression in 17th-century southern region as well.

However, the human propensity to play could not be stifled, and the narrow sanctions of the ruling class had in the long run little chance of being obeyed. Slowly but steadily, sport grew not only in New England, but also along the frontier. Hunting and fishing became not only a means for gaining food, but also a form of diversion. At the beginning of the 19th century, there was a wide diversity of amusements in the North. The principle amusements included walking, riding, shooting, track and field, card-playing, and sailing. The sports that seemed to attract the most attention in the South were cockfighting and horse-racing. The former eventually disappeared in the South except in a few isolated areas, but the latter became America's first organized sport and has remained unquestionably one of its most popular one, equaling that of the World Series (baseball) and the Super Bowl (football). At any rate, by the end of the 19th century, sports in America had not only been widely embraced and celebrated by the general public, but also developed from participant activities to spectator events. How did such changes occur? No one seems to be able to offer any conclusive answers except the human love of sports, the need for heroes, the revolution in technology, and, above all, the promotion of them by mass media.

In the U.S. of today, football is the most popular spectator sport, and baseball is in second place among the sports people most like to watch. Both baseball and football are, of course, American developments of sports played in England. Baseball does not come from cricket, as many people think; instead it comes from baseball, and is still very popular in the United States as an informal, neighborhood sport. More than one American remembers the time when he/she hit a baseball through a neighbor's window. What makes football in the U.S. so different from its European cousins, rugby and soccer, is not just the size, speed, and strength of its players. Rather, it is the most "scientific" of all outdoor team sports. Specific rules state what each player in each position may and may not do, and when. There are hundreds of possible "plays" (moves) for teams on offense and defense. Because of all this,

217

football has been called "an open-air chess game disguised as warfare." Those who don't understand the countless rules and the many possibilities for plays miss most of the game and fun.

Baseball and football have the reputation of being "typically American" team sports. This is ironic because the two most popular participant sports in the world today are indeed American origin — basketball and volleyball. The first basketball game was played in Springfield, Massachusetts, in 1891. It was invented at a YMCA there as a game that would fill the empty period between the football season (autumn) and the baseball season (spring and summer). Volleyball was also first played in Massachusetts, and also at a YMCA, in 1895. During the First and Second World Wars, American soldiers took volleyball with them overseas and helped to make it popular. Today, both basketball and volleyball are played everywhere by men and women of all ages, and they are especially popular as school sports.

Indeed, in America sports are associated with educational institutions in a way that is unique. Junior and senior high schools have coaches as faculty members, and school athletic teams compete with each other in an array of sports. Each team's entourage includes a marching band and a group of cheerleaders. In some smaller American communities, high school athletics are a focal point of the townspeople's activities and conversations. Nowhere else in the world are sports associated with colleges and universities in the way they are in the United States. College sports, especially football, are conducted in an atmosphere of intense excitement and pageantry. Games between teams classified as "major football powers" attract nationwide audiences that number in the millions. There is a whole industry built on the manufacture and sale of badges, pennants, T-shirts, blankets, hats, and countless other items bearing the totem and colors of various university athletic teams. Football and basketball coaches at major universities are paid higher salaries than the presidents of their institutions. Athletic department budgets are in the millions of dollars. While observing the university football, a recently-arrived foreign student in Iowa City uttered the following remark: "It looks like that the most important part of the University of Iowa is the football team. Maybe the team is the most important thing in the whole town."

There is an enormous amount of live broadcasting of all different types of sports events, professional and amateur, at state, national, and

Chapter Ten
Popular Culture

international levels. Americans are used to having baseball and basketball, college and professional football games, golf, tennis, autoracing, swimming meets, and the Olympics carried live and at full length. In season, college football games are shown live all day Saturday. On Sundays, there are live television broadcasts of the professional teams. Usually, one or two games are broadcast throughout the land, and many others only to regions where the teams have most of their fans. This live broadcasting of sports events has not only increased interest in the sports, but also increased actual attendance at the stadiums or arenas. In some social circles, associating with athletes is a way to achieve social recognition. A person who knows a local sports hero personally, or who attends events where famous athletes are present, is considered by some people to have accomplished something worthwhile.

Black Americans are heavily overrepresented in the major sports of baseball, football, and basketball. Sometimes, it is not uncommon to see a basketball game in which all the players on the floor are black. Equally worth mentioning is that the women's liberation movement has brought considerable attention to women's athletics in the United States, perhaps more so than in any other country. Whatever the case, sports in America have transformed tremendously over the past two centuries, attracting not only ordinary folks, but also statesmen and professional people. Indeed, sports play such an important role in American life that the sociology of sports, sports medicine, and sports psychology have become respectable scholarly specializations. Perhaps, scholars will someday be able to provide a full account for the popularity of sports in America, but it suffices to say at this point that the fact that Americans like competition at least partially explains it.

SUMMARY

(1) Comic books and the daily and Sunday comic strips are part of the reading habits of millions of people at all educational and social levels in the United States. The comic art may be defined as an open-ended dramatic narrative about a recurring set of characters. In many ways, they serve as revealing reflectors of popular attitudes, tastes, speaking directly to human desires, needs, and emotions.

(2) Advertising has been described as a business, an industry, a profession, and an art. For better or worse, advertising has been attacked and defended by almost every segment of society, one lauding it as being

informative, the other condemning it as being deceptive. America has probably done more than any other nation to use and foster advertising, making it the most pervasive form of popular culture.

(3) While the actual inventor of the first American automobile may remain a mystery, it was not until the 1910s that the automobile emerged as a commercially practical business and industrial venture. For the automobile culture, Henry Ford, whose mass production made family cars possible, deserves all the credits. With virtually every family owning at least one car, America is truly a nation on wheels.

(4) Dance at its most popular level in America has served as a form of social, participational recreation. Country or folk dancing and city or social dancing together describe the major patterns. In early America, dance was discouraged, if not forbidden. But as America became modernized and urbanized, dance gained not only acceptance, but also popularity. To it, Blacks and Latinos have made very great contributions.

(5) Although popular music is relatively new, the music itself has been vigorously alive in America for a long time. Some of the music was seriously academic, brought to America by the colonists; and some was folk music, passed down through generations by tradition. Popular music, however, is typically America, which includes, among other things, rag, blues, jazz, rock and roll, rap, hip hop, and grunge.

(6) In early America, sport was largely viewed negatively, for the Puritans did not believe it was doing any good to the general welfare. Slowly but steadily, sport grew and prospered in America, beginning with individual sports like walking, riding and sailing, and culminating in such big team games as baseball, football, and basketball. Apart from professional games, there are also amateur and college sport events.

ESSAY QUESTIONS

(1) Comic art is consumed by readers of all types in America, young and old, men and women, white and black. From day one when it made its first appearance, comic art as a form of popular culture has never failed to attract its readership. Describe the basic features of comic strips and explain why comics have such a strong appeal to the American reading public across age, class, gender, and race.

(2) Given that advertising is so indispensable in modern America, no Americans can escape from its influence. Whether one likes it or not, he/she has to live with it. Trace the evolutionary process of advertising in

Chapter Ten
Popular Culture

America and discuss the role it plays not only in meeting the needs of consumers, but also in creating desires for consumption by potential customers, noting, in particular, the consumer culture it helps to create.

(3) Since the invention of the automobile, particularly since the automobile became necessity rather than luxury in America, people's life has significantly changed. From business activity to private life, from residential location to grocery shopping, and from tourism to courtship, virtually every aspect of an American's life has been affected by it. Examine how Americans organize their life around the automobile.

(4) Although recreational dance initially raised eyebrows among the Puritan settlers in the New World, it soon found its supporters and enthusiasts. With the rising wave of immigrants throughout the 19th and 20th centuries, dance not only was given fresh life, but also took on new forms and styles. Eventually, dance caught on and spread across the land. Examine the way(s) dance evolved and diversified.

(5) Both music and sports are popular culture, having fans primarily among the young people. Of these two forms of popular culture, rock and roll and American football and basketball have the largest audiences. Pick up any one form of music or any one kind of sport and discuss its social and cultural implications.

American Society and Culture
美 国 社 会 文 化

Chapter Eleven
Capitalist Economy and Business Civilization

American Society and Culture
美 国 社 会 文 化

LEARNING OBJECTIVES

- Know the strengths and weaknesses of American capitalism
- Learn the way(s) the businessman commands respect and admiration in America
- Be informed of the process in which the corporate empire was built
- Understand the organizational structure of the American economy
- Be aware of the relationship between capital and labor in America

It is often said that the American economy had to be built from the ground up, because prior to the arrival of European settlers, there was, except for the Indians living scattered around, virtually no form of modern economy. In the beginning, there were simply no farms or houses or factories. Whatever was needed had to be made by the settlers themselves. Or it had to be imported at great expense. The tremendous ingenuity and inventiveness of Americans has been traced to this pioneer time and spirit. "Do-it-yourself," in other words, is hardly a recent trend or a middle-class hobby in America. There were few skilled craftsmen available and no established class of agricultural workers, or peasantry. Therefore, if a new way to do the work couldn't be found, it just didn't get done. What has been achieved since the settlement of North American continent is amazing. By 1900, for example, the U. S. had become the greatest industrial nation, and its citizens enjoyed the highest standard of living in the world. By the post-World-War-II era, the United States was producing 50 percent of the "gross world product." Today, while no longer dominating the world as it did then, America still produces around 25 percent of the world's industrial products, agricultural goods, and services. Evidently, its capitalist economy and business civilization deserve more than a casual look for anyone interested in understanding American civilization.

Chapter Eleven
Capitalist Economy and Business Civilization

11.1 American Capitalism

When colonial settlement started in North America, the present-day America was then the outpost of British capitalism, carrying on trade and commerce with England and other European countries in exchange for manufactured products. After the founding of the United States, capitalism not only found fertile soil in the New Land, but also flourished in this socially and culturally congenial environment. Due to its rapid and reckless development, capitalism has been subject to criticisms and denunciations of all kinds, particularly by progressive and liberal-minded people as well as radical groups in the United States. However, voices of defense and applause have been much stronger and more frequently heard, mostly from people of conservative mind and vested interest groups. While criticisms and denunciations are useful for our understanding of the nature of American capitalism, defense and applause are also helpful in that they tell us how capitalism as a system has been supported and sustained in the United States by the people who believe in and benefit from it, helping us to appreciate its enduring value and sustaining power in this most developed country in the world.

The defense of American capitalism runs largely in broad abstractions like "the American system," "the free-enterprise economy" or "the free market economy." Underlying these catchwords are some basic arguments. One is the argument from incentive. It argues that men's brains and energy work best when they have no hampering restrictions, and when they see an immediacy of relation between effort and reward. The second is the argument from a free market. It states that an economy runs best as the result of millions of individual decisions made through the operations of a free production, wage and price system. Further, it believes that should it go out of kilter, it can generally set itself right again by individual adjustments within a frame of government spurs and checks. Beyond that, the argument continues, even government regulation is best accomplished by the indirect methods of inducements and pressures on the free market, rather than the direct methods of planning and control. The third is the argument from managerial efficiency. According to this view, the corporate managerial group is recruited from the men with the best skills, who deal with the problems of industrial production more flexibly than a governmental bureaucracy could, thereby improving the efficiency of business management.

These arguments, though vulnerable, are basically valid, for capitalism, by definition, has its origin and essence in private property ownership and free market economy. It can be easily imagined that when property could be acquired through individual's effort in the free market, people will be highly motivated to apply their intellect and energy to the pursuit of property to the maximum degree. Similarly, since each and every individual is convinced that he is as capable as anybody else, free market economy obviously offers the best opportunity for all participants to compete with each other, bringing forth the optimal results of the operation of market economy. Finally, the need for maximum profits as well as the desire for greater share of the market will serve as a source of constant pressure to improve management efficiency. Still, the essence of American capitalism does not lie only in all these three elements. After all, the fundamental basis of American capitalism is the means of production in the hands of a small number of people, which makes it difficult, if not impossible, for everyone to enjoy full freedom in the so-called free market economy. In other words, those who possess means of production or other resources will have access to free market, while those without all this will be denied such opportunities. In this sense, American free market is not free to all, nor is American capitalism open to all. For this and many reasons, American capitalism has been plagued by a host of operational strains—the periodic breakdowns, the sense of insecurity, the shadow of monopoly, the dependence upon war expenditure, and the question of distributive justice.

However, to say that American capitalism has not changed its fundamental basis does not mean no changes have taken place in the structure and functioning of American capitalism, for over the past century, significant and far-reaching changes have taken place there. The profit incentive, for example, does not operate in corporate management as it used to operate in individual enterprise, after the split between ownership and management, though it still functions as a strong driving force within the manager to make the best possible profit record for the corporation. Additionally, the idea of private property has suffered a change as well, since industrial ownership is now widely scattered in the form of stock ownership, some of the stocks being owned by trusts, investment trusts, other corporations, life insurance companies, and even trade unions. More significantly, the earlier picture of capitalism as a

Chapter Eleven
Capitalist Economy and Business Civilization

competitive system has also had to be changed. To some extent, competition has been inhibited by price agreements and "oligopoly"—the control of an industry by a handful of big corporations competing only partly in price and mainly in packaging, advertising, and brand-names, as in meat packing, automobile, cigarette, computer or software industries. Still, despite all this, the impressive fact about the American economy is the extent to which it has effectively resisted the monopoly tendencies. In present-day America, the concept of bigness is not the same as the concept of monopoly, and something that can be fairly called competition is still a power regulator of the economy, providing the necessary dynamics for the development of American capitalism.

In assessing American capitalism as a going concern, one important test is the test of productivity. Here, it is fair to say that American capitalism shows the most impressive facet of its record. Arguments might be made that, given the resources of America and the accidents of its history, some other countries could have attained the same productivity with a better distribution of the products. This is one of those "if" questions that can never be resolved. On the other hand, it is hard to sustain the claim that the creative force in the American record of increased productivity is the capitalist entrepreneur and manager, and he alone. Science, technology, the legal and governmental framework, and the skill of the worker—all belong in the larger pattern along with the supplier of risk capital and the business organizer. Yet, the remarkable increase of productivity in the history of American economy must be counted one of the overall achievements of American capitalism. Nor has this production record been only a matter of technology and resources. The drive toward productivity has also been due to the elements within the social structure which have stimulated and mobilized the productive forces of the whole society. In this sense, American capitalism has been largely a successful story.

However, judged by another test—that of income spread and distribution, American capitalism as a going concern has evoked strong criticism not only from American critics, but also from international commentators. The extremes of wealth and poverty, the gap between Whites and Blacks, the discrepancies between "the affluent society" and "the other America," the sharp contrast between the fabulous and glamorous life of the superrich class and the miserable and impoverished life of the ghetto and slum residents, all this bears testimony to the lopsided income distribution of this richest country in the world. According to the statistics released by US Census Bureau, nearly 36 million Americans live below the official poverty line, accounting for about 13% of the nation's population. More alarmingly, *USA Today* recently reported that as many as 727,304 Americans were homeless in 2007, suggesting that about one in every 400 Americans had no home. Equally significant, in this most developed country in the world, nearly 46 million Americans, or 18% of the population under the age of 65, were without health insurance, an increase by almost 8 million people since 2000. Evidently, all these hard evidences easily demystify the miracle of American capitalism, giving the lie to its claim that American capitalist system has been largely a story of success.

11.2 *The Cult of the Businessman*

Every civilization has its characteristic flowering in some civilization type, that is, the persona of the social mask on which the ordinary man in the civilization models himself. In the Athenian civilization, for example, the persona was the leisure-class citizen with a turn for art and philosophy. With the Jews, it was the lawgiver-prophet, but in the Roman Empire, it was the soldier-administrator. In the Middle Age, the cleric dreaming of sainthood was the unquestionable persona, yet in ancient China, the mandarin-scholar was the indisputable persona, and in Indian, the ascetic. At the height of French power, the courtier was the persona, but at the height of British power, it was the merchant-adventurer and empire builder that was the persona. Most interestingly, in both German and Japanese history, it was the elite soldier of the Junker and samurai classes that was held as the persona.

But unlike any other country in the world, the United States has its persona quite differently. Throughout the course of its civilization, the American persona has been the businessman—the "Titan" as the writer Dreiser called him, the "Tycoon" as *Fortune* called him, or the Giant as the present-day media call him. Where other civilization types have pursued wisdom, beauty, sanctity, military glory, and asceticism, business civilization type pursues the magnitudes of profit with a similar single-minded drive. When confronted in business by appeals to nonpecuniary values, the businessman's comment is likely to be that he is not in business for altruistic purposes. Probably, such a business-interest-based value finds its best expression in a

Chapter Eleven
Capitalist Economy and Business Civilization

concise statement made by U. S. president Calvin Coolidge: "The business of America is business." Given the great importance Americans attach to business, it comes as no surprise that a halo has been put on successful businessmen in American history. Such figures as John D. Rockefeller, Andrew Carnegie, Henry Ford, J. P. Morgan, and Bill Gates, to name just a few, have all been comfortably placed in the pantheon of business giants. To be fair, some have been honest according to the standards of business honesty, but some have not hesitated to use force, guile, and bribery. Yet, all have been unsentimental and hard in business, even they have been pious in the church, devoted in the home, softhearted in friendship, and generous in the philanthropic work.

Of course, the business spirit was not indigenous to America. It grew out of the history of European capitalism, and when the U. S. was founded it had already found ample expression in Italy, England, and Holland. During the first half century of American national life, the American business spirit lagged behind the European. While there were land speculators, a shipbuilding and commercial group, an incipient factory system, the type-figure of America well into the Jacksonian era was the farmer-turned-artisan or the artisan-farmer. However, beginning in the 1850s, a hard materialist spirit could be found everywhere in the United States. The spread of a railway network in the 1850s, the triumph of Northern capitalism over the Southern plantation system in the 1860s, the rise of investment banking and the process of rapid capital formation in the 1870s, the trust movement of the 1880s, the harvests of money and power reaped from the technology throughout this period, all this combined to make of America a paradise for the new business fortunes and a stamping ground for the business spirit.

The result was the emergence of the Big Money and the Big Business man. For quite some time, the Titan was treated with servility and often lauded to the skies. On the whole, the successful businessman was said to have afforded "an example of industry, energy, and business talents of the highest order, combined with a sense of personal honor and unimpeachable integrity." For this reason, he should "be long spared to enjoy the fruits of his industry, and to share in advancing the kingdom of Christ on earth, not merely by his Christian use of the large wealth of which God has made him steward, but also by his living example of peaceful but active piety." By the early 20th century, after the work of the muckrakers, the mood of the press and the reading public became more realistic. The businessman was still a legendary figure, to be sure, but in a manner different from the sugar-loaf legends of the early admirers. By and large, he was believed to have a daring vision, able to make reckless use of his resources to gain his ends. Equally important, he was said to have a quick sense for estimating and using people and an ability to see his lucky change and grasp it. Driven by a compelling desire for success, he was engaged in a restless search for novelty, taking joy in the creation of means rather than the outcome of his risk-taking activity itself. Most of all, there was in him a quality of tenacious single-mindedness of purpose, pushing him forward toward the building of his business empire.

What happened in the Great Depression significantly changed the image of the Titan. Before that time, if there had been any serious criticism, the indictment against the businessman had stressed the enormity of his power, the charge being that he used it to betray the early ideals of the Republic. Many of American critics were disillusioned at the chasm between the Jeffersonian dream of a spacious and egalitarian American democracy and the actual power of Big Business, protesting against the wasteland of American moral and cultural life brought about by the formidable power of Big Money. After the Depression, these so-called "Lords of Creation" were stripped of a good deal of their stature and grandeur. Rather than being the figure of production, the businessman was now viewed with suspicion: a man of dubious character who knew only the magic of extracting something from nothing, and who knew only how to take advantage of other people's naivety.

However, the greater transformation of the businessman was wrought not so much by the Great Depression as by the corporation. The type-figure who carved out the great industrial empires was almost submerged in the impersonality of the corporate form. In the new and highly specialized technology-based economy after WWII, experts have taken over virtually every phase of the corporation's activity, such as engineering, financing, production, promotion, advertising, marketing, public relations, and R&D. In place of the heroic adventurism of the Titans has come a contingent of technocrats with managerial skills, often known as "Organization Men." If entrepreneurs became American heroes because they mostly began as common people and later on turned into "self-made" men, organization men become heroes to Americans because of their managerial expertise, running business in a cost-efficient way.

Chapter Eleven
Capitalist Economy and Business Civilization

They acquire power and wealth not by creating business, but by managing it. In this sense, they serve as role models of success in contemporary American society, though their image has been constantly compromised and sometimes even irreparably tarnished by the revelations of business scandals involving high-salaried corporative executives, the most recent of which is the sub-prime loan financial crisis on Wall Street in 2008. Taken as a whole, the businessman, be he the entrepreneur or the organization man, still commands respect and admiration from the majority of the American population.

11.3 The Corporate Empire

Since American economy has long time ago shifted from small and family-based enterprise to large and corporate-based business, it is necessary for us to take a closer look at the corporation as a major form of present-day American economy. In a way, the corporation in America can be viewed as a social contrivance, for it plays a central role in shaping people's life in society. Reaching into every area of life, it has become the instrument by which Americans organize any project demanding group effort, impersonality, continuity beyond the individual life, and liability. It is striking that in such a highly individualistic society as the United States, people should accept a transformation of their life wrought by so impersonal a social invention.

The early American corporations were wards of the state, chartered only in rare cases and supervised by the state in every phase of their operation. When a group of men received a charter to build a railroad or canal, or run a toll bridge, or organize a college, the assumption was that the state was grudgingly signing away one of its inherent functions, retaining only the responsibility of supervision. The corporation thus began as a state instrument, to be kept within the ambit of the state power. But such was the dynamism of American business enterprise within it that it ran away with the original intention. It helped gather vast blocs of capital by subdividing and dispersing business ownership and collecting the savings and hopes of many. By consolidating a number of enterprises and tapping the profits from their combined future growth, it anticipated these future profits and expressed them in the immediate market value of stocks. The corporate form thus suited a business spirit which sought always to capitalize the future, and in turn it created the stock market as a way of mirroring men's shifting calculations about future earnings and values.

In those ways, the corporation built vast power blocs whose size and impersonality daunted the social critics of the early 20th century. Some felt that when Wealth was concentrated, it would destroy the Commonwealth; others believed that the corporation behaved like the Octopus, whose impersonal power blasted personal life and hopes; still others worried about the alliance of corporation and political machine, leading eventually to corruption. However, regardless of these social criticisms and worries, these corporate power blocs make possible the industrial concentration. Such a trend toward the big corporate unit is partly explained by low production and distribution costs. The big corporations are in a real sense the children of competition. In the fierce struggle for survival and profits, the payoff is in efficiency, and those who triumph in the competitive struggle quite naturally drive their rivals to the wall, where they are willing to be bought out. This is especially true in the case of brand competition in an era when economic success depends on the psychic contagion among buyers as much as it does on the quality or utility of the product itself.

But the persistent question is: "How big is too big?" American businessmen know that the steel industry, once the leader in technological advance, has fallen behind such newer industries as aviation, chemicals, and the electrical industries. Clearly, corporate bigness has as much to do with the strategic capture of power as with possible efficiencies of production. Current technology involves outlays so huge that only the big producers find them compassable. Moreover, the big firm has more resources to carry out Research and Development to maintain its competitive edge in the market. Similarly, the bigger the company is, the more money it has to spend on advertising campaign, putting a bigger and more aggressive sales force into the field. Indeed, the corporate power bloc has command of raw materials often not available to its smaller competitors, especially in an armament economy, where procurement officials are hurried and harassed, and tend to give the priority allocations as well as the contracts to the big firms. Equally, because of its research laboratories and its ability to buy up promising inventions, it has command of patents and processes with which it can freeze others out of the market. In short, with its financial power, it can attract scientists,

Chapter Eleven
Capitalist Economy and Business Civilization

engineers, technicians; it can set up elaborate marketing and advertising structure; it can surround itself with the artfulness of "public relations"; it can control a big enough portion of the market so that its voice is heard loud and clear in the price agreements, a standard practice in the corporate world; and it can apply pressure to the government itself by lobbies in the capital and by its influence over party managers, candidates, and local machinery.

Thus, the advantages of corporate bigness may come after the established fact, not before. By the very fact of their bigness, corporations may achieve a strategic power that sometimes makes it unnecessary for them to pursue efficiencies which can cut costs. They, instead, become tired and unwilling to take risks, and in some cases grow backward in their response to technological change. In this way, the corporation which started as a legal device has ended by carving out an empire for itself. It is for this reason that John Dewey called it "the corporateness of society," W. J. Ghent, "the New Feudalism," and Max Lerner, "private governments." Their decisions influence the size and distribution of the national product, the channeling of investment, the levels of employment, the rise and fall of the stock market, and purchasing capacity of the workers.

Operating basically for private purposes, with public consequences secondary, corporations can not only divide the market, but also determine price levels and production volume. In a number of the mass-production industries, corporate prices tend to be set "administratively" by the action of a small number of corporations with an eye to costs, profits, volume of sales, and what the transportation will bear. This is modified somewhat by the fact that while the prices are set administratively, say by the auto-makers, the retail dealer makes adjustments to a variable market through discounts and by varying the turn-in allowance for the older car. However, this should not obscure the fact that the functions described above affect the public interest deeply, yet they are being carried out by holders of corporate power who are not chosen by the people, not responsible to them, and not replaceable by them. It can be argued that without the corporate form, America could not have probably developed industrialism so rapidly or on so large a scale, nor could it have accumulated capital and plowed it back into industry as dramatically as it did. In the early 19th century, an economy of small firms was possible, but in the 21st century, where both

233

industries and markets are globally connected, such a possibility scarcely exists. The only alternative to such monstrous corporations is national ownership with big-scale enterprise under government trusts. But this is to change American capitalism, and would have raised even more far-reaching issues of power than the corporate empires have done. Whatever group owns or runs the economic plant of the United States has vast power vested in it, and so long as capitalist system provides the basic structure of American economy, corporations will remain unchanged and continue to build and expand their empires in and outside the United States.

11.4 Business and Its Satellites

Like any imperial force, the corporate empires have opened hitherto untapped areas of American life and added to their domain a whole array of satellite activities. Even the barest profile of the business pattern in 21st-century America shows it vastly different from what it was at the beginning of the 19th century. Now, operating at the center of the American economy, corporations have a galaxy of satellites around them to serve a variety of purposes. In many ways, it is these satellites that help corporations function smoothly and effectively in the American economy.

The first important satellite is, of course, the stock market, which in fact serves as the barometer both for the corporation executive and for the large massive investors. The struggle of "bulls" and "bears" has become an American form of bread-and-circuses. In the boom of the late 1920s, during the prosperous decade of the 1950s, and throughout much of the 2000s, there had been a scramble for speculative profits by clerks, school teachers, university professors, mill-hands, industrial workers, truck drivers, and even veterans and pensioners. But again and again, they were slaughtered by "insiders, who bid up stocks and unloaded them on the unwary outsiders for a profit of several millions." The great market crash of 1929 has become part of the folklore of America, an image of tangled ticker tape, desperate men, and ruined lives, sadly remembered by a burned generation of inexperienced speculators. But Americans seem to be forgetful. In 2008, driven by insatiable desires for easy money and spurred by soaring value in real estate industry, they risked their present

Chapter Eleven
Capitalist Economy and Business Civilization

and future wellbeing on the uncertain and oftentimes unpredictable stock and property markets, losing their life time savings and in many cases even seeing their houses foreclosed. If the market crash of 1929 was largely a result of wild speculations, the once-in-a-century economic recession of 2008 resulted more from ill-conceived U. S. monetary policy as well as irresponsible behavior on the part of U. S. financial and banking institutions.

 The history of the stock market, whose ups and downs are read on commuters' trains, public screens and computer terminals, has shown violent fluctuations over the course of the past decades, resulting in what business circles know as "brokers' blood pressure." Stock speculation—the exchange of present money for an expectation of future money—expresses the impatient desire of many Americans to get rich quick, at least quicker than the normal process of work and savings will allow, and thus provide security for the future and some kind of the luxuries. It also gives scope to the risk element that is being crowded out of the society, and it has a special appeal for those who lead humdrum lives on rarely fluctuating incomes. The peaks, troughs, and plateaus of the market, as shown on plotted charts, are for them the only landscape worth watching. Some of the stock market professionals have the cool nerve of a great gambler as well as the courage of a lion. They have made fortunes, often by selling "short," or getting out at the right time. But the mass of the people have generally shown a talent for being perversely wrong. Still, there is also the large, undramatic group of real investors, who are less concerned with short-range fluctuations than with long-range trends, who have a basic confidence in continued corporate prosperity and wish to share in it. Stocks enable them to become the "owners" of the majority stocks corporations, although they are like the passive spectators of mass sports and cannot control what takes place in the ring or field. They get a stake in the success and survival of the corporate system itself, which is one of the strongest psychological facts about the hold of business on the American mind. Even for those who do not invest, the stock market has continued to be a register of hopes and fears for the capitalist economy.

 A more crucial form of corporate business magic is salesmanship or marketing. There has been a well-marketed transformation of the art of the older personal seller, who either owned his own shop or had a group of customers whom he knew well, into an impersonal or synthetically personalized salesmanship. In an economy of the Big Technology and the

Big Corporation, it is not surprising that Americans have developed Big Marketing. Indeed, one of the lessons American businessmen have learned during the past half of century is a paradoxical one: while mass production makes mass distribution necessary, it is even truer to say that mass distribution makes mass production possible, and marketing is the key art of the whole structure of mass distribution. In this sense, it is the core activity of the American economy, with technology, production, and financing all subsidiary to it. An American magazine describes it as "the biggest man-made force to keep the economy going. When it falters, recession follows." Even though competition has been drastically modified within any one mass production industry, there is brand and product competition and, most of all, the need to keep the assembly-line going. The role of productivity is to set the pace: where machines are pouring out so much commodity volume, and the high profits are being plowed back into the new technology, the problem is to continue unloading the products on the consumers. Consequently, the sales manager is in some way the key figure of the American corporation, more so than the engineer, the production manager, and even the financial executive.

The salesman may operate in the shop itself or "on the road, selling to shops, department store buyers, and manufacturers." Over the past several decades, however, the salesman has been operating on an international level, traveling from one country to another and sometimes from one continent to another. Virtually on every level, American business has developed marketing/salesmanship into the "art of planned persuasion." The elements of this art include the right kind of packaging (this is notably true in cosmetics, which stress seductive and glamorous mystery), systems of installment buying and consumer financing, an effective sales "theme," sales "line," or sales "angle" (the "line" of the insurance salesman has become part of American folklore), and the stress on the personality of salesman or salesgirl, whose smile behind the counter is commercialized lure and who have become part of the personality market, where the skills are skills in selling people rather than producing things. One of the less attractive by-products of the stress on salesmanship has been the development of personality courses, charm schools, and a popular literature of self-improvement that teaches the art of manipulating people.

The third important satellite in American business is advertising. Like the corporation, advertising was not invented by the Americans, but

Chapter Eleven
Capitalist Economy and Business Civilization

it has been carried furthest and is most at home within the American frame. The go-getting temper which used to be associated with the personal salesman has been transferred to advertising copy, the singing commercials on the radio, and the "selling pitch" on television. Their purpose is not so much the immediate selling of the product as the creation of a favorable climate within which either the sale becomes easy or the customer is induced to ask for the product himself. Of course, advertising does more than help sell the products on which business is built: it has also provided a special kind of language for the people as a whole. Even before American children learn the language of the primer and the schoolroom, they mimic the language of the commercials on TV, and of the world of comic little Disneylike men and animated packages that accompany the commercials. Even more important, as the sociologist David Potter has pointed out, is the fact that advertising speaks in highly charged symbolic terms and surrounds Americans with a universe of images of plenty. This conditions them not only to the act of purchase, but also to a view of the American economy as a cornucopia abounding in good things, urging them to consume and consume hard.

Finally, there is the player of "public relations," probably the youngest of the corporate satellites in the world of corporations. Unlike other satellites, "public relations" brings into the corporate world a spanking brashness and an appetite for power. The theory behind public relations is that a corporation is judged not only by the products it turns out, but also by the total impression it leaves on public opinion. In the business world, there is a long-held belief that today's business formula is to make a product the public wants and an impression the public likes. To achieve all this, corporations have to rely upon "public relations" to make them possible. For that, corporations have paid handsomely the "public relations counsel," "publicity consultants," and others who would dry-clear their public wash and give them a general valet service so as always to appear in public at their best.

Because of its enormous importance, some of the shrewdest and most imaginative brains of the business world have moved into the orbit of this corporate satellite. They help write speeches of the big corporate executives, cushion the impact of bad news, issue public statements for them, see that they are on the right public committees, and most important of all try to get the right kind of stories "planted" and the wrong kind excluded from the mass media which may represent life or death in the race for markets and profits. Their techniques are based on an unsentimental assessment of the hidden springs of belief, gullibility, and action in men. As an approach not only to business but also to the whole of life, this mentality has come to be known as the "Madison Avenue" mind, thus adding another symbolic street to Wall Street in the demonology of business.

11.5 Capital and Labor

While capital, corporations, and businessmen are essential to the development of American capitalism, labor is equally indispensible. After all, it is labor that provides the necessary forces to dig out raw materials, turn them into products, and eventually ship them to the market. It is inconceivable that profits can be made, capital can grow, and corporations can expand without the contribution of labor.

However, it is important to keep in mind that although American labor may share similarities with labor in many other countries, labor laws, labor relations, and labor unions have a somewhat different history in the United States than they have had in other western industrialized countries. The main reason is that in America, employer and employee relations were not as much a battle between classes and sociopolitical philosophies as they were in other countries. Throughout American history, the American worker has usually fought for "a bigger piece of the pie," better working conditions, better health and retirement benefits, and greater job security, rather than social status, political power, or control of means of production. Oftentimes, due to relatively higher social mobility and more economic opportunity, the employee's boss did not have a socioeconomic background significantly different from his. In many cases, the major difference between the employer and the employee was neither accent nor social class, but money and what it could buy.

Partly for this reason, and partly for reasons to be explained below, the sociologist Max Lerner argues that the real revolution in American labor has been the impulse to see the worker not just as a union member or a ward of the welfare state, and certainly not as a serf in the hierarchy of corporate power, but as an industrial man who is part of his society. In other words, American workers have rarely attempted to storm the gates of capitalist power, but instead, they have been making every bit of effort to fight for their legitimate rights as well as their share of the capitalist economic benefits. In addition to such factors as economic opportunity and social mobility, other developments particular to American history were also important. For a long time, there had been a shortage of labor, especially of skilled workers. As a result, wages were usually much higher in the United States than they were in Europe. As many employers were in competition for employees, workers were often able to get better wages and better working conditions. While it gave some advantages to workers in the short run, it delayed the organization of labor, and thereby slowed down the process of collective action by organized workers in the long run.

In the mid-19th century, the rapidly growing industries were able to employ the hundreds of thousands of immigrant workers who poured into the American cities, but before long the situation quickly changed. Many workers had to take whatever jobs they found at whatever wages were offered. Bad working conditions and overcrowded housing often sparked protest and confrontation between employers and employees, and between workers and the police. As protests and walkouts increased, so did the labor movement, which gained its greatest momentum between 1860 and 1900, the period in which the U.S. started moving from the towns to the cities, from the farms to the factories. The first labor movement impulse expressed itself through the Knights of Labor in 1869, a class-wide politically conscious movement affiliated with non-labor reform groups. This movement arose as a response to the political unrest which swept the country when the vision of a nation of small farmers and artisans was shattered by the rise of corporate power. But the Knights of Labor were sprawling in their organization, and probably made the mistake of seeking political power before establishing a strong economic and political base. With the emergence of the American Federation of Labor in 1886, the American version of labor movement started its mature but more conservative phase. Under Gompers, the AFL sought to rechart labor's course, devoting itself to lobbies and pressures, and at election time to the policy of "rewarding labor's friends and punishing labor's enemies." During this period, there appeared a clear shift on the part of the organized labor from the decision to challenge corporate power drastically to the decision to bargain with the corporations for a larger share of economic gains. In other words, the AFL's position on labor problems was "bread and butter," rather than political influence and power.

The industrial unions were most powerful in the period immediately following World War II. In virtually all major industrial areas and industries in the United States, union membership was required. Nothing was built, made, manufactured, transported, shipped or moved without the agreement of the unions. States that were not fully unionized, where workers did not have to become union members to do certain jobs, might try to attract industries with the promise of lower wages and taxes. But in 1947, when Congress passed the Taft-Hartley Act, dramatic changes took place with regards to labor unions. One of its provisions outlawed the "closed-shop" which required employers to hire only union members. It also permitted the states to pass "right to work" laws which forbade agreements requiring workers to automatically join a union after they were hired. Equally significant, a major offensive against the American working class was launched in the 1950s under the name of automation. It was the period of technological innovation, when old concentrations of workers were broken up or reduced and new plants were built embodying the new technology, resulting in job loss of many industrial workers. This was also the period when theories about the disappearance of the working class or theories about the "new" working class appeared. In point of fact, the industrial working class did not decline in size, although it did decline in numbers relative to the population as a whole. Infinitely more crucial than size was the fact that the industrial working class still resided at the points of production and transportation and communication and thus could play an important role in areas decisive for all of society.

Today, some industrial firms have been attracted to locations in states where labor unions are not so strong, where wages are often lower, and where safety and pollution regulations are not so strict or so strictly enforced. More likely, many big corporations have moved to the developing countries to tap into their cheap labor market and take advantage of their lax safety and environment laws The decline of some industries, such as the textile and steel industries, along with the rise in the number of white-collar, technical and service jobs, has also harmed the traditional, blue-collar unions. Yet, at the same time, groups such as teachers, firemen, and even policemen have formed unions of their own. Twenty or thirty years ago, it would have been inconceivable for these civil servants to strike for their demands. Now, Americans have learned to get accustomed to their strikes. Most shocking of all, firemen and policemen have also gone on strike in many areas in the United States, the

Chapter Eleven
Capitalist Economy and Business Civilization

most well-known of which is the "Blue Flu" strike, where the policemen in their traditional blue uniforms all became "ill" on the same day, leaving enough "healthy" policemen to carry out their daily functions.

Although there are more and more professional and technical unions, the many other industrial unions face the same problem that other unions in the western world do. Problems include what can be done about those jobs that will no longer exist in companies adopting new technology, or what should be done about those industries that are no longer competitive. Some unions have decided that job security is more important than pay increase, but most unions still demand agreements which include a short work week, together with such fringe benefits as medical and life insurance, profit-sharing, pensions, and health care plans. Although much smaller compared with their peak membership in the 1950s, unions still remain an important political factor in the United States, especially within the Democratic Party. Today, most unions are aligned with one of two large umbrella organizations: the AFL-CIO and the Change to Win Federation. Currently, unions are trying to diminish employers' opportunities to run anti-union campaigns by advocating new federal legislation that would allow workers to elect union representation by signing cards, a process often referred to as card check recognition. This proposed legislation is known as the Employee Free Choice Act, according to which, once a majority of employees in a workplace have signed a card, the employer will be obligated to make a good-faith effort to bargain a contract with the union. Since the 2008 elections, the Employee Free Choice Act has got the support of majorities in the House and Senate, and of the President.

SUMMARY

(1) American capitalism, from its inception, has been more defended and applauded than criticized and denounced in its own country. In various terms, American capitalism has been referred to as "the free-enterprise economy" or "the free market economy." In a sense, the essence of American capitalism is twofold: private property ownership and free market economy, where profit comes first and distribution second.

(2) Every civilization has its characteristic flowering in some civilization type, i.e., the persona of the social mask on which the ordinary man/woman models him/herself. Unlike any other nation in the world, America has its persona quite differently. Throughout the course

of its civilization, the American persona has been the businessman: self-made entrepreneurs in the past, organization men now.

(3) The early American corporations were wards of the state, charted only in rare cases and supervised by the state in every phase of their operation. Later, in the fierce struggle for survival and profits, some companies strengthened their share of resources and market, others weakened or driven out of market. Consequently, big corporations emerged, establishing corporate empires in their respective domains.

(4) In order to maintain their domination in the American economy, the corporate empires need to have a whole array of satellite activities to serve a variety of purposes. Without these satellites, big corporations can hardly function so effectively. They include the stock market, marketing, advertising, and finally public relations.

(5) In America, capital and labor historically were not as much a battle between classes and sociopolitical philosophies as they were in other countries. Throughout American history, the American worker has usually fought for "a bigger piece of the pie," better working conditions, better health and retirement benefits and greater job security rather than social status, political power, or control of means of production.

ESSAY QUESTIONS

(1) Although American capitalism has experienced ups and downs in its history, it has been basically quite successful in developing the American economy. What do you think are the chief reasons for the success of the American economy? Also, what changes have taken place in the structure and function of American capitalism over the past century that have speeded up the development of American capitalism?

(2) It is often said that American civilization is basically business civilization. Subsequently, in the history of American civilization, heroes are often those from the business world. Examine the creation of business heroes in America and discuss the key criteria in measuring up a business hero in American culture, paying particular attention to the change of benchmarks for heroes from the past to the present.

(3) The proverb has it that Rome was not built in a day. Nor was the corporate empire in America. While fair competition is believed to be the key principle in the American economy, it does not mean that competition is always conducted in the spirit of fairness. The rise of monopoly and the subsequent corporate empire out of it are two cases in point. Examine and

Chapter Eleven
Capitalist Economy and Business Civilization

discuss the process of empire-building in America.

(4) Business satellites, as their names indicate, primarily serve the purpose of satisfying the needs of the key economic players in the American economy. Describe two or three major business satellites and explain their specific functions in securing the smooth operation of the American corporate economy, noting, in particular, their role in expanding the capital market and the production scale.

(5) The relationship between capital and management in America has not been as confrontational and conflicting as in other western industrialized countries. Trace the development of American labor and labor unions from the 19th to the 21st centuries and carefully examine the characteristics of American labor and labor unions, paying special attention to the purposes and demands of labor union organizations.

American Society and Culture
美 国 社 会 文 化

Chapter Twelve
Social Services

LEARNING OBJECTIVES

- Be aware of American values in social welfare
- Be informed of the general development of social services in America
- Be knowledgeable about the key elements in public social services
- Understand the services provided by public and private health care institutions
- Know the difficulties in government-funded public housing projects

Any society needs social services of every kind, which include health care, retirement pensions, unemployment payments, housing, disability allowances, and welfare benefits. They are provided for individuals and groups by both the private and public sectors. The availability of these services varies from time to time, and often in line with the attitudes of people and politicians of a given time. They are also conditioned by experiences with the actual workings of social institutions and demands of social life. Historically speaking, Americans have believed in self-reliance and independence in social services and the responsibility of the family or individuals, rather than of state or federal government. The private enterprise market is theoretically supposed to supply necessary services for which individuals should pay. But since the 1930s, there has developed an awareness that some people in society are unable to benefit from free enterprises, and therefore are in need of assistance from government. Additionally, many people also feel that the provision of essential social services like unemployment compensation and health care should be made a national responsibility, thereby slowly but steadily pushing America in the direction of a welfare state.

Chapter Twelve
Social Services

12.1 American Values in Social Welfare

Social welfare in any society has two major purposes: social helping and social control. Americans easily agree with the helping purpose but are generally almost unaware of the social control function of social welfare because it is hidden in ideas about equality and what Americans consider their "right" to change their clients. However, society needs certain social control, for some behaviors must be regulated so that interdependent people can live and work together. Of course, not all such control is positive, and social welfare controls aim at America's most vulnerable citizens. Seldom do they participate in social welfare decisions that affect their lives, and the price they pay for such help is often their personal dignity and individual freedom. In this sense, American personal, societal, and social work values are perhaps the most important factors in the practice of social work.

It is generally held in America that all people are equal, but those who do not work are less equal; that individual life has worth, but only the fit should survive; and that people are responsible for each other, but those who are dependent upon others for their living are of less worth. It can be said that such values permeate American social welfare, whatever the perspective, culture, or period of history. It is generally agreed that every perception or reaction is value-laden and value-based, and no one can be truly objective. In other words, Americans are very clear about what they "ought to" provide and how they "ought to" deal with deviants. For instance, as social helpers, people have no right to impose what they believe on the lives of others. They may and can empathize, but they cannot understand the lives of their clients, for the life situations and life experiences of the two are vastly different from each other. To assume that they do and to make decisions for them is unethical. Society has a right to control dangerous or destructive behaviors, but most of social work does not involve those problems. For this and many other reasons, Americans tend to believe that they should not enforce conformity to norms that may not be relevant to the life situations of others, for doing so often creates or perpetuates their problems.

American attitudes towards social services and values in social welfare are often couched in religious, moral, or patriotic terms. These attitudes and values are so much a part of their lives that most Americans think they are facts rather than beliefs. We know that a fact is the quality of being actual or having objective reality, whereas a value is something intrinsically desirable. In more practical terms, a fact is the way things are and a value is how people wish they were. People tend to believe that they know both facts and values, but they may confuse them and base important judgments on what we wish rather than on what is. Americans will be able to make far better social welfare policies if they could often test what they know by remembering that fact is something that has existed throughout history and in every culture, and everything else is value.

To understand where American values come from, or the reasons for the way they treat/help others, we may trace our way to two human characteristics. The first is mutual aid, and the second is protection from others and otherness. These characteristics are, respectively, the bases of values concerning social treatment and social control. Often contradictory, they have caused major dilemmas in the way American social welfare institution operates. Whatever the case, based on these two characteristics, values have affected American social welfare programs and even human services itself. These values all seem positive; so positive indeed that Americans rarely question them even when they contradict one another. What is worth noting is that even though they may be positive for society in general, they can be intensively negative for certain groups in American society, such as women, children, the unemployed, and people of minority groups. Specifically speaking, the most basic values include Judaeo-Christian charity values, democratic egalitarianism and individualism, the Protestant work ethic and capitalism, social Darwinism, the new Puritanism, and family values.

Judaeo-Christian values basically refer to Judaic teachings of social justice and the teachings of Jesus as practiced in the early centuries of Christianity. They are non-sectarian and social rather than religious, and their major thrust is that those in need have a right to help and society has an obligation to provide for them. As primary social ethics in the Christian world, they are the bases for social altruism, and their prescriptions of love and charity are the reasons that people enter the human services. Democratic egalitarianism was a primary tenet in the founding of the United States: all citizens are equal before the law and no one has privileges based on class, heritage, wealth, or other factors irrelevant to citizenship. Related closely to egalitarianism is

Chapter Twelve
Social Services

individualism: the ideal of individual effort and personal motivation by which any American can achieve success. The Protestant work ethic is the moral basis for American capitalism: an economic system in which profit through business enterprise is mostly uncontrolled by governments. A social rather than an economic creed, the Protestant ethic is a value accepted by most Americans regardless of religion. Its complex of values includes individualism, personal achievement and worth, the morality of wealth, and patriotism. Work for economic gain is the way to success, a sign of personal morality, and a moral obligation. Conversely, poverty and public dependency demonstrate immorality.

As for social Darwinism, it is an application of Darwin's biological theory (natural selection and the survival of the fittest) to economic and social problems. According to social Darwinism as applied to social welfare, the state support of the poor is against the law of "the survival of the fittest" and that the lives of people who were "economically unfit" should not be saved by giving them public assistance. Moreover, it claims that they are poor by choice, because of their moral degeneracy, and therefore should perish. Also against social welfare programs is the New Puritanism, which is now permeating American society. Essentially, it is a political thrust of the Christian Coalition, a powerful lobby group for legislation to enforce compliance to the patriarchal and Puritan values of the past. Puritan values include chastity, particularly for women, honesty in dealing with others; abstinence from things denied by religion and custom as immoral, such as promiscuity, gambling, and the use of alcohol or drug to excess; and proper behavior. Puritan morality also emphasizes the sanctity of marriage and family and patriarchal authority in the homes and condemns life-styles such as communal living and homosexuality. According to the New Puritanism, those who do not live a moral life as defined by the New Puritanism do not deserve the state support in the form of social welfare. Finally, to most Americans, family values emphasize marriage as a social, sexual, and economic relationship in which a man and a woman are legally joined to set up and maintain a family. In light of this perspective, singleness, particularly for women, homosexual people, non-married heterosexual couples living together without marriage should all be viewed with suspicion, if not stigmatized by society.

Of all the American values in social services described above, two lines of thought stand out in sharp contrast to each other. One stresses independence, self-reliance, and hard work, and self-responsibility; the other emphasizes interdependence, empathy, love, and caring community. Throughout the U.S. history, American social welfare policies have been torn between these two sets of values, shaped and reshaped by these deep-rooted concepts and their powerful influence, which explains, in part at least, why American social welfare programs have not been able to develop to the same level as other developed countries have.

12.2 Social Services: A Brief History

Before the industrialization process began, America was primarily a rural society in which most Americans worked in the fields and there were few urban centers. The essence of life for most Americans was self-reliance in social, health, employment and housing needs. Based on these early experiences, there has emerged the image of the independent farmer and frontier in American mythology. Paradoxically, however, the pre-industrial American society of farmers and pioneers was also one of cooperation and mutual help, providing not only emotional support but also communal protection. Such contrasting images illustrate the tension in U.S. value system between individualism and communalism, affecting the way Americans later would respond to the issue of social services.

With the development of industrialization and urbanization of the late 18th and 19th centuries, new problems were created when many people lost jobs, got injured, or could not find shelter. Social services at that time were still either largely private and individualistic, or provided mostly by voluntary charity organizations. Although there were some kinds of aid by state and local governments, they were neither systematic nor sufficient. By and large, most Americans at that time were unwilling to give too much power to the central government over such matters as social services, jealously protecting their independence and continuously taking pride in their ability to cope with difficulties in life. Influenced by the prevailing public opinion, politicians avoided stepping in, leaving social services largely in the hands of private charity groups. Consequently, no adequate national system of social services developed in America in the late 19th and early 20th centuries. Only when it became obvious that private measure needed to be supplemented by governmental actions did federal, state, and local governments get involved.

The social services program improved significantly in the mid-1930s under the Franklin D. Roosevelt administration when U. S. Congress passed a series of social welfare legislation. With a large number of people out of job and numerous families without food, Roosevelt was concerned to rectify faults in the social welfare system by providing a framework for a measure of social protection. Subsequently, Social Security legislation was passed in 1935, which made benefits for workers and their families dependent on employment status and the payments that employees contributed during their employment. Additionally, two more important federal welfare programs, AFDC (Aid to Families with Dependent Children) and GA (General Assistance), were passed to help the needy, children, single parents and the handicapped. On the whole, however, these programs were not comprehensive, and publicly financed non-contributory welfare was still unpopular in the 1930s. Indeed, there was antagonism towards those who would not work or help themselves.

Reformers, however, did not stop their efforts. Arguing that the above-mentioned measures needed to be supplemented by further action, they urged federal, state, and local governments to be more involved in social services. As publicly funded programs expanded considerably during World War II, government position began to change in the direction of the welfare state. Meanwhile, individuals and groups, encouraged by the New Deal programs, began to agitate for more assistance and put pressure on the federal government. War veterans, for example, were soon given federal medical, educational, and housing benefits by the GI Bill of Rights. Soon afterwards, a new element of "rights" to public social services became apparent, giving rise to the feeling that the U. S. government should care more for its citizens, particularly those who were in need. Gradually, on the basis of programs like GI Bill, the federal government took a more positive position in providing social services, though they were still piecemeal and largely in response to public pressure.

From the 1960s to the early 1980s, more federal and state money was spent on public social services. President Lyndon Johnson (1963—1968) introduced new programs as part of his "Great Society" plan, designed to alleviate poverty and suffering. Medicare, for example, provided health care for the elderly, Medicaid supplied health care to the poor, and the Food Stamp program gave coupons to the needy to buy food in specified shops and grocery stores. Additionally, Johnson also introduced a range of other initiatives which were intended to attack poverty and unemployment through education, job training, and regional development. Still, by European standards, impressive though they were, these policies were not directed towards establishing a welfare state. Instead, they were meant to provide opportunities for those who were prepared to work and improve themselves. Nevertheless, the Johnson reforms laid the good foundation for future public social services in America. Not only were a range of government agencies established to implement these new programs, but also a growing number of people came to regard non-contributory welfare and health care as a right.

Public spending on social services increased in the 1970s, but presidents after Johnson differed in their attitudes toward social services and welfare schemes. President Reagan (1981—1988), for example, tried to reduce the cost of welfare and public programs, asking Americans to be responsible for their own lives through self-help and depend less on government aid. Similarly, the Bush administration (1989—1992) attempted to reduce social and public spending, but was forced to meet increased demand by raising taxes. When Clinton was elected to the White House, he tried to introduce proposals for universal health care financed mainly by individuals and corporate contributions. But this reform collapsed and the return of Republican majorities in Congress in 1994 led to proposals for more cuts in public spending. Under pressure from a Republican-controlled Congress, President Clinton in 1996 decided to change American welfare policy by cutting and restructuring federal public spending, emphasizing workfare over welfare. During the George W. Bush administration, public spending on social safety net programs like Medicaid and Medicare was cut quite significantly. As a "compassionate conservative," President Bush was committed to reducing the role of government in social welfare provision by emphasizing market forces and philanthropy as well as cutting taxes. As a result, American welfare programs experienced some setbacks and retrogression during his administration, waiting for new directions and restructuring under the new administration of President Barack Obama.

12.3 *Public Social Services*

Public social services in the United States can be conveniently divided into two categories. The first is the contributory Social Security System, through which benefits are earned and distributed. The second is a program that provides assistance to people incapable of financially supporting themselves. Such assistance is given on the basis of income, but is not tied to the contributory system. Programs of this kind are generally known as social welfare programs.

Governmental provision for Social Security is a large and expanding part of public social services. In 2007, for example, the U. S. federal budget for Social Security amounted to $623 billion, which was composed of retirement insurance payments ($369 billion), survivors insurance ($113 billion), disability insurance ($105 billion), and supplemental security income payments ($36 billion). Social Security contributes about 33.9% of federal government's total tax revenue in the form of social insurance and retirement taxes, and its payments account for about 21% of federal spending, close to the expenditure for defense (20%).

Social Security derives from the programs contained in the 1935 Social Security Act. It now refers to three main areas: the old age, survivors, disability and health insurance program; Medicare; and Unemployment Compensation. Employees and the self-employed contribute financially (some 7% of earnings) to these programs during their employment. In return, they and their families receive benefits from the system on the basis of their contributions. Such benefits include: pensions on retirement, which are relatively low, representing about a quarter of one's average earnings; medical care for the elderly and disabled under Medicare; disability payments; illness and accident provisions; and finally unemployment payments. In many ways, it is more like a social insurance program, by European standards at least.

However, Society Security does not cover all the bills incurred, and therefore provision for old age, illness, and unemployment often has to be supplemented by additional private resources, such as savings, investments, and insurance policies. In many cases, employers and trade unions also provide additional retirement, unemployment, health care, and life insurance services for employees. These are mainly paid by employers or unions, but can also include financial contributions from workers.

Welfare programs are designed to provide financial help for the needy and poor. Additionally, they also provide job training and rehabilitation programs for those in need, such as the unemployed and the sick. Furthermore, for those homeless and foodless people, welfare institutions are responsible to shelter and feed them. For all these programs, government of all levels, federal, state, and local, is involved with varying level of financial resources. Local community institutions, churches, charitable groups, and voluntary service organizations also play a large part. In this sense, there is no single welfare system, but rather a mosaic of measures created to assist those in need.

The cost of welfare programs has been traditionally shared by federal, sate, and local governments. Generally, federal funds are distributed to the states, which are supposed to spend equal amount of money to match the federal funds. At the state level, however, in addition to the funds for federal-state revenue-sharing or revenue-matching welfare programs, states may provide additional funds for their own welfare programs, depending on their financial capability, public opinion, and political leadership. On the whole, welfare programs are better provided in northern states than in southern states. Whatever the case, each state devises and organizes its own program, defines the threshold for welfare relief, and decides, on the basis of its budget, which families and individuals are qualified for assistance.

Until 1996, the U. S. federal welfare consists of the following four programs: Medicaid, Aid to Families with Dependent Children, Food Stamps, and General Assistance. Medicaid is a health scheme and is the largest direct federal aid program for citizens under 65. It is meant to provide health care for those who do not have private health insurance or do not have the financial ability to pay for a range of medical requirements. Aid to Families with Dependent Children (AFDC) used to be the second largest federal aid program to the poor. Payments to the disabled and families with children were based on need and the official poverty line was used as a guideline. Like other welfare programs, AFDC payments varied from state to state, with southern states paying less than northern states. In 1996, AFDC was abolished, and the responsibility was passed on to the states, which receive federal grants to run their own programs. There is a five-year lifetime limit on this welfare benefit and most recipients will have to enroll in workfare schemes. The third largest welfare program derives from the 1964 Food Stamp Act. It provides coupons that are used by eligible needy people to buy food in approved shops at an average national rate of some one-third of its normal price. Finally, the General Assistance scheme provides income support, cash grants, aid for housing, school meals, Supplemental Security Income for the elderly poor and help with other basic necessities.

Seemingly comprehensive and well-developed, the federal welfare system does not provide adequate help for the most needy. People who are unemployed for long periods, for example, may receive little help form the government. Similarly, those who do not enroll in workfare may find their benefits greatly curtailed or even completely denied. Clearly, except for the disabled, employment is a crucial factor for most Americans, without which they cannot receive much public assistance. Take the restructured AFDC, for example, those who receive help from it must find a job after two years, or all the benefits will automatically discontinue right away. This is the so-called "workfare" (work+welfare) programs, by which recipients are required to work or to participate in job training programs while still on welfare. By providing remedial education, vocational training, and child care, state governments want to encourage welfare recipients to get jobs with decent wages and prospects for long-term employment. Although certain exemptions have been made for families with preschool children, for most Americans, however, it is a matter of sink or swim situation. In other words, Americans want the recipients of welfare to be temporary rather than permanent, demonstrating their long-held values in social services, namely Protestant work ethic, self-reliance, self-responsibility, and social Darwinism.

12.4 Health Care Services

American health care system has long been a subject of debate and criticism, both from home and abroad. Europeans, for example, have quite negative views about the health care system in America, pointing out that as a public service it is insufficiently funded, and seriously flawed. As a result, a significant number of people are uninsured, creating a large degree of inequality among Americans in health care. In a much sharper tone, American critics categorically denounce the misconceptions of health care system itself as well as serious flaws built in this system. They point out that the availability and adequacy of health care in America largely depends upon the financial ability of the patient, rather than upon the actual need of the person involved. Consequently, those living in affluent neighborhoods are well covered, while those of low income groups, such as single-parent families, ethnic minorities, and rural and inner city residents, often have difficulties obtaining adequate health care. Over the past several decades, efforts have been made time and again to reform the health care system, but each time high-profile political talks and moves ended in failure. Not until 2010 did the health care reform finally succeed under the Obama administration.

As of now, American health care services are divided between the private and public sectors. Private hospitals, clinics and surgeries are in general well equipped and quite efficient. They may be run by commercial organizations, or by religious groups. By contrast, the public sector is financed by state or federal funds, and oftentimes, hospitals and clinics in the public sector lack resources and adequate funding. As can be imagined, physicians and surgeons in private hospitals usually work longer hours, and, almost as a rule, have much higher incomes. But doctors in the public sector also enjoy decent salaries and high prestige. Both the private and public sectors are available for health care coverage for individuals and institutions, with the former usually providing better health care than the latter.

Most employees and their families are normally insured for health care through private insurance schemes. Insurance premiums, which tend to be expensive even by American standards, are purchased by companies, trade unions or individuals. Companies (or employers) make the payments by deducting money from employees' wages and salaries, unions by union membership fees, and individuals by personal contributions. However, no one health insurance policy, private or public, covers all possible eventualities, and as a result, whenever financially possible, people subscribe to several policies in order to provide adequate health care for themselves. Still, even if people have purchased several health care schemes, they may still end up paying for some of the medical treatments that are not covered by the insurance policies. Of course, those who have no health insurance live the most precarious lives, worried all the time what they can do should they fall seriously ill. It is estimated that presently there are over 44 million Americans medically uninsured, either because they can not afford it or because they do not want to buy it even if they have the money. Thus, an irony is created: although the U. S. has high quality and extensive medical facilities, particularly in the private sector, gaining access to them remains a problem for a substantial proportion of the population. Now, with the health care bill passed by U. S. Congress in 2010, these uninsured people will be covered by the new law.

Chapter Twelve
Social Services

American anxieties about possible illness are conditioned not only by relatively high insurance premiums, but also by the high cost of medical treatment. For this reason, the medical profession has long been suspected of being the culprit to push up medical costs for its own profit. Also for this reason, the American public has plenty of resentment against the medical profession for its profit-driven services, particularly in the private sector. In the public sector, things are only relatively better, for at least health care is available there to those in need of it but lack money and insurance to pay for the service. The federal non-contributory Medicaid programs, for example, provides grants to states for the free treatment of the poor and needy, blind and disabled people and dependant children. However, because of the mandatory nature of the federal matching-fund policy, the scope of Medicaid varies from state to state, with some states providing more than other states. More importantly, Medicaid covers only about 40% of the poor nationwide in the United States.

Another big federal health program is called Medicare, which was established in 1965 to cover much of the cost for the medical treatment of the elderly and disabled. Such health care is dependent upon Social Security contributions made by the pensioner during his/her employment. Like any other health insurance, Medicare does not provide complete coverage, and therefore many elderly people have to buy other health insurances. Those who cannot afford often find themselves unable to pay for some types of medical treatment, particularly the most expensive ones. For these reasons, Americans would normally try to put aside some of their savings for the balance of their medical fees in case of emergence. But, with the increasing cost of medical care, most elderly people find difficult to catch up with it, even with the full amount of their lifetime's savings.

Of course, it is not only senior citizens who find medical cost prohibitively high. People across the board in the United States feel the pinch of its soaring cost. It is estimated that in recent years over 15% of U. S. GDP derives from the provision of public and private health care services, which is considerably higher than that of most other developed countries. Much of it stems from the high salaries of doctors, management and the expense of equipment and drugs. Critics argue that the American public is not receiving the full benefit of such expenditure, particularly when medical services vary so greatly between urban and rural areas, and between affluent and poor neighborhoods. Additionally, critics have also commented on other serious developments that have contributed to the rising costs of medical care, such as well-publicized lawsuits against doctors and hospitals for alleged wrong treatment. Lawyers can profit enormously by fighting such personal injury lawsuits on a contingency fee basis. But the rise in such cases forces doctors to insure themselves against the risks of being sued. Medical care and vital decisions can be consequently influenced by these considerations, driving the cost of health care to rise higher.

Nevertheless, despite all these shortcomings and limitations, American federal, state and local governments do provide a range of public health facilities for many categories of people, ranging from the poor to war veterans. They make funds available for hospitals, mental institutions, retirement homes and maternity and child health centers. These public facilities may also be supplemented by voluntary organizations, universities and other public institutions that provide free health care for the local population. But, ultimately, public medical and care services in the United States suffer from inadequate coverage of the needy, varying standards in different areas, and finally the rising cost of medical services.

12.5 *Housing*

Homes and houses are very important for most Americans and their families. They give a sense of possession, material satisfaction, personal identification and individual lifestyle, around which family activities take place. Indeed, the lives of most Americans revolve around their homes and houses. Most Americans still live in "single-family dwellings," that is, houses which usually have a front and a backyard. Contrary to a common belief, only about 5 percent of all Americans live in mobile homes. For all practical purposes, most of these homes are not actually mobile but function as prefabricated housing units in stationary settings.

The average American may move home many times in his/her lifetime. Under normal circumstances, over 20 percent of American population move from one place to another within a county. Even when the economy does not perform particularly well, the annual rate at which people move still stays above 10 percent. The U. S. Census Bureau reported in 2009 that in 2008, 11.9 percent Americans, compared with 13.2 percent in 2007, moved within a county, the lowest rate since the

Chapter Twelve
Social Services

Bureau began measuring mobility six decades ago. There may be plenty of factors for people to move around, but one of the key factors is homeownership. In the United States, homeownership is very closely associated with socio-economic mobility. A young family unit will move more frequently in the early years from apartments to houses and up the housing market. There may be further moves in middle age from urban areas to the suburbs. Some people may restrict themselves to a particular location, but many Americans move long distances across the country, some even from coast to coast. On the whole, the percentage of Americans owing the houses and apartments they live in is the highest among western nations. The reasons for that are manifold. For one thing, homeownership to the American is part of the American Dream, which makes many people feel very bad and even ashamed for not being able to own a home. For another, most Americans are of middle class, and therefore to buy a house or an apartment unit is not particularly difficult. For still another, private houses and apartment units are in general reasonably priced across a broad band, although they are subject to price fluctuations in the housing market. In the United States, the housing market is divided between the private sector for those who are able to buy or rent a house and the public sector for those who need governmental assistance to obtain low-rent property.

Private houses or apartment buildings are usually of good quality, with many amenities. When buying them, most owners borrow money from a bank (such a loan is called a mortgage) which is secured by the value of their house and income in order to pay for them. In 1995, for example, a median-sized house cost $109,000 and had an average mortgage of 8 percent. This entailed a monthly repayment on the mortgage of $643, which amounted to 19.9 percent of average family incomes in the 1980s, but the housing market then suffered from the economic recession of the early 1990s, which means that the owner of the house would find it harder to pay for the mortgage should he lose his job or have his salary cut. If he could not pay at all, he could face foreclosure right away, which means that he and his family would be driven out of the house, which would be put for sale in the housing market.

Public sector housing in the United States is meant to provide for a minority of Americans who are unable to buy property or afford high-rent private accommodation. Efforts to provide such housing for the needy have been both slow and piecemeal in the United States, primarily because of cultural biases against public funding for private citizens. In American value system, individuals are expected to be responsible for themselves, including responsibility for their housing arrangements, rather than expecting these to be a public responsibility. However, due to the growth of urban slums as well as substandard housing in both urban centers and rural areas, the Federal Housing Administration was created in 1934 to deal with housing problems. The Federal Housing Administration, generally known as "FHA," provides mortgage insurance on loans made by FHA-approved lenders throughout the United States and its territories. FHA insures mortgages on single family and multifamily homes including manufactured homes and hospitals. It is the largest insurer of mortgages in the world, insuring over 34 million properties since its inception in 1934.

Specifically for public housing, the Administration provides loans to organizations willing to build low-rent accommodation for needy people. Similarly, local and state governments also build public housing for people without financial ability to buy homes for themselves. However, even though federal funds for such public housing have never been enormous, attempts to build more low-cost public housing projects have been frequently opposed by property developers. More significantly, while many states and cities have implemented fair-housing laws and fair-housing regulations, a large number of low-income families, particularly low-income minority groups in urban areas, continue to live in barely inhabitable housing conditions. Worse still, since local, state and federal governments have failed to provide sufficient numbers of low-cost accommodation for the needy, quite a significant number of Americans are homeless. Estimates of homeless people vary from unofficial figures of up to the millions to official figures of half a million. In 2008, for example, *The New York Times* reported that the number of chronically homeless people living in American streets and shelters dropped by about 30 percent—to 123,833 from 175,914—between 2005 and 2007. But the same report also said that about 1.6 million people experienced homelessness and found shelter between Oct. 1, 2006 and Sept. 30, 2007, suggesting that many of these homeless people shuttled between shelters and the street. Voluntary or charity organizations attempt to help the homeless by providing shelter and food, but their help is often limited both in scope and length, making the issue of the homeless a sticking sore in this land of abundance.

SUMMARY

(1) In general, a set of values permeates American social welfare: all people are equal, but those who do not work are less equal; individual life

Chapter Twelve
Social Services

has worth, but only the fit should survive; people are responsible for each other, but those who are dependent upon others for their living are of less worth. Specifically, American attitudes toward social services are often couched in religious, moral, or patriotic terms.

(2) In pre-industrial America, farmers and pioneers provided not only emotional support, but also communal protection, making government-sponsored social welfare unnecessary. As people lost jobs or became homeless in the industrialized and urbanized society, social welfare became imperative. But for a long while, it was done by charity organizations. The U.S. government did not intervene in it until the 1930s.

(3) Public social services in America can be divided into two categories. The first is the contributory Social Security System, through which benefits are earned and distributed. The second is a program that provides assistance to people incapable of financially supporting themselves. Such assistance is given on the basis of income, but not tied to the contributory system. These programs are called welfare programs.

(4) American health care services are divided between the private and public sectors. Private hospitals, clinics and surgeries are generally well equipped and quite efficient, run by commercial organizations of religious groups. The public sector is financed by state or federal funds, which are often inadequate in proportion to the needs. Both the private and public sectors for health care are available for individuals and institutions.

(5) Homes and houses are important for most Americans, for owning a home/house is part of the American Dream. On the whole, the percentage of Americans owning a house or an apartment unit is the highest among western nations. Private houses or apartment buildings are usually of good quality. Public sector housing in America is meant to provide for the people unable to buy a house or rent an apartment room.

ESSAY QUESTIONS

(1) American social welfare programs are heavily influenced by their cultural values regarding Protestant work ethics and individual moral responsibility. Examine all these values that undergird American welfare programs, and explain to what extent they have contributed to the social services provided by private charity and to what extent they have impeded state-run welfare programs for the underprivileged people.

(2) In general, social services in America have gone through several

stages: from communal support and protection to private voluntary charity organizations to state-sponsored social welfare programs. Trace the evolutionary process of social services in America and identify the forces that brought about these changes in both people's perceptions and government actions regarding social welfare programs.

(3) Public services in America are of two categories, one is contributory, and the other social welfare. Describe each of them in detail and compare and contrast them in their concept and approach, paying particular attention to their advantages and disadvantages as well as their limitations in actual operation. Also, take note of the key disagreements and debates over the U.S. government social welfare policies.

(4) American health care system has long been a subject of debate and criticism. America is the most developed country in the world, and yet has the least developed health care system in the industrialized countries, leaving millions of Americans uninsured. Describe and analyze the flaws inherent in the American health care system, noting, in particular, the arguments of both pros and cons over this issue.

(5) Owning a home/house has always been part of the American Dream. The great majority of Americans are able to see this dream come true, but a sizable portion of the population can never find their dream materialized. While the U.S. government has been making some efforts to help these people, such as launching government housing projects, such efforts have been slow, piecemeal, and inadequate. Examine the chief reasons behind U.S. government' reluctance to do it on a larger scale.

American Society and Culture
美 国 社 会 文 化

Chapter Thirteen
Law and Legal System

LEARNING OBJECTIVES

- Know the sources of American law
- Understand the operating procedure of the U.S. federal judicial system
- Understand the operating procedure of the U.S. state judicial system
- Be aware of the criminal court process in the U.S.
- Be aware of the civil court process in the U.S.

American law has its roots in the method and body of the common law which the American colonists brought over with them from England. There was still a chance in the 17th century that the new settlements might develop their own system of law. But in the 18th century, the English common law, which had served as a weapon in Parliament's struggle against the absolute monarchy, began to be taken over as a colonial weapon in the struggle for freedom. Although the process was by no means inevitable, the fact that the common law became dominant in the American legal system was due mainly to the influence of the great American judges and treatise writers of the pre-Civil War generation. With the rise of a business economy, the new American business class was glad to have an instrument like the common law to deal with the problems of commercial litigation and justice. Eventually, an American legal system was fashioned out which has a continuity with the English much like the continuity of the American language with the English. There are local variants in usage, but the frame and tradition are the same. Thus, a legal system has emerged embodying a number of master ideas interwoven with those of politics and economics of American experience as well as the American mind itself.

13.1 The Sources of the Law

The sources of contemporary U. S. law mainly come from the common law, the statute law, and the doctrine.

The common law of England is the body of rules declared by the royal courts to be common to the customs of England, in theory at least. It was brought to the American continent by the first settlers, though not without qualifications. At the very beginning, the common law was more or less ignored by early settlers, for their priority at that time was to survive, not to apply the common law of England. Later, as life in the New World became more normal and as the number of settlers increased, the application of the common law became not only possible but also desirable. When the colonies declared their independence, they drafted constitutions in which they adopted the common law in various laws. In most cases, the formula of adoption was not a clear one: the new states wanted to retain their law, but nobody knew with certainty what had been the sources of the law in colonial times. When new states joined the Union, they adopted again, with the exception of Louisiana, the common law applicable in all states across the land.

Such is still the situation. Louisiana excepted, all states are governed by the common law as well as such statutory law as have been adopted. However, each state is sovereign in its power to declare the content of the common law. As a rule, its common law is administrated by its courts, and its supreme court has the sovereign power to declare such and such a rule is or is not a part of the common law of the state. The common laws of the states, therefore, while being close to each other, remain quite different from each other. By definition, the common law should be found in the decisions of the courts, which, in turn, ought to be followed in subsequent cases, according to the rule traditionally known as *stare decisis*. They have "authority of precedents" in similar cases. More precisely, what has authority is the *ratio decidendi* of the precedent, the rule on which the decision is based, as opposed to the *obiter dicta*, the mere explanations or examples given by the court.

In addition to the common law, present-day U. S. law also derives from the statute law. In the United States, as far as federal law is concerned, statute law, in a broad sense, is almost the only one. By "statute law," it refers to laws passed by state legislatures and U. S.

Congress. It grew considerably from the 19th century as state and federal governments intruded increasingly into everyday life of American citizens. Federal laws basically consist of the Constitution, treaties, acts of Congress, presidential proclamations, executive orders and rules of the various departments or commissions. In many ways, the role of the statute law in the U.S. is comparable to what it is in Great Britain. For instance, while the bulk of the law still remains the common law, the rules of the common law, in many cases, are superseded by legislation. More importantly, if the traditional function of the statute law was to amend the solutions of the common law on points of detail, legislation now covers a wide range of areas in social, economic, and even family matters. In this case, state legislation is valid in areas already covered by federal legislation as long as they do not conflict with each other. Most important of all, the tradition of applying to the statute a literal and narrow construction has now been abandoned by most of the courts both at federal and state levels.

As for the doctrine, it refers to the body of books and commentaries published on legal problems, though they are not of the same importance as the common law or the statute as source of law. In other words, its authority is only a persuasive one, rather than a decisive one. For instance, unlike the common law or the statute law, the doctrine takes a different form. It exists in the form of handbooks, casebooks, law reviews, and encyclopedias. Judges and practicing lawyers play a significant part in the formulation of doctrine. The main center, however, is the law school, where cases of all kinds are not only discussed carefully, but also reviewed and argued over critically. Out of class discussions, moot-courts, and law reviews of these law schools, there have emerged some of the most persuasive legal doctrines in the United States. Students trained in such intellectual environments will later on help shape new interpretation of laws, or even help make new laws, when they become lawyers, judges or government officials after graduation. In short, the doctrine serves as a source of law not so much by writing laws as in the case of the statute law, or by setting precedents as in the case of the common law. Rather, it does so by formulating ideas and making arguments in the form of publications, such as casebooks and law reviews, indirectly exerting its impact on the people making laws (law-makers) and interpreting laws (judges).

Chapter Thirteen
Law and Legal System

13.2 The Federal Judicial System

U. S. courts operate at separate federal and state levels and have their own areas of authority or jurisdiction. State and local courts handle most of the legal cases and are the most immediate for Americans. The federal courts only account for some two percent of cases tried annually. Together, federal and state and local courts make up the structure of the judicial system in the United States.

As the word "federal" indicates, federal courts deal with cases which arise under the U. S. Constitution, treaties or federal law and any disputes involving the federal government. They also hear matters involving governments or citizens of different states, and thereby play a part in state law as well. Besides, if a case in the highest state court of appeal involves a federal question, it can be appealed to the U. S. Supreme Court.

The federal judicial system forms a hierarchy, including three main levels of courts, namely the United States District Courts, the United States Courts of Appeal, and finally the United States Supreme Court. Usually, a case involving federal jurisdiction is heard first before a federal court. If not solved, an appeal may be made to the United States Courts of Appeal. Most federal cases begin and are settled in the U. S. District Courts. Some ninety-four district courts are situated across the United States and various U. S. territories such as Puerto Rico, with each state having at least one district court. The jurisdiction of a court sometimes extends over the territory of a state, usually over one-half, but sometimes one-third of it. The number of judges assigned to each court varies greatly with the needs of the court. Some courts have only one judge, or two or three, while other courts may have more than twenty.

Like all other judges, the district judges are appointed by the President with the advice and consent of the Senate. They always come from the bar. The selection of judges should be made on the basis of the technical merits of the candidates. It is generally believed that the politics should not interfere in the process, or perhaps that Presidents should strive for a political equilibrium between the affiliation of judges. However, experiences demonstrate that Presidents usually appoint persons of their party. This is not to mean that the federal judges are not of satisfactory caliber. In most cases, they are. Besides, appointments are generally made after consultation between the Attorney General and the American Bar Association, the weight of the latter organization's recommendations varying with the President and the Attorney General. Moreover, once they are appointed, the judges definitely consider themselves above party divisions and interests, even though they cannot always rid themselves of the prejudices of the community to which they belong, and in some instances, have shown themselves stern segregationists.

As a rule, federal District Courts try cases involving breaches of criminal law, such as bank robbery, drug dealing, kidnapping, currency fraud and assassination. However, most of the work of the District Courts is in areas of civil law, such as taxation, civil rights, administrative regulations, disputes between states and bankruptcy. The Courts of Appeals, as the name indicates, hear appeals from decisions of the U.S. District Courts within the circuits. Altogether, the territory of the United States is divided into eleven judicial circuits, each under the jurisdiction of a court of appeal, with three to five judges sitting in session. Critics maintain that the Appeal Courts are the most important judicial policy-makers in the United States, because most of their decisions are final and set a precedent for future similar cases. However, they are not the ultimate authority, for their decisions can be overturned by the U.S. Supreme Court, which, as the name suggests, is the highest court in the U.S. judicial system. The federal Supreme Court is composed of a Chief Justice and eight Associate Justices, having jurisdiction in all cases affecting ambassadors, other public ministers and consuls and those in which a state shall be a party. However, its main role is that of an appeal court that hears cases from lower federal and state courts. These appeals usually involve constitutional issues, questions of federal law and conflicts between two or more states. Although not explicitly given by the U.S. Constitution, the Supreme Court has developed the so-called "judicial review" authority to review any executive and legislative action or law passed by government of all levels, and can declare it unconstitutional if it is found incompatible with the U.S. Constitution and federal laws. Such authority has enabled the Court to exert profound influence on American society.

Appointments to the Supreme Court are made by the President of the United States with the advice and consent of the Senate. The judges of the Court constitutionally hold their office during good behavior. It has long been a traditional saying that Justices of the Court seldom resign and rarely die. Normally, the Court rules on some 150 cases each year, and decides for itself whether or not it will hear a particular case. Although the Court does not have the power to actually make laws, its decisions on many important issues such as segregation and abortion often have profound legislative or policy-making implications. In general, the Court plays a restrained or conservative role, following legal tradition and previous precedent. But from time to time, it can assume an image of liberal activism. Over the past four decades, its caseload has increased significantly due to new legislation in civil rights and federal regulation. Consequently, its political profile has become increasingly larger in American life.

13.3 The State Judicial System

To average Americans, the state courts are more important than the federal ones, for the former are more immediate to their life and therefore more directly related to them than the latter. Indeed, in comparison with the federal courts, the state courts have a wider jurisdiction and consequently have heavier workloads They are the normal judges of contracts, torts, property, domestic affairs, corporation problems, and criminal laws. They pass over 95 percent of all cases made in the United States. Moreover, when a federal court has jurisdiction by reason of the diversity of citizenship of the parties involved, it ought to apply state law as it has been applied by the state courts.

According to the U. S. Constitution, the states have areas of authority (or sovereignty) outside the federal judicial system. They have their own criminal and civil legal systems, laws, prisons, police forces, courts and associations of lawyers. Court systems and laws are similar in most cases, but there are differences in many areas such as court structure, sentences for murder, capital punishment, marriage age, drinking age, and possession of a driver's license. As self-contained legal units, the states jealously guard their independence, and their courts deliver judgments from which there is often no appeal. Of course, if an issue has federal implications, jurisdiction can be shared between federal and state courts. To a great extent, the sovereignty of the states explains the diversity of the state judicial system, a diversity which does not permit an accurate general description. Still, a broad scheme of organization may be found among the state courts in the United States.

At the bottom of the hierarchy are the local courts with a limited jurisdiction. They hear minor civil and criminal cases (misdemeanors) that often cannot be appealed and may not have a jury. Justice in local courts is administrated by justices of the peace or, in the cities, by magistrates. The names of local courts vary from one locality to another, and often have something to do with the nature of the case. So, they may be known as Police Courts, Town or City Courts, or Justice of the Peace Courts. Above the local courts are the trial courts. They are so called because the facts of the case are ascertained before them. Sometimes, they are also called courts of record, because they must keep records of their decisions. Usually, such courts have a general jurisdiction. In some states, however, distinctions are made between civil and criminal courts, or between courts of law and of equity. At any rate, due to their diversity, trail courts may consist of the following courts in one way or another: District, County or Municipal Courts which hear civil suits and criminal cases; Juvenile or Family Courts which decide domestic, juvenile and delinquency cases; Probate Courts which decide on wills and hear claims against estates; and Criminal Courts which determine criminal cases. Most of the criminal and some civil cases will be heard by a jury.

In a number of states, perhaps three-quarters of them, some kind of intermediate appeal courts have been set up between the courts of first instance and the States Supreme Court. They hear appeals from lower courts to relieve the State Supreme Court of its load of appeals, which hears civil and criminal appeals from inferior state courts and can employ judicial review. Judges on the State Supreme Court are appointed or elected for a long period of time, sometimes nine or twelve years during good behavior. In the lower courts, judges in some states are publicly elected, but in others appointed by state governors or by special bodies such as judicial councils. Some judges hold office for fixed periods, while others are installed for life or up to a retiring age. In some cases, there may be provision for "recall," meaning a group of people dissatisfied with a judge may collect signatures on a "recall" petition, and if the signatures reach the required figure, the people of the state will then vote to decide whether to keep the impugned judge in office or remove him from it.

Chapter Thirteen
Law and Legal System

13.4 *The Criminal Court Process*

The criminal process begins when a law is first broken and extends through the arrest, indictment, trial, and appeal. However, an act is not automatically a crime because it is hurtful or sinful. An action constitutes a crime only if it specifically violates a criminal statute duly enacted by Congress, a state legislature, or some other public authority. A crime, then, is an offense against the state punishable by fine, imprisonment, or death. The sanctions of imprisonment and death cannot be imposed by a civil court or in a civil action. In the United States, there is no single criminal, or civil, court process. Instead, the federal system has a court process at the national level, and each state and territory has its own set of rules and regulations that affect the judicial process, though norms and similarities do exist among all of these governmental entities.

Crimes in the United States come in many forms. Most crimes constitute sins of commission, such as embezzlement; a few consist of sins of omission, such as failing to file an income tax return. The state considers some crimes serious, such as murder and treason, but other crimes only mildly reprehensible, such as double parking or disturbing the peace. Some crimes, such as kidnapping or rape, constitute actions that virtually all citizens consider outside the sphere of acceptable human conduct. The most serious crimes in the United States are felonies. In a majority of the states, a felony is any offense for which the penalty may be death (in the states that allow it) or imprisonment in the penitentiary (a federal or state prison). In other states, and under federal law, a felony is an offense for which the penalty may be death or imprisonment for a year or more. All other offenses are misdemeanors, which are regarded as petty crimes by the state, and their punishment usually consists of confinement in a city or county jail for less than a year. Public drunkenness, small-time gambling, and vagrancy are common examples of misdemeanor offenses.

Broadly speaking, there are five categories of criminal offenses in the United States today, namely conventional, economic, syndicated, political and consensual. By conventional crimes, they refer to property crimes such as theft and burglary, and violence against the person such as murder, forcible rape and robbery. Of these two, property crimes make up the lion's share of the conventional crimes. As for economic crimes, they include (A) personal criminal activities like writing a bad check and cheating one's income tax, (B) breach of trust by employees against their employer such as commercial bribery, embezzlement and filling out false expense accounts, (C) business crimes incidental to its operation such as misleading advertising and violations of the anti-trust laws, (D) white-collar criminal activities committed under the guise of a business like confidence games. Regarding syndicated/organized crimes, they refer to groups of people engaged in such lucrative activities as trafficking in illegal drugs, gambling, prostitution, and loan-sharking. With respect to political crimes, they are usually committed against the government, offenses of which include treason, armed rebellion, sedition, and assassination of public officials. Finally, so-called consensual crimes are also known as victimless crimes, because both perpetrator and client commit the forbidden activity with consent. Prostitution, gambling, illegal drug use, and unlawful sexual practices between consenting adults are all of this type.

When a crime is believed to have occurred, a series of legal procedures quickly follow, including arrest, trial and sentencing. The arrest is the first substantial contact between the state and the accused. The U.S. legal system provides for two basic types of arrest—those with a warrant and those without. A warrant is issued after a compliant, filed by one person against another, has been presented and reviewed by a magistrate who has found probable cause for the arrest. Arrests without a warrant occur when a crime is committed in the presence of a police officer or when an officer has probable cause to believe that someone has committed (or is about to commit) a crime. Such a belief must later be established in a sworn statement. In the United States, up to 95 percent of all arrests are made without warrant. After a suspect is arrested for a crime, he/she is booked at the police station, where the facts surrounding the arrest are recorded and the accused may be fingerprinted and photographed. Next, the accused appears before a lower-level judicial official whose title may be judge, magistrate, or commissioner. Such an appearance is supposed to occur without unnecessary delay.

This appearance in court is the occasion of several important events in the criminal justice process. First, the accused must have been informed of the precise charges and must be informed of all constitutional rights and guarantees, including the right to remain silent. Second, the magistrate will determine whether the accused is to be released on bail and, if so, what the amount of bail is to be. Constitutionally, the only requirement for the amount is that it shall not be excessive, and bail is considered to be a privilege, not a right, and it may be denied altogether in capital punishment cases for which the evidence of guilt is strong or if the magistrate believes that the accused will flee from prosecution no matter what the amount of bail. An alternative to bail is to release the defendant on recognizance of a pledge by the defendant to return to court on the appointed date for trial. In minor cases, the accused may be asked to plead guilty or not guilty. If the plea is guilty, a sentence may be pronounced on the spot or at a later date set by the judge. If the defendant pleads not guilty, a trial date is scheduled.

At the federal level, all persons accused of a crime are guaranteed by the Fifth Amendment to have their cases considered by a grand jury. However, the Supreme Court has refused to make this right binding on the states. Today, only about half of the states use grand juries. Those states that do not use grand juries employ a preliminary hearing or an examining trial. Regardless of which method is used, the primary purpose of this stage in the criminal justice process is to determine whether there is probable cause for the accused to be subjected to a formal trial. Grand juries consist of 16 to 23 citizens, usually selected at random from the voter registration lists, who render decision by a majority vote. At a preliminary hearing, the prosecution presents its case, and the accused has the right to cross-examine witnesses and to produce favorable evidence. Usually, the defense elects not to fight at this state of the criminal process.

After that, the legal process moves on to the arraignment in which the defendant is brought before the judge in the court where he/she is to be tried to respond to the grand jury indictment or the prosecutor's bill of information. The defendant is informed that he/she has a constitutional right to be represented by an attorney and that a lawyer will be appointed without charge if necessary. At this stage, the defendant has several options about how to plead to the charges. The most common pleas are guilty and not guilty. At both the state and federal levels at least 90 percent of all criminal cases never go to trial, because before the trial date a bargain has been struck between the prosecutor and the defendant's attorney concerning the official charges to be brought and the nature of the sentence that the state will recommend to the court. In effect, some form of lenience is promised in exchange for a guilty plea. And, since plea bargaining seals the fate of the defendant before trial, the role of the judge is simply to ensure that the proper legal and constitutional procedures have been followed. If no plea bargain has been struck and the accused maintains his/her innocence, a formal trial will take place.

During the trail, the accused is provided many constitutional and statutory rights guaranteed by the Sixth Amendment and the Fifth Amendment. The former stipulates: "In all criminal prosecutions, the accused shall enjoy the right to a speedy and public trial," as well as the right to an impartial jury. The latter declares that no person shall be tried twice for the same crime by any state government or by the federal government. Another important right guaranteed to the accused at both the state and federal level is not to "be compelled in any criminal case to be a witness against himself." The guarantee serves to reinforce the principle that under the U.S. Constitution the burden of proof is on the state, and the accused is presumed innocent until the government proves otherwise beyond a reasonable doubt. Finally, as a way of protection for the accused, the Supreme Court has interpreted the guarantee of due process of law in the Fourth Amendment to mean that evidence procured in an illegal search and seizure may not be used against the accused at trial. The Court's purpose is to eliminate any incentive the police might have to illegally obtain evidence against the accused.

During the trial, the judge's role, although very important, is a relatively passive one. He/She does not present any evidence or take an active part in the examination of the witnesses. The judge is called upon to rule on the many motions of the prosecutor and of the defense attorney regarding the types of evidence that may be presented and the kinds of questions that may be asked of the witnesses. In some jurisdictions, the judge is permitted to ask questions of the witnesses; in other states, the judge is constrained from such activity. If the accused elects not to have a bench trial, that is, not to be tried and sentenced by a judge alone, his/her fate will be determined by a jury, whose role during the trial is passive. Their job is to listen attentively to the cases presented by the opposing attorneys and then come to a decision based solely on the evidence that is set forth. They are ordinarily not permitted to ask questions either of the witnesses or of the judges, nor are they allowed to take notes of the proceedings. This is not because of constitutional or statutory prohibition but primarily because it has been the traditional practice of courts in America. At the federal level, 12 persons must render a unanimous verdict. At the state level, such criteria apply only to the most serious offenses. In many states, a jury may consist of fewer than 12 persons and render verdicts by other than unanimous decisions.

At the close of the criminal trial, generally two stages remain for the defendant if he/she has been found guilty: sentencing and an appeal. Sentencing is the court's formal pronouncement of judgment upon the defendant at which time the punishment or penalty is set forth. At the federal level and in most states, sentences are imposed by the judge only. However, in several states, the defendant may elect to be sentenced either by a judge or by a jury, and in capital cases states generally require that no death sentence shall be imposed unless it is the determination of 12 unanimous jurors. At both the state and federal levels, everyone has the right to at least one appeal upon conviction of a felony, but in reality few criminals avail themselves of this privilege.

13.5 The Civil Court Process

Civil actions are separate and distinct from criminal proceedings. The American legal system observes several important distinctions between criminal and civil law. Criminal law is concerned with conduct that is offensive to society as a whole, while civil law pertains primarily to the duties of private citizens to each other. In civil cases, the disputes are usually between private individuals, although the government may sometimes be a party in a civil suit. By contrast, criminal cases always involve government prosecution of an individual for an alleged offense against society. Furthermore, in a civil case, the court attempts to settle a particular dispute between the parties by determining their legal rights. The court then decides upon an appropriate remedy, such as awarding monetary damage to the injured party or issuing an order that directs one party to perform or refrain from a specific act. But in a criminal case, the court decides whether the defendant is innocent or guilty, and a guilty defendant may be punished by a fine, imprisonment, or both.

Virtually any dispute between two or more persons may provide the basis for a civil suit, and that is why civil cases far outnumber criminal cases in both the federal and state courts in the United States. Generally speaking, they fall into the following five basic categories of civil law: contract law, tort law, property law, the law of succession and family law. As the name indicates, contract law is primarily concerned with voluntary agreement between two or more people. Some common examples include agreements to perform a certain type of work, to buy or sell goods, and to construct or repair homes or businesses. Basic to these agreements are a promise by one party and a counter promise by the other party. Although many contracts are relatively simple and straightforward, some complex fields also build on contract law, such as commercial law, which focuses primarily on sales involving credit or the installment plan. Tort law may be generally described as the law of civil wrongs. It concerns conduct that causes injury and fails to measure up to some standard set by society. Actions for personal injury or bodily injury claims are at the heart of tort law, and automobile accidents have traditionally been responsible for a large number of these claims. One of the most rapidly growing subfields of tort law is product liability. This category has become an increasingly effective way to hold corporations accountable for injuries caused by defective foods, toys, appliances, automobiles, drugs, or a host of other products. Besides, medial malpractice is also rapidly growing as a subfield of tort law, when patients believe that doctors or hospitals have failed them and decide to file a malpractice suit.

Regarding property law, a distinction has been traditionally made between real property and personal property. The former normally refers to real estate, such as land, houses and buildings. Almost everything else is considered personal property, including such things as money, jewelry, automobiles, furniture, and bank deposits. Property rights have always been important in the United States, but today property rights are more complex than mere ownership of something. The notion of property now includes, among other things, the right to use that property, such as land use controls. As for the law of succession, it considers how property is passed along from one generation to another. The American legal system recognizes a person's right to dispose of his/her property as he/she wishes. One common way to do this is to execute a will. If a person leaves behind a valid will, the courts will enforce it. However, if someone leaves no will or has improperly drawn it up, and the person has died intestate, the state then must dispose of the property according to the fixed scheme set forth in the state statute. By law, intestate property is passed to the deceased person's heirs, that is, his/her nearest relatives. Occasionally, a person who dies intestate has no living relatives, in which case the property passes to the state in which the deceased resided. Finally, family law concerns

Chapter Thirteen
Law and Legal System

such matters as marriage, divorce, child custody, and children's rights, all touching the lives of a great number of Americans.

Every year, thousands of potential civil cases are resolved without a trial because the would-be litigants settle their problems in another way or because the prospective plaintiff decides not to file suit. When faced with a decision to call upon the courts, many people resort to a simple cost-benefit analysis, that is, to weigh the costs associated with a trail against the benefits they are likely to gain if they win. In practice, few persons make use of the entire judicial process. Instead, most cases are settled without resort to a full-fledged trial, because in civil cases, a trial may be both slow and expensive, taking sometimes three to five years for a case to come to trial. For these two reasons, from major corporations to attorneys to individuals, support for alternative dispute resolution (ADR) has been growing. Corporate America is interested in avoiding prolonged and costly court battles as the only way to settle complex business disputes. Additionally, attorneys are more frequently considering alternatives such as mediation and arbitration. And individual citizens are also increasingly turning to local mediation services for help in resolving family disputes, neighborhood quarrels, and consumer complaints.

However, while a number of disputes are resolved through some method of alternative dispute resolution either in a specialized court or by an administrative body, a large number of cases each year still manage to find their way into a civil court. Generally speaking, the adversarial process used in criminal trials is also used in civil trials, with just a few important differences. First, a litigant must have standing, meaning that the person litigating the suit must have a personal stake in the outcome of the controversy. Otherwise, there is no real controversy between the parties and thus no actual case for the court to decide. Second, the standard of proof used in civil cases is a preponderance of the evidence, not the more stringent beyond-a-reasonable-doubt standard used in criminal cases. The preponderance of the evidence is generally taken to mean that there is sufficient evidence to overcome doubt or speculation, meaning that less proof is required in civil cases than in criminal cases. Thirdly, many of the extensive due process guarantees that a defendant has in a criminal trial do not apply in a civil proceeding. For instance, neither party is constitutionally entitled to counsel, though the right to a jury trial is guaranteed.

The person initiating the civil case is known as the plaintiff, and the person being sued is the defendant. In a typical situation, the plaintiff's attorney pays a fee and files a complaint or petition with the clerk of the proper court. Once the appropriate court has been determined and the complaint has been filed, the court clerk will attach a copy of the complaint to the summons, which is then issued to the defendant. The summons directs the defendant to file a response, known as a pleading, within a certain period of time, usually 30 days. These simple actions by the plaintiff, clerk of the court, and a process server set in motion the civil case. What happens next is a flurry of activities that precedes an actual trial and may last for several months. Approximately 75 percent of cases are resolved without a trial during this time. When the trial does get underway, the right to a jury trial in a civil suit in a federal court is guaranteed by the U.S. Constitution. State constitutions likewise provide for such a right. A jury trial may be waived, in which case the judge decides the matter. Although a jury traditionally consists of 12 persons, today the number of jurors varies. Most of the federal district courts now use juries of fewer than 12 persons in civil cases. A majority of states also authorize smaller juries in some or all civil cases.

After the jury has been chosen, the trial begins, with each side presenting its case. Following that, the judge informs the jury that it must base its verdict on the evidence presented at the trial. Additionally, the judge also informs the jurors about the rules, principles, and standards of the particular legal concept involved. With all this in mind, the jury retires to the seclusion of the jury room to conduct its deliberations. The members must reach a verdict without outside contact. In some instances, the deliberations are so long and detailed that the jurors must be provided meals and sleeping accommodations until they can reach a verdict. The verdict, then, represents the jurors' agreement after detained discussions and analyses of the evidence. Sometimes, the jury deliberates in all good faith but cannot reach a verdict. When this occurs, the judge may declare a mistrial, in which case a new trial may have to be conducted. But when the verdict is reached, the jury is conducted back into open court, where it delivers its verdict to the judge, who, in turn, informs the parties of it. If the losing party feels that an error of law was made during the trial, it may appeal to a higher court. In most cases, the most common grounds for appeal are that the judge admitted evidence that should have been excluded, refused to admit evidence that should have been introduced, or failed to give proper jury instructions.

Chapter Thirteen
Law and Legal System

SUMMARY

(1) Contemporary American law derives from three sources: the British common law, the statute law, and the doctrine. The common law of England is the body of rules declared by the royal courts to be common to the customs of England. The statute law refers to laws passed by state legislatures and U. S. Congress. As for the doctrine, it refers to the body of books and commentaries published on legal problems.

(2) The U. S. federal judicial system has a hierarchical structure, including three main levels of courts, namely the U. S. District Courts, the U. S. Courts of Appeal, and the U. S. Supreme Court. Accounting for some two percent of cases tried annually in America, federal courts deal with cases which arise under the U. S. Constitution, treaties or federal law and any disputes involving the federal government.

(3) Every American state has its own state judicial system, in parallel to the federal judiciary in organizational structure. State and local courts handle most of the legal cases and are the most immediate for everage Americans. Comparatively, the state courts have a wider jurisdiction and subsequently have heavier workloads. They hear cases involving contracts, torts, property, divorces, corporation problems, and crimes.

(4) The criminal court process begins when a law is first broken and then extends through the arrest, indictment, trial, sentencing, and appeal. Broadly speaking, there are five categories of criminal offences in America: conventional, economic, syndicated, political and consensual. In America, there is no single criminal court process. Rather, the federal and state systems have their own different court processes.

(5) Civil actions are separate and distinct from criminal proceedings, for civil law pertains primarily to the duties of private citizens, and civil cases usually involve disputes between private individuals, though the government may sometimes be a party in a civil suit. In general, civil cases in America involve five basic categories of civil law: contract law, tort law, property law, the law of succession, and family law.

ESSAY QUESTIONS

(1) American law has its origins in the method and body of the English common law, the statute law, and the doctrine. Describe the main ideas of each one of them and discuss how they are reflected in contemporary American law, paying particular attention to the changes

and modifications of these laws made necessary by the changed or changing circumstances of modern American life.

(2) U.S. courts operate at separate federal and state levels and have their own areas of authority or jurisdiction. First, describe the structure of the federal court system, then discuss different functions and jurisdictions of these federal courts at each level, and finally analyze how so far the federal court system has played its role in defending and safeguarding the U.S. Constitution both in letter and in spirit.

(3) It is often said that to average Americans, the state courts are more important than the federal court, for the former are more immediate to their life and therefore more directly related to them than the latter. Assuming this is the case with the American court system, please explain in detail how and why the state courts have a closer bearing on average American life than the federal court.

(4) When a crime is committed in America, the criminal process begins right away, involving a series of complicated steps. Describe each step in the criminal process and discuss how one step leads to another in the whole procedure, paying particular attention to the devices in the proceeding that were designed or intended to protect the constitutional rights of the individual involved in the case.

(5) Civil cases in the American judiciary are separate and distinct from criminal proceedings. First, make distinctions between criminal and civil law in the American court system, and then describe in specific terms the five basic categories of civil law, and finally explain how and why each one of them is so carefully structured, paying particular attention to the way(s) the involved parties are respected and protected.

American Society and Culture
美 国 社 会 文 化

Chapter Fourteen
American Women

American Society and Culture
美 国 社 会 文 化

LEARNING OBJECTIVES

- Be aware of the role played by the founding mothers in early America
- Understand the implications of the Republican motherhood
- Learn how the first wave of feminism was initiated in America
- Be informed of the cult of domesticity and the so-called feminine mystique
- Know the causes of the second wave of feminism in America

Rarely in historic civilizations have women been as free, expressive, and powerful as in America, and yet rarely also has the burden of being a fulfilled woman been as heavy to carry. That is one of the many paradoxes that characterize the social role of the American woman. Everything in American life seems to conspire to make her a glittering, bedecked, and almost pampered creature, yet also one bedeviled by a dilemma that reflects the split both within herself and her culture. The American woman is torn between trying to vie with men in jobs, careers, business, and government, and finding her identity as wife, mother, and woman. The tussle between them accounts in great measure for the ambiguous place she holds in American society and for the frustrations and depressions commonly associated with American women in general, career women in particular.

14.1 Founding Mothers

The fate of the European women who came to the New World in the early days of colonial settlement was a life of nearly ceaseless hard work. The demands of the New World allowed colonial women more freedom to

Chapter Fourteen
American Women

do than was often available to women of later generations. This latitude was the product not of ideology, but of necessity. Colonial society did not support the idea of equality between men and women. Indeed, European men brought with them to America the tenet that woman was man's inferior. This belief in female inferiority, however, was minimized by the conditions of the New World, where women were an integral part of all permanent settlements. When men traveled alone to America, they came as fortune hunters, adventurers looking for a pot of gold. Such single men had no compelling reason to establish communities. When women came, they acted as civilizers for men living along in the wilderness. For the simple reason is where there were women, there were children who had to be taught, and there was a future—a reason to establish laws, towns, churches, and schools. In many cases, women actually emigrated together with their men, especially those who settled in New England.

The lives of colonial women and men tended to center around farm and family. For the most part, a traditional division of labor was observed, whereby men did the outside work—planting and harvesting crops, while women worked inside, transforming the raw products into usable commodities. Virtually, all of women's work on the farm came under the general heading of "housewifery." What it included varied somewhat from region to region. The wives of southern planters rarely did their own weaving and spinning, while in the northern colonies these tasks took up many hours of a woman's day. However, despite local variations, women's activities were much the same throughout the colonies. First came supervision of the house. Women swept, scrubbed, laundered, polished, and made their own brooms and soap. Secondly, they carried water, built fires, and made candles. Above all, they sewed everything—sheets, clothing, table linen, and diapers, and were responsible for food preparation and cooking. On top of all this, colonial women also worked outside the home. In the villages, towns, and small cities, they performed every kind of job held by men. Women ran taverns, inns, and boarding houses. In fact, not a few women were blacksmiths, silversmiths, wheelwrights, sail-makers, tailors, printers, teachers, shopkeepers of every sort. Throughout most of the colonial period, more women practiced medicine than men. Women were nurses, unlicensed physicians and midwives. Clearly, since women played such a crucial role in shaping the New World, there is no reason not to regard them as the founding mothers of the new nation.

However, even though women were central to colonial America in all walks of life, they were not treated as men's equals. In religion, for example, the Holy Scripture told woman that she, like man, was created in God's image, and to this degree recognized a spiritual equality between the sexes. Yet, throughout Old and New Testament literature, woman was also told that her duty and responsibility was to be subservient to men. For Christians in general, and Calvinists in particular, the story of Adam and Eve was of extreme importance. By being the first to fall under the serpent's spell, Eve was believed to have unloosed the devil in the world. Subsequently, Eve's fall was taken as proof that women were more susceptible to the devil than men, and hence she should be watched over by man. More significantly, colonial women were deprived of almost all legal rights. Under Common Law, as we know, married women were treated not as persons, but as property belonging to their husbands, and most colonies based their legal codes on the Common Law system. For the single woman, with the exception of the right to vote and the right to sit on a jury, she was treated more or less as man, because she had no man to "protect" her property. However, once married, she would no longer need these legal rights, for they would be covered by her husband. The basis of this assumption was the Common Law belief that husband and wife are one flesh, one unit, and one person, and that the "one person" was the husband. Later on, most of American colonies made alterations in the Common Law code granting women three important rights married women in Britain did not possess. Specifically, colonial courts recognized a wife's right to share her husband's home and bed; a wife's right to be supported by her husband, even if abandoned; and a wife's right to be protected from violence at her husband's hand.

Viewed from hindsight, these legal rights were very trivial. But given the fact that colonial American women were so constrained in their legal protection that their single most autonomous decision was their choice of a husband, these rights were quite significant. For colonial American women, their legal disability not only made them non-existent as human beings entitled to property ownership, but also invisible as social members with access to political process. Indeed, as far as political rights were concerned, American women had to wait for more than a century and a half before they could enjoy voting rights as equal citizens.

Chapter Fourteen
American Women

14.2 Women in the New Republic

To say that American women were denied legal and political rights does not mean that they did not think about it or demand it. As early as 1776, when America declared independence from Great Britain, for example, Abigail Adams wrote to her husband John Adams: "To be adept in the art of government is a prerogative to which your sex lay almost exclusive claim." It was not so much a comment as a complaint, for when American Revolution broke out, some women like Abigail Adams became excited by it, thinking that just as America was struggling for freedom from Britain, so should women begin to fight for their political freedom from men. But, Abigail Adams' political consciousness was not shared by many people, and women were not given a public role to play. Indeed, for most women and almost all men in the 1780s, a woman's duty was to maintain her household and raise her children.

Apart from the fact that some states eased women's difficulties in obtaining divorces, the Revolution did not significantly affect the legal position of women. More importantly, women did not gain any new political rights, although New Jersey's 1776 constitution did not exclude white female property holders from voting and a law in force in that state from 1790 to 1907 referred to voters as "he and she." The assumption that women were naturally dependent—whether as children subordinate to their parents or as wives to their husbands—continued to dominate discussions of the female role. As with African Americans, the Revolutionary era witnessed the beginnings of a challenge to traditional attitudes toward women. Massachusetts' women, for example, began to write political satires to ridicule local politicians. In other states, women started to demand for property rights, arguing that they were entitled to family property right like any other member of the family.

Gradually, the subordination of women, which once was taken for granted, became the subject of debate. The Massachusetts essayist Murray contended in 1779 that the genders had equal intellectual ability and deserved equal education. Murray hoped that "sensible and informed" women would improve their minds rather than rush into marriage, and would instill republican ideals in their children. After 1780, the urban upper class founded numerous private schools, or academies, for girls, and these provided to American women their first widespread opportunity for advanced education. Massachusetts also established an important precedent in 1789, when it forbade any town to exclude girls from its elementary schools. Furthermore, American women who chafed at the restrictions of their domestic role took heart from the publication in 1792 of the English radical Mary Wollstonecraft's *Vindication of the Rights of Women*. Although feeling obliged to condemn Wollstonecraft's intemperate language and sexually liberated lifestyle, many American women approved her passionate defense of female moral equality.

Although the great struggle for female political equality would not begin until the 19th century, the frequent Revolutionary-era assertions that women were intellectually and morally men's peers provoked scattered calls late in the 18th century for political equality. In 1793, Priscilla Mason, a young woman graduating from one of the female academies, blamed "Man, despotic man" for shutting women out of the church, the courts, and government. In her salutatory oration, she urged that a woman's senate be established by Congress to evoke "all that is human—all that is divine in the soul of woman." Unmistakably, Priscilla Mason had pointed out a fundamental problem in republican egalitarianism: what, besides being a virtuous wife and mother, should a woman do with her education?

For tradition-minded people, women should be contented with their role of wife and mother, but for women baptized by the republican ideals of the Revolution, this argument was no longer persuasive. Indeed, towards to the end of the 18th century, the major signs of a post-Revolutionary change in women's status were already manifesting themselves. Taken as a whole, they emphasized a new ideal of companionate marriage, the new legitimacy of women's education, a new rhetoric of female self-esteem, and an enhanced regard for motherhood. These signs were class-based, for republican motherhood was a concept that essentially served the interests of the emerging elite and helped to consolidate a middle-class gentry. Equally important, the early years of nationhood also brought the claim that women might serve a civic function, according to which female virtues might comfortably coexist with civic virtues, reconciling politics and domesticity. However, as a political concept, republican motherhood was a limited one, for it was a role played solely in the home. In other words, by assigning women the role of Republican motherhood, American women would be confined to the narrow sphere of the home. Still, changes had taken place. Before the Revolution, women had been excluded from political life; afterward, they remained on the periphery of the political community. Therefore, it is possible to read the subsequent political history of women in America as the story of women's efforts to accomplish for themselves what the Revolution failed to do.

14.3 Women's Rights Movement

The position of American women in the 1830s contained many contradictions. For one thing, women could not vote; for another, when married, women had no right to own property (even inherited property) or to retain their own earnings. Yet the spread of reform movements of the era provided women with unprecedented opportunities for public activity without challenging the prevailing belief that their proper sphere was the home. By suppressing liquor, for example, women could claim that they were transforming wretched homes into nurseries of happiness. Evidently, the argument that women were natural guardians of the family was double-edged. It justified women's reform activities on behalf of the family, but it also undercut women's demands for legal equality. Let women attend to their sphere, the opposition forces countered, and leave politics and finance to men. So deeply ingrained was sexual inequality at that time that not even serious feminists seriously thought about attacking it. Rather, it was their experiences in other reform movements, notably the abolition movement, that eventually led women to embark on the women's rights movement in 1848.

Among the early women's rights advocates who started their reform careers as abolitionists were the Grimké sisters, the Philadelphia Quaker Lucretia Mott, and Lucy Stone. Indeed, as early as 1837, Angelina and Sarah Grimké embarked on an antislavery lecture tour of New England. During the 1830s, women were deeply involved in antislavery societies, but always in female auxiliaries affiliated with those run by men. What made the Grimké sisters so controversial was that they drew mixed audiences of men and women to their lectures at a time when it was thought indelicate for women to speak before male audiences. Clergymen chastised the Grimké for lecturing men rather than obeying them. Such criticism got backfired, because the Grimké increasingly took up the cause of women's rights. "Men and women," Sarah Grimké wrote, "are created equal. They are both moral and accountable beings, and whatever is right for man to do, is right for woman." The most articulate and aggressive advocates of women's rights, however, tended to gravitate to William Garrison, a militant abolitionist and vigorous feminist at once. In the early issue of *The Liberator*, edited by Garrison, there contained a "Ladies' Department" headed by a picture of a kneeling slave woman imploring: "Am I not a woman and a sister?" It was common knowledge that slave women were vulnerable to the sexual demands of white masters. Garrison denounced the South as a vast brothel and described slave women as "treated with more indelicacy and cruelty than cattle."

Although their involvement in abolition aroused advocates of women's rights, the discrimination they encountered within the abolition movement infuriated them and impelled them to make women's rights a separate cause. In the 1840s, Lucy Stone became the first abolitionist to lecture on women's rights. When Lucretia Mott and other American women tried to be seated at the World's Anti-Slavery Convention in London in 1840, they were relegated to a screened-off section. The incident made a sharp impression not only on Mott but on Elizabeth Cady Stanton, who had elected to accompany her abolitionist husband to the meeting as a honeymoon trip. In 1848, Mott and Stanton organized a women's rights convention at Seneca Falls, New York, that proclaimed a Declaration of Sentiments. Modeled on the Declaration of Independence, the Seneca Falls Declaration began with the assertion that "all men and women are created equal." The convention passed twelve resolutions, including rights to property and education, and only one, a call for the right of women to vote, failed to pass unanimously; but it did pass. Ironically, after the Civil War, the call for women suffrage became the main demand of women's rights advocates for the rest of the century, transforming women's rights movement to women's suffrage movement.

Although its crusaders were resourceful and energetic, women's rights had less impact than most other reforms. Temperance and school reform were far more popular, and abolitionism created more commotion. Women would not secure the right to vote throughout the nation until 1920, 72 years after the Seneca Falls Convention. One reason for the relatively slow advance of women's rights was that piecemeal gains, such as married women securing the right to own property in several states, satisfied many women. The cause of women's rights also suffered from a close association with abolitionism, which was unpopular at that time. In addition, the advance of feminism was slowed by the competition that it faced from the alternative ideal of domesticity. By sanctioning activities in reforms such as temperance and education, the cult of domesticity provided many women with worthwhile pursuits beyond the family, thereby blunting the edge of female demands for full quality.

14.4 The Cult of Domesticity and New Women

The Victorian world view on morality and culture, coupled with rising pressures on consumers to make decisions about a mountain of domestic products, had a subtle but important impact on middle-class expectations about women's role within the home. Throughout the second half of the 19th century, members of the clergy and other promoters of the so-called cult of domesticity had idealized the home as "the women's sphere," a protected retreat where she could express her special maternal gifts, including a sensitivity toward children and an aptitude for religion. "The home is the wife's province; it is her natural field of labor... to govern and direct its interior management." During the 1880s and 1890s, advocates of this cult of domesticity added a new obligation to the traditional woman's role as director of the household: to foster an artistic environment that would nurture her family's cultural improvement. For many Victorian Americans of the comfortable classes, houses became statements of cultural aspiration. Elaborately ornamented architectural styles were popular, and women took charge of arranging the furniture and the overflowing decoration of the front parlor, turning it into a treasure house whose furnishings and curios would reflect the family's social standing and refinement. Souvenir spoons and other knickknacks collected during family travels were displayed to demonstrate the household's cosmopolitanism. Excluded from the world of business and commerce, many middle-and upper-class women devoted considerable time and energy to decorating their home, seeking to make it, as one advice book suggested, "a place of repose, a refuge from the excitement and distractions of outside... provided with every attainable means of rest and recreation."

As if in response to the cult of domesticity, by the turn of the century, the middle-class home had been transformed. "The flow of industry has passed and left idle the loom in the attic, the soap kettle in the shed," one magazine commented in 1908. The urban middle class could now buy a wide array of food products and clothing—baked goods, canned goods, suits, shirts, shoes, and dresses. Technology improvements changed the rest of domestic work. Middle-class homes had indoor running water and furnaces, run on oil, coal, or gas, that produced hot water. Stoves were fueled by gas, and delivery services provided ice for refrigerators. Electric power was available for lamps, sewing machines, irons, and even vacuum cleaners. Indeed, no domestic task was unaffected. One innovation after another changed the middle-class homemaker's responsibilities; each removed a different aspect of physical labor and household drudgery. Of course, not all homes benefited from this new household technology. Technological advances always affected the homes of the wealthy first, and then filtered downward into the urban middle class. But women who lived on farms and in urban slums were not affected by household improvements. In this sense, the household technology drew a sharp dividing line among women according to class and region.

Still, as America became increasingly industrialized and urbanized, the home had become a center of consumption. Since household appliances replaced menial labor, each household needed a trained executive to manage it. Seemingly if not actually, it was the homemaker's job to make the home "a more interesting place... and the possibilities of doing this today are almost endless." However, if the middle-class homemaker had less menial work than her grandmother, her mental work had increased. Some tasks required special insights into science, such as the job of preventing family members from picking up germs in public places and spreading contagious diseases around the home, or of avoiding items made in contaminated sweatshops. In short, according to the cult of domesticity, the homemaker must now be an educated one, knowing how to buy appliances to foster efficiency, and capable of mastering techniques of scientific management. More importantly, she also had to adopt a self-critical posture, constantly asking herself such questions as "Can I do better than I am doing?" "Is there any device which I might use?" "Is my house right as to its sanitary arrangements?" "Is my food the best possible?" "Have I chosen the right colors and best materials for clothing?"

The elevation of the homemaker to professional status had allure in many quarters. It appealed to many woman magazines' readers for whose patronage advertisers now competed. It appealed to the colleges, which established departments of domestic science and degree programs in home economics. It won applause in suffragist circles, ready to endorse any enhancement of women's status. However, not all middle-class women

Chapter Fourteen
American Women

pursued the domestic ideal. For some, the cult of domesticity was no more than continuity of the so-called true womanhood of the mid-19th century. For others, women should never limit their activities to the home only. For still others, the meaning of life for women should be found far beyond the sphere of domestic life. It was from this group of feminists that American women would blaze out a new path for themselves, pursuing an entirely new lifestyle, following a completely uncharted career, and taking on a totally new image.

The new image women projected came in many forms and shapes. Some women advocated that women should participate in politics so as to protect family and improve public morality. Some women expanded women's organization activities to include welfare work, prison reform, labor arbitration, and public health, becoming what many people called "social housekeepers." Many young college girls took full advantage of their higher education to learn traditionally "masculine" strategies for gaining power, such as college organizations, athletics, and dramatics. More significantly, Victorian constraints on women were further loosened at the beginning of the 20th century, when many young American women followed the vogue of the day—bicycling as a new way of female exercise. Most important of all, during the Jazz Age of the 1910s—1920s, American women began to seek freedom in virtually every possible way. They threw noisy parties, consumed bootleg liquor, flocked to jazz clubs, danced the jitterbug and the Charleston, and discussed sex freely and in some cases indulged in premarital sexual experimentation without much hesitation. In short, female sexuality was acknowledged more openly, with dating, necking, petting, kissing, and partying becoming the common topics among young women. Together with the feminist "social housekeepers" at the turn of the century, they fashioned out a new image of women in the early 20th century, laying the groundwork for the emergence of sexual revolution of the 1960s.

14.5 Housewifery and Domesticity

While new women appeared as driving force for social, economic and political changes, old traditions die hard, particularly those regarding women's functions as wife and mother. During WWI and WWII, American women participated in large numbers in the war efforts, making considerable contributions to the victory of these two great wars. However, even though their contributions were reasonably recognized, traditional values about women's role still prevailed in much of the country, particularly among the ruling elites and the mass media under their control. *McCall's* magazine, for example, coined the term *togetherness* in 1954 to celebrate the "ideal" couple: the man and woman who married young had a large family, and centered their lives on home and children. The message could not be clearer: despite or because of political, economic, and social competence displayed by women during the two wars and their strong determination to assume an image of new women, the conventional wisdom remained very much unchanged: the women's place is the home and their happiness can be found only in their role as wives and mothers.

In fact, the campaign to recast women's role back to housewifery began as early as 1950, when a female journalist wrote an article in *The Atlantic* magazine. She claimed: "No job is more exciting, more necessary, or more rewarding than that of housewife and mother." In the era of consensus and conservatism, countless others echoed that sentiment in various ways. Popular culture glorified marriage and parenthood and depicted a woman's devotion to life in the home with her children as the most cherished goal. Television almost always pictured mother at home—usually in the kitchen. Hollywood films perpetuated the stereotype of career women as neurotics and of loving mothers and wife-companions as happy. As the "girl next door" star Debbie Reynolds explained in the film *The Tender Trap* (1955): "A woman isn't a woman until she has been married and had children." Virtually without exception, American culture emphasized that women found their truest fulfillment, and made their greatest contributions to national life, as wives and mothers.

Even the educational system promoted the same notion. Whereas girls learned typing, etiquette, and cooking, boys were channeled into carpentry, auto mechanics, and courses leading to careers. Extracurricular activities reinforced the belief in males as leaders and females as assistants. Guidance counselors cautioned young women not to "miss the boat of marriage" by pursuing a higher degree. "Men are not interested in college degrees, but in the warmth and humanness of the girls they marry," stressed one textbook on family living, "because men still want wives who will bolster their egos rather than detract from them." Overall, women constituted a smaller percentage of college students in the 1950s than in the 1920s or 1930s, and received fewer advanced degrees than women in those decades. Indeed, almost two-thirds of the college women in the 1950s failed to complete a degree, and except in the most prestigious colleges, most of these who did graduate concentrated in such fields as home economics and primary education. Likewise, popular psychology insisted that a contented woman accepted her natural role as wife, mother, and homemaker. Only "neurotic" woman or "imitation men" avoided marriage and motherhood, and feminists suffered from penis envy or some other psychological sexual disorder. It is no wonder that the Baby Boom became the label of the age.

Yet even as the culture celebrated domesticity, profound changes were under way. Despite the layoffs of women immediately after WWII, women quickly returned to the labor force. By 1952, 2 million more women worked outside the home than had been employed during the war, and by 1960 nearly 40 percent of American women would hold full-or part-time jobs. The proportion of working wives, moreover, rose from 15 percent in 1940 to 30 percent in 1960. Reversing earlier patterns, some 40 percent of all working women in 1960 had school-age children. Most worked to add to family income, not to challenge stereotypes. To help pay for family expenditures of every kind, they took low-paying, low-prestige jobs where women remained "girls" whatever their age. Although the rise in female employment fostered conditions that would lead to a feminist resurgence in the late 1960s, the great majority of women responded to prosperity and atomic jitters by concentrating on private satisfactions and trying to make the home a haven in an uncertain world.

14.6 *A New Wave of Feminism*

Although the feminist movement as a whole hit a low point in the 1950s, the undercurrents of women's dissatisfaction with housewifery and domesticity were bubbling. With the rising tempo of activism sparked by the civil-rights movement, a new spirit of self-awareness and discontent began to stir among middle-class women. The result was a revived women's view of themselves and their role in American life.

Several events coalesced the stirrings of discontent into a movement. Firstly, John F. Kennedy established the Presidential Commission on the Status of Women. The panel's 1963 report on sexual discrimination in employment documented occupational inequalities suffered by women. Women received less pay than men for comparable or even identical work and had far less chance of moving into professional or managerial careers. Although women composed 51 percent of the population, only 7 percent of the nation's doctor's and less than 4 percent of its lawyers were female. The women who served on the presidential commission successfully urged that the Civil Rights Act of 1964 prohibit sexual as well as racial discrimination on employment. Secondly, when these women found that the Equal Employment Opportunity Commission had failed to handle discrimination complaints by women, they formed the National Organization for Women (NOW) in 1966. Defined itself as a civil-rights group for women, NOW lobbied for equal opportunity, filed lawsuits against gender discrimination, and mobilized public opinion "to bring American women into full participation in the mainstream of American society *Now.*" Thirdly, the publication of Betty Friedan's *The Feminine Mystique* captured the attention of many women activists. Calling it "the problem that has no name," Friedan condemned the narrow postwar view that women should seek fulfillment solely as wives and mothers and "desire no greater destiny than to glory in their own femininity." *The Feminine Mystique* revealed to disillusioned women that they were not alone in their unhappiness. Friedan's demand for "something more than my husband, my children, and my home" rang true to many educated middle-class women who found the creativity of homemaking and the joys of motherhood exaggerated. Finally, the involvement of younger women in the civil-rights and anti-Vietnam movements helped them gain confidence in their own potential. From these engagements, they formed an ideology to describe oppression and justify revolt; from these participations, they acquired valuable experience in the strategy and tactics of organized protest.

Throughout the second wave of feminism, NOW remained the largest and most enduring organization in America's contemporary women's movement, though it was often challenged by both "conservative" and "radical" feminists. During its first decade, NOW changed direction a number of times, but it never veered from its basic reformist course, always trying to seek "rights" for women within "establishment" institutions. At its second national convention in 1967, NOW's Bill of Rights incorporated a resolution supporting "the right of women to control their own reproductive lives." This was the first time a woman's

Chapter Fourteen
American Women

group had supported abortion as a feminist issue. Following the lead of NOW, many other women's organizations also joined the fight against sex discrimination. Together, they lobbied, litigated, and propagandized for equality in education, employment, and political organizations. Their goals included government-supported child care centers, paid maternity leaves for working women, and tax reforms that recognized the value of homemaking.

The women's rights approach to feminism, which relied on steady organizational work and traditional reform tactics, was only one part of the contemporary woman's movement. A second center of the emerging feminism was far more controversial, for its focus was on the underpinnings of sex discrimination, claiming that unequal laws and customs were the effect, not the cause, of woman's oppression. Underlying sex discrimination was sexism, that is, the male assumption that woman's different biology made her inherently inferior. Guided by this understanding, this group of radical feminists employed a variety of publicity-generating techniques and confrontation tactics to fight sexism. In 1968, for example, radical feminists crowned a live sheep Miss American to dramatize that such contests degraded women, and set up "freedom trash cans" in which women could discard high-heeled shoes, bras, curlers, and other items that they considered demeaning. They invaded all-male bars and social clubs and sat in at lawyer's associations and medical societies to dramatize discrimination against women in professional careers. At some points, these radical feminists also challenged the moderate goals of women's-rights groups such as NOW, arguing that formal rights for women were not enough. Instead, they called for a transformed society in which neither women nor men would be assigned or restricted to roles on the basis of sex.

However, despite the gulf between radicals and reformers, quarrelling factions set aside their differences in August, 1970 to join in the largest women's rights demonstration ever. Commemorating the 50th anniversary of women suffrage, the Women's Strike for Equality brought tens of thousands of women nationwide to parade for the right to equal employment and safe, legal abortions. In sharp contrast to the 1950s, when the ideology of domesticity and "togetherness" had sought to force all women into a single mold, the changed consciousness born of the second feminist wave opened up for millions of young women as well as many older women a larger world of choices and opportunities.

14.7 Gains and Uncertainties

One legacy of the 1960s was a revitalized women's activism and basic changes in the status of women in American life. With the feminist movement's growth came political clout. The National Women's Political Caucus, for example, promoted a feminist agenda in Washington and state capitals. By 1972, many states had liberated their abortion laws and outlawed gender discrimination in hiring. That same year, U.S. Congress passed an Equal Rights Amendment (ERA) to the Constitution ("Equality of rights under the law shall not be denied or abridged by the United States or any State on the basis of sex."). In *Roe v. Wade* (1973), the U.S. Supreme Court proclaimed women's constitutional right to abortion.

The women's movement remained strong in the later 1970s and the 1980s, and movement activists also remained overwhelmingly middle-class and white. However, as the movement gained visibility, its opposition hardened. In 1972, President Nixon vetoed a bill that would have set up a national network of day-care centers. More seriously, after the initial spurt of support for the ERA, the ratification process bogged down. Most important of all, in the wake of *Roe v. Wade*, a well-organized "Right to Life" movement pressed for a constitutional amendment outlawing abortions. This effort, led by Roman Catholic and conservative Protestant groups, generated intense controversy, with "pro-life" advocates pitting themselves against "pro-choice" supporters in a "tug of war."

Meanwhile, the proportion of women working outside the home leaped from 35 percent to about 58 percent in 1990. While the women's movement contributed to the rise of women in the work force, the soaring cost of living in these years also helped push the trend upward. Many families found they could not get ahead, or even maintain their standard living, on a single income. Although many women workers remained at the low end of the pay scale, this pattern was changing as well. From 1977 to 1987, the proportion of corporate-management position held by women rose from 24 percent to 37 percent, though top management still remained an overwhelmingly male preserve. The ratio of female lawyers and physicians edged upward after 1960, reaching about 18 percent by 1986. Steeply rising female enrollments in medical schools, law schools, and Ph.D. programs guaranteed a continuation of this trend.

Chapter Fourteen
American Women

Some conservatives worried that women's changing roles would lead to a weakening of the family. Working women themselves acknowledged the stresses of their situation in the 1980s. Torn between career and family pressures, some yielded to the "superwoman" syndrome, pushing themselves to be successful professionals, attentive mothers, super cooks, efficient housekeepers, and seductive wives all at the same time. Additionally, older feminists worried that younger women, benefiting from opportunities won in earlier struggles without having participated in those struggles, were losing sight of the movement's original goals. Could women function as equals in the male world, they asked, without absorbing the competitiveness, the preoccupations, and the careerism characteristic of that world? Feminists recognized, too, that a long road lay ahead in overcoming ingrained patterns of gender discrimination. As late as the 1990s, working women's average earnings still lagged well behind those of men. Although the pattern was shifting, the workplace remained largely gender segregated. Such fields as nursing and secretarial work overwhelmingly employed women, whereas men dominated the higher-prestige professions like law and medicine, particularly at the upper ranks. Still, as the 1980s ended, feminist leaders and women generally could take legitimate satisfaction in many gains achieved.

By the late 1990s, American women had smashed through many sexist barriers to higher education and in the workplace. In many fields that were long virtually closed to women, such as medicine, law, engineering and business management, large numbers of women energetically pursued productive careers. There also were huge increases in the number of women holding public office in the 1980s and 1990s. In 1996, the number of working mothers with children exceeded the number of mothers with children not working outside of the home. In 1998, one-fourth of all doctors and lawyers were women. By 1999, women constituted almost half of the total work force. But as increasing numbers of women moved into formerly male-dominated occupations and professions, disparities continued in the pay women received for performing comparable work. Women who worked full time in 1999 earned about 73 cents for every dollar a man earned. Many working-class women still confronted a segregated job market in the late 1990s, with about 60 percept women holding "pink collar" jobs. Many women who had reached managerial positions in business in the late 1990s felt that they were paying too high a personal price for professional successes.

Others complained they could not fulfill family obligations at home and perform their jobs at the highest levels. What is particularly worth mentioning is that long-term structural changes in the economy adversely affected working women. The rise of service industries and the implementation of new technologies created millions of new jobs for women but also created new limits and liabilities. In many ways, automated offices were the sweatshops of the 1990s. More significantly, cultural traditions still remain quite strong. In spite of all changes in social, political, and economic life, traditional values and stereotypes still exhibit strong staying power. Advertisers no longer celebrate domesticity as a woman's only appropriate realm but still insist that the busy woman has to keep her weight down and be attractive. Women spend far more of their incomes on clothes, beauty aids, and diets than men. In other words, while explicit gender discrimination may have significantly diminished, implicit or subtle one still exists, and sometimes quite persisfentfy and pervasively.

SUMMARY

(1) In the founding of the United States, women played a role as important as that of men. Although men did the outside work and women worked inside, their respective contributions to the survival and prosperity of colonial economy were equally important, when economic activity was primarily centered on farm and family. In spite of all this, women were denied equality in virtually everything.

(2) During the American Revolution, women began to think about their freedom as America was trying to win freedom from Great Britain. However, their demand for political equality was rebuffed. After the founding of the new Republic, women were cast in the role of Republican motherhood, assuming the responsibility of fostering Republican virtues in the younger generation to make them good citizens.

(3) In the first three decades of the 19th century, American women were provided with unprecedented opportunities for public activity without challenging the prevailing belief that their proper sphere was the home. Thanks to their involvement in the social reform movements of the 1830s, women's political consciousness rose significantly, which eventually led to their organized efforts to fight for their suffrage.

(4) Despite women's efforts to play a bigger role in social and political life, traditional values still prevailed throughout 19th-century America. Along

with the Victorian values, the male-oriented American society tried hard to compel women to conform to the cult of domesticity. Nevertheless, encouraged by opportunities brought about by industrialization and urbanization, women started assuming a new image.

(5) With the emergence of "New Women" pushing for social, economic, and political changes, male chauvinism, together with its gender prejudices, reasserted itself, making fresh efforts to put women back to where they supposedly "belong"—the home. Around the turn of the 20th century, housewifery and domesticity became the two catchwords in the mainstream culture.

(6) The feminist movement hit a low point after the passage of the 19th Amendment, but the undercurrents of women's discontent with housewifery and domesticity never stopped bubbling. Spurred by the social reform movements of the 1960s, women organized themselves and launched the second wave of feminism, demanding equal rights in every aspect of American life, economic, political, legal, social and cultural.

(7) The new wave of feminism brought about many gains for American women: growing political clout, abortion right, greater participation in the workforce, no-fault divorce law, child custody right, equal access to higher education (professional schools in particular), and fairer division of housework. Still, in spite of all this, women fall behind men in many areas: income, promotion, career, profession, and power.

ESSAY QUESTIONS

(1) For a long time, when describing the early settlement of the New World, historians tended to regard men as the key players in the whole process, ignoring altogether the role played by women. This is especially so when they used the term "Founding Fathers" to refer to those who led the American Revolution. What are the significance and implications of the term "Founding Mothers" in all this?

(2) While the phrase "Republican Motherhood" seemingly elevated women to a high status in society by putting them on a pedestal (placing upon their shoulder the responsibility of maintaining Republican virtues through the education of children), it could be a double-edged sword in that, by assuming the role of Republic Motherhood, women could thereby be confined to the home. Discuss the paradox of this notion.

(3) The first feminist movement in America had many origins, the most direct of which was women's involvement in the reform movements

of the time, particularly their engagement in the abolitionist movement. Describe the relationship between the reform movements and the emergence of the feminist movement, noting the growing consciousness and organizational skills of women through all these involvements.

(4) Throughout American history, different terms have been used to describe, or rather prescribe, the role of women in society, such as Republican Motherhood, the Cult of True Womanhood, the Cult of Domesticity, Housewifery, and Feminine Mystique, all of which carry the same message: women can find their happiness best by playing the role of mother and wife at home. Try to demystify all these images.

(5) In comparison with the first feminist wave, the second one is larger in scale and broader in scope, resulting in a wider array of achievements, both in terms of new legislation about women's rights and in terms of public perception of women's role in American society. Examine the important issues fought by the second feminist wave and discuss their long-term impacts on American people, men and women alike.

American Society and Culture
美 国 社 会 文 化

Chapter Fifteen
Who Is an American?

American Society and Culture
美 国 社 会 文 化

LEARNING OBJECTIVES

- Know the basic arguments in the Puritan Thesis
- Be Informed of the essence of the Frontier Thesis
- Understand the central thrust of the Melting-Pot Thesis
- Be aware of the metaphorical meanings of the Salad Bowl Thesis
- Appreciate the political, social, and cultural implications of multiculturalism

Ever since Michel-Guillaume Jean De Crévecoeur, an emigrant French aristocrat turned farmer, posed the famous question in his *Letters from an American Farmer* in 1782: "What, then, is the American, this new man?" Americans have been wrestling with their national identity. According to Jean De Crévecoeur, this new man "is either an European, or the descendant of an European, hence that strange mixture of blood, which you will find in no other country. I could point out to you a family whose grandfather was an Englishman, whose wife was Dutch, whose son married a French woman, and whose present four sons have now four wives of different nations. He is an American." Jean De Crévecoeur may well have been right, because in 18th-century America, the vast majority of Americans were of European origin. But, as a nation of immigrants, Americans almost have a perpetual impulse or urge to define what is American. And one of the most dynamic forces of the United States is that their shared ideas and identity are always in flux and perpetual redefinition. Each generation offers a new answer to Crévecoeur's question: "What is the American, this new man?" and each generation redefines, reclaims, and reassesses American identity to make the definition fresh and ever new. So far, many theories or theses have been offered to answer the famous question: Who is an American?

Chapter Fifteen
Who Is an American?

15.1 The Puritan Thesis

Many nations have a creation myth that suggests that the beginnings of that nation were accomplished with the active assistance of the Almighty. That the Pilgrims—and their later descendants, the Puritans—came here seeking to escape religious persecution and found the "New Jerusalem" probably helped make this particular group of European immigrants a more popular and likely choice for the role of America's "forefathers" than did other groups that were settling in other parts of America at about the same time. The mundane fact that many Europeans came to America seeking free estate or to avoid military service or to escape imprisonment for crimes or debts is not the stuff of which national myths are made.

Implicit in the Puritan thesis is the belief that Puritan values, ideas, and customs are usually credited with having given Americans the Protestant work ethic, which laid the moral basis for America's economic growth. It is often argued that the city of Boston and Harvard College were the intellectual and cultural leaders of the nation, for Harvard was both America's first university and has remained the most eminent. Such New Englanders as William Bradford created the nation's first literature, and later others — Henry Hawthorne, Ralph Waldo Emerson, Henry David Thoreau, Henry Wadsworth Longfellow— lifted that literature to a place from which it could seriously rival the work of Europe's finest writers. New England's "Boston Brahmins" later proclaimed themselves the nation's cultivated, educated, and wealthy elite, and to some extent the claim was justified. From John Adams to Calvin Coolidge, the Calvinist belief in hard work, self-reliance, and stern morality heavily influenced the familiar image of the "hardworking, hard-driving American" in hot pursuit of what Henry James once called the "bitch Goddess of America, Success."

At the core of Puritanism was the notion of individual responsibility for the well-being of society. As "the Elect of God," the Puritans bore a heavy sense of duty to improve both themselves and their community. This sense of duty can been seen in the dilemma of John Winthrop, who had serious misgivings about leaving England for the new World in 1963, even though Puritans were being persecuted in England. Winthrop finally convinced himself that in going to the New World he would ultimately be

303

helping reform English society rather than abandoning it. When he landed in Massachusetts Bay, he is reputed to have said, "Men shall say of succeeding plantations: 'The Lord make it like that of New England.'" That is, Puritan New England would be an example for the rest of the world to follow.

In a sense, Winthrop's prophecy may be said to have been fulfilled when Winston Churchill, leading embattled Great Britain against Nazi Europe in the darkest days of World War II, called on "the new world to come to the rescue of the old." Moreover, Winthrop's theme is reiterated throughout U.S. history: in George Washington's Farewell Address, in Abraham Lincoln's Gettysburg Address, in John F. Kennedy's inaugural address, and in Barack Obama's presidential victory speech. The Puritan notion that it was America's duty to serve as an ideal for all humankind was at once noble and audacious. It gave America a sense of historic mission, but it would inevitably cause disappointment, for no matter how much of an example Americans wanted to be for the rest of the world, America could never be perfect either in their own eyes or in the world's, and many countries simply do not want an American way of life to be imposed upon them. Moreover, along with the Puritan commitment to a better world came a certain smug self-righteousness implicit in those who, on the assumption that they were somehow better, presumed to improve other people's morals and behavior. Thus, the contemporary view of the Puritan was of a prudish person bent on controlling other people's morality.

Even today, Puritan zeal is not uncommon in America. For instance, many Americans are very desirous of, and even demand for, property tax reduction. To them, it is not merely a matter of tax reduction, but rather a matter of Puritan beliefs and principles. Out of this concern and conviction, they have time and again protested any move on the part of the federal government to raise property tax, ready to wage a latter-day crusade to purge government of waste and wickedness. In this way, they argue, they would be able to free American taxpayers from what they regard as the gaudy excesses of bureaucrats, high-living school teachers, and "welfare chiselers," that is, those who did not understand or conform to Puritan principles of hard work, self-denial and thrifty life. While such ideas and arguments are conservative, it should be acknowledged that the Puritan tradition accounts for much that is positive in American history. The early agitation against slavery, for example, was centered in New England, the founding base of the Puritans, as was the movement for free public education. Today, a good many environmentalists welcome the energy crisis as an opportunity for Americans to learn that "small is beautiful," "less is more," "saving is gaining"—in short, to turn back from the excesses of affluence and relearn the older, and Puritan, values of simplicity, thrift, hard work, self-denial, and economy.

15.2 The Frontier Thesis

If the Puritan Thesis tries to explain the national character of the United States from the perspective of Puritans' early settlement of the New England, the Frontier Thesis attempts to probe into the westward movement to find out the shaping forces of American personality. As the United States passed from the Revolutionary War period to continental expansion and conquest, it was clear that the ideas and doctrines of New England no longer described the actual experience of the American people, particularly that portion of people who engaged in building railroads across a continent, who took California and Texas from Mexico by force, and who steadily pushed their way west, removing all the obstacles in their way and leaving behind them a tail of murdered native Americans and slaughtered buffalo.

As they created new farms, towns, and territories, the people of the West were also creating new heroes, new values, a new literature, and a new culture. Andrew Jackson and Abraham Lincoln redefined American democracy in terms of homespun cloth rather than broadcloth. Davy Crockett became the first great popular hero of the new "coonskin democracy," to be followed later by a gaudy and colorful procession of western guides, gunslingers, and bad men such as Buffalo Bill, Wild Bill Hickok, and Jesse James. Mark Twain, hailed by the eminent New England critic William D. Howells as the "Lincoln of Our Literature," became the definitive voice of this new America.

Twain's most memorable literary creation, Huck Finn and Tom Sawyer, came somehow to embody certain American characteristics: youth, simplicity, native shrewdness, scorn for theory and mere bookishness, self-reliance, and above all, the perennial quest for a new and better life, symbolized by Huck's search for happiness on the breast of the "Brown River God" (the Mississippi River) or their desire to "light out for the territory." The vast stretch of the western region provided unprecedented opportunities for such resourceful and dynamic youths as Huck Finn and Tom Sawyer to bring out their desires and potentials to the fullest extent.

As a hypothesis, the Frontier Thesis found its most coherent and articulate spokesman in historian Frederick Jackson Turner, who argued that "the existence of an area of free land, its continuous recession and the advance of American settlement westward, explain American development.... [It is] to the frontier that the American intellect owes its striking characteristics. That coarseness and strength combined with acuteness and inquisitiveness; that practical, inventive turn of mind, quick to find expedients; that masterful grasp of material things, lacking in the artistic but powerful to effect great ends; that restless, nervous energy; that dominant individualism, working for good and for evil, and withal that buoyancy and exuberance which comes with freedom—these are traits of the frontier." In Turner's view, as can be easily inferred from his arguments, most of Americans' positive traits such as self-reliance and practical-mindedness were forged in the westward movement experience.

However, if the frontier left Americans with a heritage of positive characteristics like individualism, equality, and respect for the "common person" (and scorn for "the Elect of God"), it also helped accentuate certain other less attractive traits. Waste, violence, contempt for authority, and a monumental disrespect for the natural beauty and harmony of the physical environment, as well as the artistic deficiency noted by Turner, were also characteristic of frontier civilization. Van W. Brooks called the West "a gigantic, overturned garbage can," full of waste. Vernon L. Parrington noted that between 1871 and 1875, a million head of buffalo a year were slain, "their skins ripped off and the carcasses left for coyotes and buzzards..." "Freedom," Parrington observed, "had become the inalienable right to preempt, to exploit, to squander." The freedom of the frontier, he noted, "was the freedom of buccaneers. The new America was an anarchistic world of strong, capable men, selfish, unenlightened, and amoral."

Actually, many of the traits that Turner had associated with the westward expansion of the United States had been noted by a French nobleman a century earlier when the eastern seaboard was still being settled. Jean De Crévecoeur, like Turner, noted that the availability of cheap or free land inevitably meant a more fluid class structure and a more

Chapter Fifteen
Who Is an American?

open society: "This [American] devoid of society learns more than ever to center every idea within his own welfare." Impressed by American prosperity and freedom, Crévecoeur nevertheless noted that Americans were not truly civilized in the sense that they rarely understood the limits of individualism, as opposed to the needs of society. Although there was no caste system as in Europe, neither was there much concern for the poor and the unfortunate, except the concern and help from charity organizations. In short, it was individual achievements and the wealth that came with it, not family name or social position, that brought power and prestige in this New World.

Implicit in the frontier thesis were many of the ideas and values most often cited by those who wish either to attack or to defend America. When former Vice-President Spiro Agnew attacked his critics in the press and on television, he labeled them part of the "effete eastern establishment," suggesting that it was the old story of the sissified East versus the manly West. Similarly, former Alabama Governor and frequent presidential candidate George Wallace, was also fond of assaulting the "pseudo-intellectual snobs," referring to the liberals in the East. Additionally, the Frontier Thesis may also be heard dimly echoed in the arguments of certain right-wing American political groups such as the John Birch Society, which tends to equate any international reverses that Americans suffer with the dominance of certain eastern-liberal-establishment groups such as the Council on Foreign relations and the Tri-Lateral Commission, both influenced by eastern banking and business interests. Crévecoeur found the frontiersmen lacking respect for intelligence, learning, and wisdom two hundred years ago: "Who," asked him, "can be wiser than himself in this half-cultivated country?" The debate continues over whether the frontier brought Americans individualism, self-reliance, and democracy or crime, waster and intolerance. In all likelihood, the answer seems to be that it did both.

15.3 The Melting-Pot Thesis

There is no denying that both the Puritans and the Frontier had played an instrumental role in shaping the character of Americans as a people. But as the Puritans became increasingly secularized and turned into Yankees, and as the Frontier gradually vanished and eventually transformed into a settled region, what would be the forces there to shape and forge American character? Does it mean that once they were gone, American character would remain as it was? Or does it mean that American character needs to be redefined by new forces or new theories?

In the late 19th century, Andrew Carnegie, having built one of the world's mightiest industrial and corporate empires and having acquired an immense personal fortune, turned to writing books. He set forth in plain English the philosophy that had made him rich and America great. "Fortunately for the American people, they are essentially British," he began one essay. By watching and emulating their Anglo-Saxon superiors, argued Carnegie, the flood of Irish people, Italians, and Eastern Europeans pouring into the country could learn to become true Americans and thus share in the nation's material abundance and spiritual grandeur. In this way, Carnegie affirmed, the immigrant's children would be as good as—even indistinguishable from—the real Americans.

This was an early and somewhat crude expression of the underlying idea that would eventually find expression in the melting-pot thesis. According to this thesis, Anglo-Saxons seemed to embody certain traits and values that contained the genius of Americanism. People of various other races, nationalities, and cultures were welcome to come because their labor was needed for America's burgeoning farms and industries, and through education and assimilation they should be transformed from whatever they had been into true Americans. The symbol of this idea was the Statue of Liberty, with its premise that the European migrants were "poor" and "wretched," whereas New York City was the "Golden Door." For millions of Europeans, this undoubtedly turned out to be the reality. For them, America became a "land of opportunity," offering education, personal and religious freedom, and a chance to work hard and thus earn a share of the world's greatest success story. For others, however, America meant sweatshops, bigotry, and new, if more subtle, forms of exploitation.

The melting-pot thesis underscored a certain definition of American character. The "typical" Americans were middle class and middle-minded, hardworking and democratic, practical and well-intentioned, and optimistic about their own and their country's future. They were clear eyed and clear headed. They were the stuff that presidents and popular heroes were made of, in fiction as well as in fact. They were Huck Finn, Horatio Alger, and of course, Jack Armstrong, the "All-American Boy." Almost invariably, they

Chapter Fifteen
Who Is an American?

were white, male, and of Christian, Anglo-Saxon heritage. In other words, what the melting-pot thesis is suggesting is that of all the many different nationalities and ethnic groups which have gone into the making of America, those who have quickly assimilated are the ones who have been "melted" into the "pot," and those who, for whatever reasons, have not been assimilated are either unmeltable or beyond the melting-pot. For those who have been melted, it means that they have lost or intentionally given up many of those specific markers which would make them much different from their neighbors. In essence, then, this process of assimilation is, in fact, the process of Americanization, hence the term "melting-pot."

As a term describing the process of assimilation, the "melting-pot" was coined by an English Jewish playwright Israel Zangwill in his play entitled *The Melting-Pot*. It is a naive and sentimental play about American immigrants, written at the height of the large surge of immigrants at the turn of the 20th century. Played before numerous audiences throughout the country, *The Melting-Pot* captured the imagination of American theatergoers. So popular was the play that it later ran through many editions in book form. More significantly, its title has been immortalized as the classic description of the immigrant's reception and future in America. "There she lies, the great Melting Pot," exclaimed the hero, David Quexano. "East and West, North and South, the palm and the pine, the pole and the equator, the crescent and the cross—how the great Alchemist melts and fuses them with his purging flames!"

Central to the argument of the melting-pot thesis is that although "never before—and in no other country—have as many varied ethnic groups congregated and amalgamated as they have in the United States," the multi-ethnicity of America has turned into a large pot, where each and every single "ingredient" is melted and becomes one and the same. Together, they constitute a whole nation, representing the best mix in the world. In other words, anyone who comes to the New World is automatically thrown into this "pot," where a process of assimilation into the American belief systems takes place, whereby all the cultural customs and values that one brings to the New World are blended together (or melted) to form a new culture. The outcome of this long and massive process is twofold. On the one hand, there has come into existence the "melted" version of a culture, known to be typically American. On the other hand, in the process of assimilation or Americanization, the identities of each original culture are extinguished to formulate an entirely new culture.

As an analogy, the melting pot is quite suggestive, implying that a way has been found for heterogeneous societies to become more homogeneous. But just as the flavor of the stew cooked in the pot derives from the ingredients that comprise it, so does the character of a society stem from the components of social groups that make up it. The bigger portion an ingredient represents in the stew, the greater flavor it holds in the pot. By the same token, the more influential a cultural group is in the multi-ethnic society, the greater power it enjoys in political, economic and social life. In other words, since the White Anglo-Saxon Protestants have been for centuries the most influential group in the United States, they are obviously the biggest "ingredient" in the melting pot, more likely to "melt" other "ingredients" than the other way round. Even if they are melted together into something new, the final "melted" outcome of the mixed-up ingredients will always contain more of the dominant one than those of marginal ones. After all, the analogy of the melting pot is no different from Americanization, which, to all intends and purposes, is designed to assimilate all less privileged racial and ethnic groups into the mainstream culture and society. It is exactly for this reason that a significant number of racial and ethnic groups in America do not like the melting pot thesis as way of characterizing American personality, for they either do not want to be melted, or simply cannot melt into the mainstream society.

15.4 The Salad Bowl Thesis

While the melting-pot thesis is attractive as an analogy, one is nevertheless tempted to ask: is this really what happens to the immigrant in America? Do the various national traits "melt and fuse" to form a new American culture when it is clear that many of them remain untouched and persistent? Some traits, to be sure, do disappear after a while. After one or two generations most of the sharply deviant contours are worn down to the common pattern. For instance, the brassy earrings, the large mustachios, the garlicked breath, and the atrociously accented English are usually sooner or later replaced by appropriated American substitutes. Equally, while it is true that when the people of one culture move into

Chapter Fifteen
Who Is an American?

another, they often have to shed layer after layer of old habits and ways of thought, much as one peels an onion, it does not necessarily mean, however, that they want to shed all they have, just as an onion cannot be peeled indefinitely without losing its own identity. In other words, true as they may be (like disappearing of some traits), they do not necessarily make a melting pot, for the dropping of old habits for new is not fusion or melting (just as the peeling of an onion is not fusing or melting either). It is in part on this ground that the melting-pot theory is questioned and challenged by the salad bowl thesis as a way of interpreting America' national character.

Contrary to the conception implied in the metaphor of the melting pot, the salad bowl theory argues that American civilization has not been homogeneous and uniform. Rather, it was and has always been diverse and pluralistic. The evidence is abundant and irrefutable: in the varieties of languages, of foods and restaurants, of religions and festivals, of newspapers and books, of costumes and dances, of literatures and theaters. Though some immigrant habits and mores are undoubtedly lost in America, others are not. They remain, not fusing into a new cultural synthesis, but persisting as living remnants of many cultures, enlivening the broader stream of American life. As a result of these resistant, undigested bits of foreign ways within the United States, American culture has been probably more colorful, more cosmopolitan, and more diverse than any other people in the world.

Take religion as an example. Historically speaking, few of the immigrants divested themselves of their religion or church, and because they did not, they enriched the unique religious heritage of America. The churches which the immigrants brought with them have increased the diversity of sects in America. In the 1950s, for example, 60 distinct religious bodies were the direct result of immigrants. The heterogeneity of nationalities carved new sects out of old denominations, as well as creating entirely new churches. The Lutherans, for example, split into a dozen national churches; the Mennonites have thirteen varieties; the Eastern Orthodox Church is divided into nine national sects. "The tendency toward conformity with the new civilization is, strangely enough, responsible for much of the denominationalism of America," explains H. Richard Niebuhr. "It separates various generations of immigrants from each other so effectively that new schisms result." Recent immigrants finding "themselves ill at ease among their partly

Americanized kindred... feel compelled to organize new denominations which will be truer to the Old World customs," and thereby give rise to greater diversity.

As a metaphor, the salad bowl suggests that integration of the many different cultures of the United States residents combines like a salad, as opposed to the more prolific notion of a cultural melting pot, implying that people of diverse backgrounds retain their won values culturally, economically and politically instead of merging into one culture as the metaphor of melting pot seems to indicate. In a bowl of freshly tossed salad, all the ingredients are mixed together, yet they never lost their shape, form or identity. Together, however, they make up a unity, or an entity. They may be covered with the same dressing, but the green vegetables, tomatoes, lettuce and eggs can all be seen for what they are. In other words, separate as they are, all the ingredients of a salad contribute to the finished product—the salad. Viewed from this perspective, America is very much like a salad bowl where individual ethnic groups blend together, yet maintain their cultural uniqueness. Walking in various communities in America, one can spot many "towns" labeling varied cultural icons, such as China Town, German Town, and Italy Town. Those towns are an apparent epitome demonstrating diversified values of these ethnic groups despite the fact they are residing abroad. In short, preserving rather than destroying the ancestral heritage of the migrants is the essence of the salad bowl thesis.

Indeed, in the salad bowl model, various American cultures are juxtaposed—like salad ingredients—but do not merge together into a single homogeneous culture. Each culture keeps its own distinct qualities. This idea proposes a society of many individual "pure" cultures and the term has become more politically correct than melting pot, since the latter suggests that ethnic groups may be unable to preserve their cultures. Each ethnic group, argues the salad bowl theory, has its own special interests, language, food, customs and traditions to protect and defend. This is why there is so much diversity within America. Such a way of explanation is often referred to by sociologists as cultural pluralism. People against this model accuse the salad bowl thesis of being a communitarianist model, but people in support of this metaphor speak for, and indeed demand, multiculturalism. Whatever the case, in today's America, the popularity of the melting-pot thesis has declined. Both American scholars and the general public are more inclined to use the salad bowl as a metaphor to describe the variety of American cultures, though some people may prefer that of a "pizza," which, by the way, is the single most popular food in America. Put in another way, uniculturalism represented by the melting-pot thesis has been replaced by multiculturalism symbolized by the salad bowl theory.

15.5 Multiculturalism

As a historical fact, the U. S. has always been a pluralistic society. From the earliest settlement in North America, people from Europe came in large numbers, English, French, Irish, the Dutch, plus Blacks and Native Americans. But, roughly before the late 1960s, the issue of multiculturalism had seldom, if ever, been raised, or seriously thought about. The melting-pot thesis, while challenged from time to time, particularly by Korace Kallen in the 1920s and 1930s, was largely held as a near-to-the-truth description/characterization of American society.

A number of factors helped bring about the shift. For one thing, since the passage of The Immigration and Naturalization Act of 1965, American demography has undergone tremendous changes. Prior to the 1965 immigrant law, the majority of immigrants had come from Europe, whereas after that, the majority of them have come from Latin America and Asian, dramatically changing the face of the United States. For another, beginning in the late 1950s, social reform movements swept across the United States, spearheaded by the Civil Rights Movement and followed by a host of others, all of which challenged the mainstream culture of White America, that is, WASP. For still another, both in Canada and Europe, many theories were proposed to address the flaws of democracy in Western democratic societies, including Jurgen Habermas' notion of Constitutional Democracy, Charles Taylor's concept of the Politics of Recognition, and Jacque Derrida's theory of Deconstructionism. All of the three above-mentioned factors combined to help pave the way for the rise of multiculturalism. The Civil Rights Movement encouraged other social minority groups to fight for their equal rights, demanding for equal respect and equal voice. The Politics of Recognition appealed for equal recognition of all cultural groups, however numerically small they may be in the society. Finally, Deconstructionism does not recognize the authority of any established ideologies, believing that "the signifier (image) has no stable or necessary relation to its signified (referent)."

To understand multiculturalism, we need to make distinctions between cultural pluralism and multiculturalism. According to Gurpreet Mahajan, "Cultural pluralism is not a modern phenomenon," because "history provides many examples of different communities and cultures living side by side within the same society, co-existing peacefully, and sometimes even amicably." Multiculturalism, by contrast, is something quite recent, particularly when it is measured by the political theory it proposes and the political action it wants to be taken. The key difference between the two, according to Mahajan, lies in the fact that cultural pluralism just acknowledges peaceful co-existence of different cultures within the same social space, pointing to a plural social fabric. Multiculturalism, by contrast, goes far beyond cultural pluralism, for it entails something more than the mere presence of different communities. It is concerned with the issue of equality, emphasizing that culturally different groups not only co-exist peacefully, but also live and work together as equals in the public arena. When applied to American society, multiculturalism implies that each and every racial and ethnic group should enjoy equality in every aspect of life and be treated as such. No barrier should ever be allowed to exist for sub-cultural groups to access political, economic, social, and educational opportunities in America. In short, multiculturalism does not simply speak of equality of cultures, but also insists that fair treatment of all cultural groups as equals in a democracy is a matter of right.

Among other things, multiculturalism is demanding changes for education reform in higher education. Of all the proposals multiculturalism has been making regarding education reforms, four areas stand out most saliently: curriculum, admissions, faculty recruitment and education policy. Regarding curriculum, multicultural proponents argue that it should reflect the increasing diversity of American society by offering courses that different cultural groups can relate to. On the issue of student admissions, multiculturalists demand that different cultural groups should have equal representation in the student body. As for faculty recruitment policy, advocates of multiculturalism insist that voice should be given to the previously voiceless cultural groups by enlisting them on the faculty members of colleges and universities so that previously unheard-of groups would have the channel to express themselves. Finally, multiculturalists ask for structural change in higher education, insisting that only by changing power and structural relationships in colleges and universities can disadvantaged cultural groups eventually enjoy equality in every sense of the word.

Chapter Fifteen
Who Is an American?

Altogether, they represent the efforts of multiculturalists to reject the assimilation concept and replace the melting-pot theory with multiculturalism. Only in this way, in the opinion of multiculturalists, can America become a truly multi-ethnic and multi-cultural society, where equality will prevail regardless of race, gender, age, class, and sexual orientation. However, given the ingrained prejudices of the mainstream culture against sub-cultural groups, many of the things multiculturalism has been talking about are more of goals than of reality, more of prescriptions than of descriptions. Indeed, considering the enormous obstacles it is encountering, it will take many years before all these goals can be fully materialized.

SUMMARY

(1) The Puritan Thesis argues that the Puritans helped shape the American national character more powerfully than any other religious or ethnic group, with their self-imposed mission of "building a city upon a hill." Implicit in it is the belief that Puritan values and customs are usually credited with having given America the work ethics, which laid the moral basis for America's capitalist economic growth.

(2) As a hypothesis, the Frontier Thesis finds its most coherent and articulate expression in Frederick J. Turner, who argued that "the existence of an area of free land... and the advance of American settlement westward explain American development." In Tuner's view, most of American positive traits such as self-reliance, resourcefulness, practical mindedness were forged in the westward movement.

(3) The Melting-Pot Thesis describes the process of assimilation, in which "East and West, North and South, the palm and the pine, the pole and the equator, the crescent and the cross" are all melted by "the great Alchemist with his purging flames." Central to the thesis is the argument that the multi-ethnicity of America has turned into a large pot, where every ingredient is melted and becomes one and the same.

(4) Contrary to the conception implied in the Melting-Pot Thesis, the Salad Bowl Thesis argues that American civilization has not been homogeneous or uniform. Rather, it was and has always been diverse and pluralistic. Instead of fusing into a new cultural synthesis, immigrant habits and mores persist as living remnants of different cultures, diversifying and multiplying an otherwise monolithic cultural life.

(5) The Salad Bowl Thesis basically argues for cultural pluralism, but a step beyond that would be something called multiculturalism, the

former emphasizing cultures living side by side peacefully within the same society, and the latter stressing equal existence of different cultural groups in the public arena. Multiculturalism implies that each and every racial and ethnic group should enjoy equality in every aspect of life.

ESSAY QUESTIONS

(1) The Puritan Thesis tries to interpret American personality by locating its formative forces in the earliest settlers of the New World, the Puritans, believing that they laid the foundation not only for the development of the colonies, but also for the growth of America as a civilization. To what extent do you think such an argument goes to the heart of American culture as reflected in the characteristics of Americans?

(2) As Americans moved westward and started conquering the vast stretch of the West, the ideas and doctrines of the Puritanism may not fit well with the actual experiences of those settling in this vast uninhabited area. Hence, Turner proposed his Frontier hypothesis. How significant is the Frontier Thesis as a way of interpreting the national character of the United States of America forged in the westward movement?

(3) According to the Melting-Pot Thesis, WASP seemed to embody certain traits and values that contained the genius of Americanism. People of other races, nationalities, and cultures, once in America, would or should be transformed from whatever they had been into true Americans, through education and assimilation. Do you think WASP has that "melting" power? If all were melted, what would America be like?

(4) The Salad Bowl Thesis is the antithesis of the Melting-Pot Thesis in that it argues that America has always been pluralistic in its racial and ethnic composition and social and cultural make-up. Many cultural groups either refuse to be melted or live beyond the Melting-Pot. What is the central thrust of the Salad Bowl Thesis?

(5) By taking a step further beyond the Salad Bowl Thesis, multiculturalism argues that America should not merely be contented with the peaceful coexistence of different ethnic and cultural groups, but also encourage and indeed ensure that all cultural groups, big or small, should be treated equally in all areas, political, economic and social. What are the political and philosophical underpinnings of this concept?

Bibliography

Aguirre, Adalberto, Jr. and Turner, Jonathan H., *American Ethnicity: The Dynamics and Consequences of Discrimination*, New York: McGraw-Hill, third edition, 2001.

Althen, Gary, *American Way*, Maine: Intercultural Press, 1988.

Baodi, Zhou, ed., *The United States in Times of War and Peace* (conference proceedings), Beijing: Foreign Language Teaching and Research Press, 2005.

Baran, Stanley, *Introduction to Mass Communication: Media Literacy and Culture*, New York: McGraw Hill, 3rd edition, 2003.

Barnes, Gregory A., *The American University*, Philadelphia: ISI Press, 1984.

Bellab, Robert N., et al., *Habits of the Heart: Individualism and Commitment in American Life*, New York: Harper & Row, 1985.

Bigsby, Christopher, *Cambridge Companion to Modern American Culture*, London: Cambridge University Press, 2006.

Blake, Nelson Manfred, *A History of American Life and Thought*, New York: McGraw-Hill, Inc., second edition, 1972.

Boyer, Paul S., et al., The Enduring Vision: *A History of the American People*, Massachusetts: D.C. Health and Company, 1993.

Bromhead, Peter, *Life in Modern America*, New York: Longman Publishing, third edition, 1998.

Butts, R. Freeman and Cremin, Lawrence A., *A History of Education in American Culture*, New York: Henry Holt And Company, 1953.

Campbell, Neil and Kean, Alasdair, *American Cultural Studies: An Introduction to American Culture*, London: Routledge, 1997.

Corbert, Julia Mitchell, *Religion in America*, New Jersey: Prentice-Hall Inc., fourth edition, 2000.

Day, Phyllis J., *A New History of Social Welfare*, second edition, 1989.

Degler, Carl N., *Out of Our Past: The Forces That Shaped Modern America*, New York: Harper Colophon Books, revised edition, 1970.

Eck, Diana L., *A New Religious America: How a "Christian Country" Has Now Become the World's Most Religiously Diverse Nation*, San Francisco: HarperCollins Publishers, 2001.

Glazer, Nathan, *We Are All Multiculturalists*, Massachusetts: Harvard University Press, 3rd printing, 1998.

Greenberg, Stanley B., *The Two Americas: Our Current Political Deadlock and How to Break It*, New York: Thomas Dunne Books, 2005.

Hymowitz, Carol and Weissman, Michaele, *A History of Women in America*, New York: Bantam Books, 1978.

Inge, M. Thomas, ed., *Concise Histories of American Popular Culture*, Connecticut: Greenwood Press, 1982.

Lerner, Max, *America as a Civilization: Life and Thought in the United States Today*, New York: Simon and Schuster, 1957.

Luedtke, Luther S., ed., *Making America: The Society and Culture of the United States*, Washington, D. C.: United States Information Agency, 1987.

Mauk, David and Oakland, John, *American Civilization: An Introduction*, London: Routledge, second edition, 1997.

Mickelson, Joel, C., *American Personality and the Creative Arts*, Minnesota: Burgess Publishing Company, 1969.

Mitchell, Jeremy and Maidment, Richard, ed., *Culture: The United States in the Twentieth Century*, London: Hodder & Stoughton, 1995.

Moore, John A. Jr. and Roberts, Myron, *The Pursuit of Happiness*, New York: Macmillan Publishing Company, 1985.

Olson, David H., DeFrain, John, *Marriage and Families*, Boston: McGraw-Hill Higher Education, fourth edition, 2003.

Reynolds, Larry, and Henslin, James, *American Society: A Critical Analysis*, New York: David McKay Company, 1973.

Robertson, James Oliver, *American Myth, American Reality*, New York: Hill & Wang, 1980.

Skolnick, Arlene, *Embattled Paradise: The American Family in an Age of Uncertainty*, New York: Harper-Collins Publishers, 1991

Smith, Henry Nash, *Virgin Land: The American West as Symbol and Myth*, Massachusetts: Harvard University Press, 8th printing, 1981.

Stein, Peter J., Richman, Judith, and Hannon, Natalie, *The Family*, Massachusetts: Addison-Wesley Publishing Company, 1977.

Stevenson, D. K., *American Life and Institutions*, Washington D. C.: United States Information Agency, 1989.

Stewart, Edward C. and Bennett, Milton J., *American Cultural Patterns*, Maine: Intercultural Press, Inc., revised edition, 1991.

Woloch, Nancy, *Women and the American Experience*, New York: McGraw-Hill, 2000.

Zelinsky, Wilbur, *The Cultural Geography of the United States*, New Jersey: Prentice-Hall Inc., 1973.

Bureau of International Information Programs, U. S. Department of State, *U. S. Legal System*, 2004.